VOLCANOES
Fire and Life

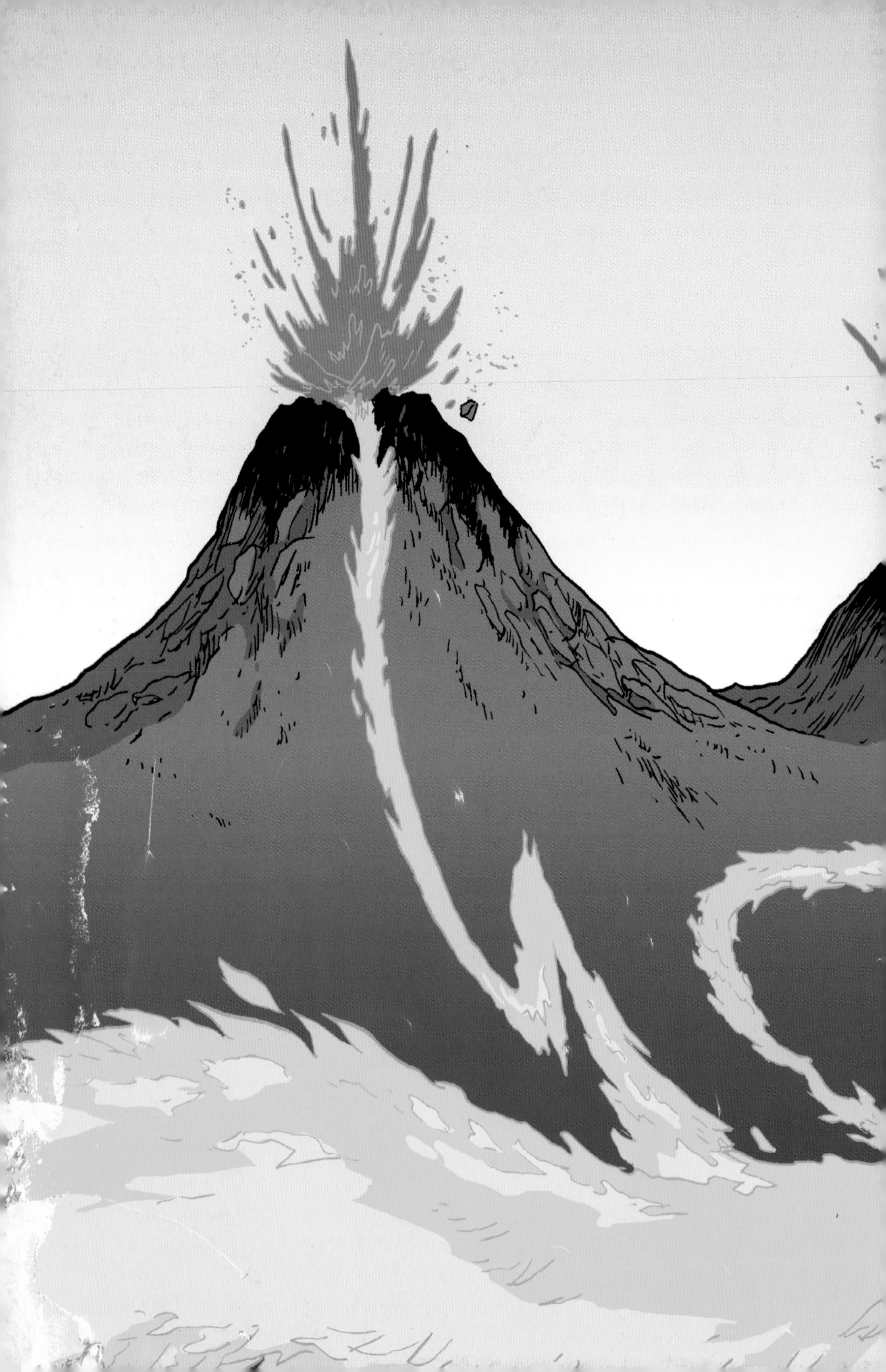

VOLCANOES

Fire and Life

JON CHAD

with color by
Sophie Goldstein

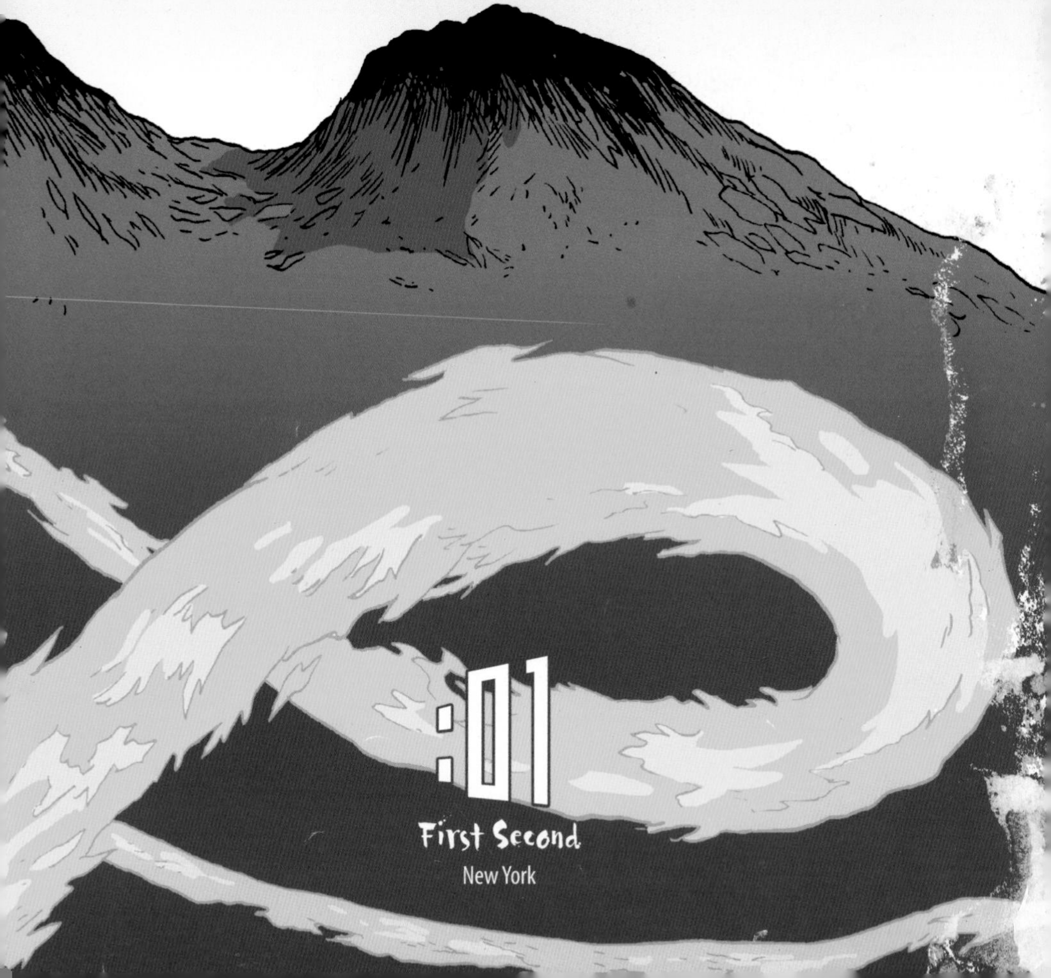

:01
First Second
New York

First Second

Drawn on Strathmore 400-series 2-ply smooth bristol board with a Staedtler 4H pencil. The panel borders were drawn with a 1.0 Copic Multiliner and the drawings were inked with a combination of Sakura Micron Pens sizes 08, 05, 03, 02, and 005, and an assortment of drawing nibs including the Hunt 102 Crow Quill, the Hunt 107 Hawk Quill, the Tachikawa No.5 School Pen, and the Tachiwara G-Pen; all dipped in Speedball Superblack ink. Colored using Adobe Photoshop.

Published by First Second
First Second is an imprint of Roaring Brook Press,
a division of Holtzbrinck Publishing Holdings Limited Partnership
175 Fifth Avenue, New York, New York 10010
All rights reserved

Cataloging-in-Publication Data is on file at the Library of Congress.

Paperback ISBN 978-1-62672-360-3
Hardcover ISBN 978-1-62672-361-0

Our books may be purchased in bulk for promotional, educational, or business use. Please contact your local bookseller or the Macmillan Corporate and Premium Sales Department at (800) 221-7945 ext. 5442 or by e-mail at MacmillanSpecialMarkets@macmillan.com.

First edition 2016
Book design by John Green

Printed in China by Toppan Leefung Printing Ltd., Dongguan City, Guandong Province
Paperback: 10 9 8 7 6 5 4 3 2 1
Hardcover: 10 9 8 7 6 5 4 3 2 1

If you take a hike on a mountain trail, it may feel like the landscape around you has been there forever—mountains look permanent and rivers seem like they have been babbling since the dawn of time. Take a hike with a geologist, however, and you'll hear a different story—one of constant motion and change. We can see our planet's long history in the rocks around us. The rocks tell a story of continents colliding, of Earth's crust ripping, tearing, and grinding, of volcanic explosions and massive earthquakes. The type, size, and shape of rocks can tell us about the slow, gradual changes that create new land and shift continents, and about catastrophic events like asteroid impacts that have altered the entire planet.

Volcanoes are perhaps the most visible and dramatic evidence of these constant changes to the Earth's surface. Volcanic eruptions shape our planet in amazing ways. The very continents we live on have grown and formed because of the movement of magma. Some of Earth's most beautiful natural landmarks like Yosemite National Park, the Rocky Mountains, and Yellowstone National Park are the result of the constant movement of magma from the Earth's interior toward the surface. And let's not forget that many islands, like Hawaii, are the result of volcanic activity on the seafloor!

When you think of volcanoes, you may imagine dangerous eruptions, but volcanic activity benefits us in many ways too. Soil in volcanic regions is often nutrient-rich, making it ideal for growing food. The next time you eat a kiwifruit from New Zealand, keep in mind that the volcanic soil there formed from lava from massive ancient eruptions. Near areas of recent volcanic activity, heat in the crust—known as geothermal energy—can be harnessed to heat homes and generate electricity. Iceland, for instance, is a particularly active volcanic island. And a lot of their electricity and heat is provided free of charge thanks to volcanoes!

As you read, you will learn that each volcano has its own unique personality, just like the characters in this book. When Aurora examines different types of volcanoes—from small flowing eruptions in Hawaii to the massive "super-eruptions" of Yellowstone—she begins to see how different factors like the chemistry of magma and the gasses it contains affect a volcano's eruptions. Aurora takes the time to see beyond volcanoes' intimidating exteriors. She discovers their potential. She learns that volcanoes are sources of land, power, heat, and life! We hope you learn to look at volcanoes a little differently, like Aurora does. Volcanoes may be super hot but the science is super cool!

—Gwyneth Hughes, PhD in Geology, MS Geophysics,
and Michael Cardiff, Assistant Professor in Geoscience, UW–Madison

METRIC MEASUREMENT CONVERSIONS

METRIC		IMPERIAL (US)
1 Millimeter (mm)	≈	0.039 (in)
1 Centimeter (cm)	≈	0.39 (in)
1 Meter (m)	≈	3.28 (ft)
1 Kilometer (km)	≈	0.62 (mi)
1 km per hour	≈	0.62 m per hour
1 Gram (g)	≈	0.002 (lbs)
1 Kilogram (kg)	≈	2.20 (lbs)
1 Liter (l)	≈	0.035 Cubic Feet (ft³)
1 Cubic Meter (l³)	≈	35.31 Cubic Feet (ft³)
1 Cubic Kilometer (km³)	≈	0.24 Cubic Miles (mi³)
0° Celsius (C)	≈	32° Fahrenheit (F)
100° Celsius (C)	≈	212° Fahrenheit (F)
1000° Celsius (C)	≈	1832° Fahrenheit (F)
2000° Celsius (C)	≈	3632° Fahrenheit (F)

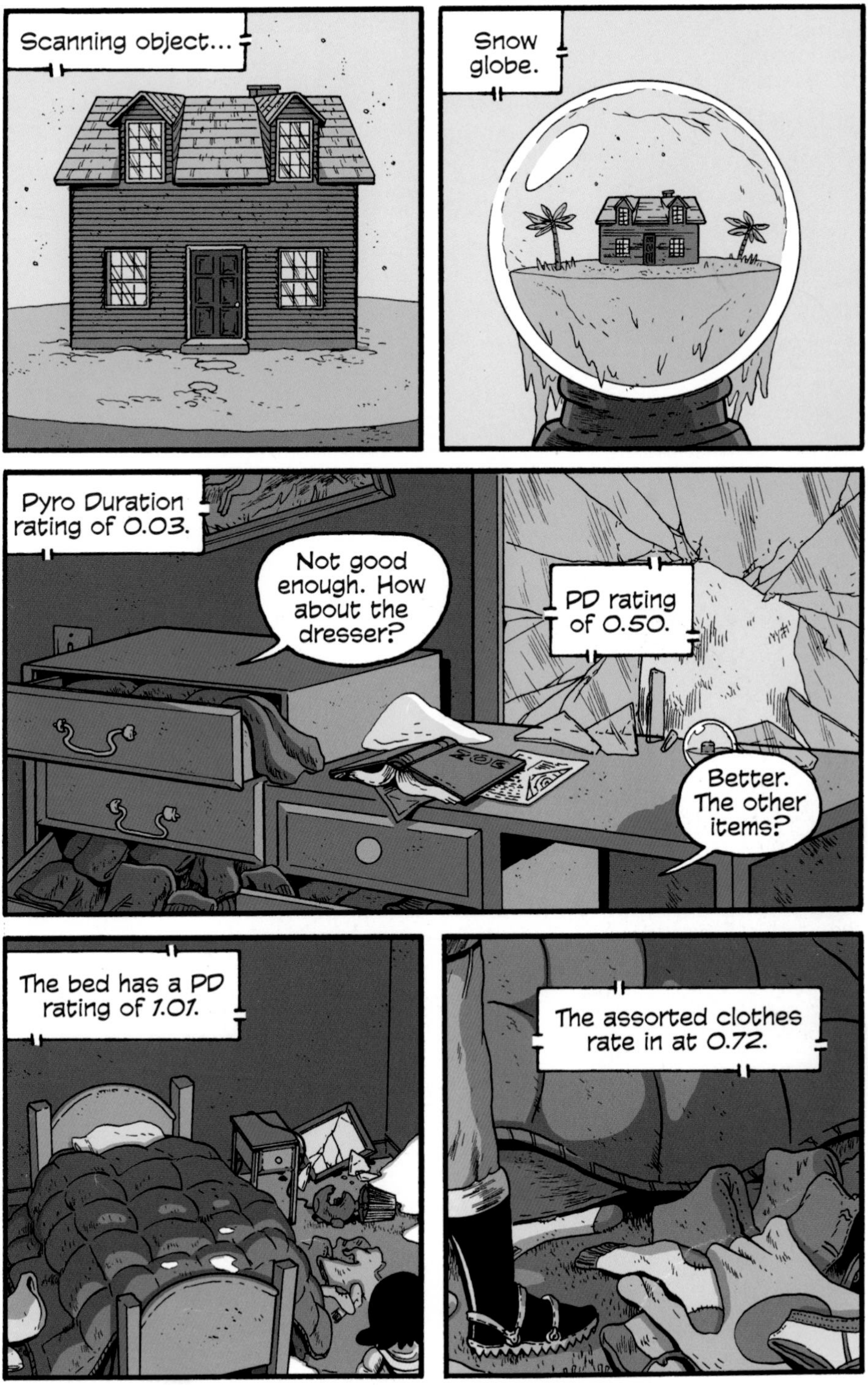
Scanning object...
Snow globe.
Pyro Duration rating of 0.03.
Not good enough. How about the dresser?
PD rating of 0.50.
Better. The other items?
The bed has a PD rating of 1.01.
The assorted clothes rate in at 0.72.

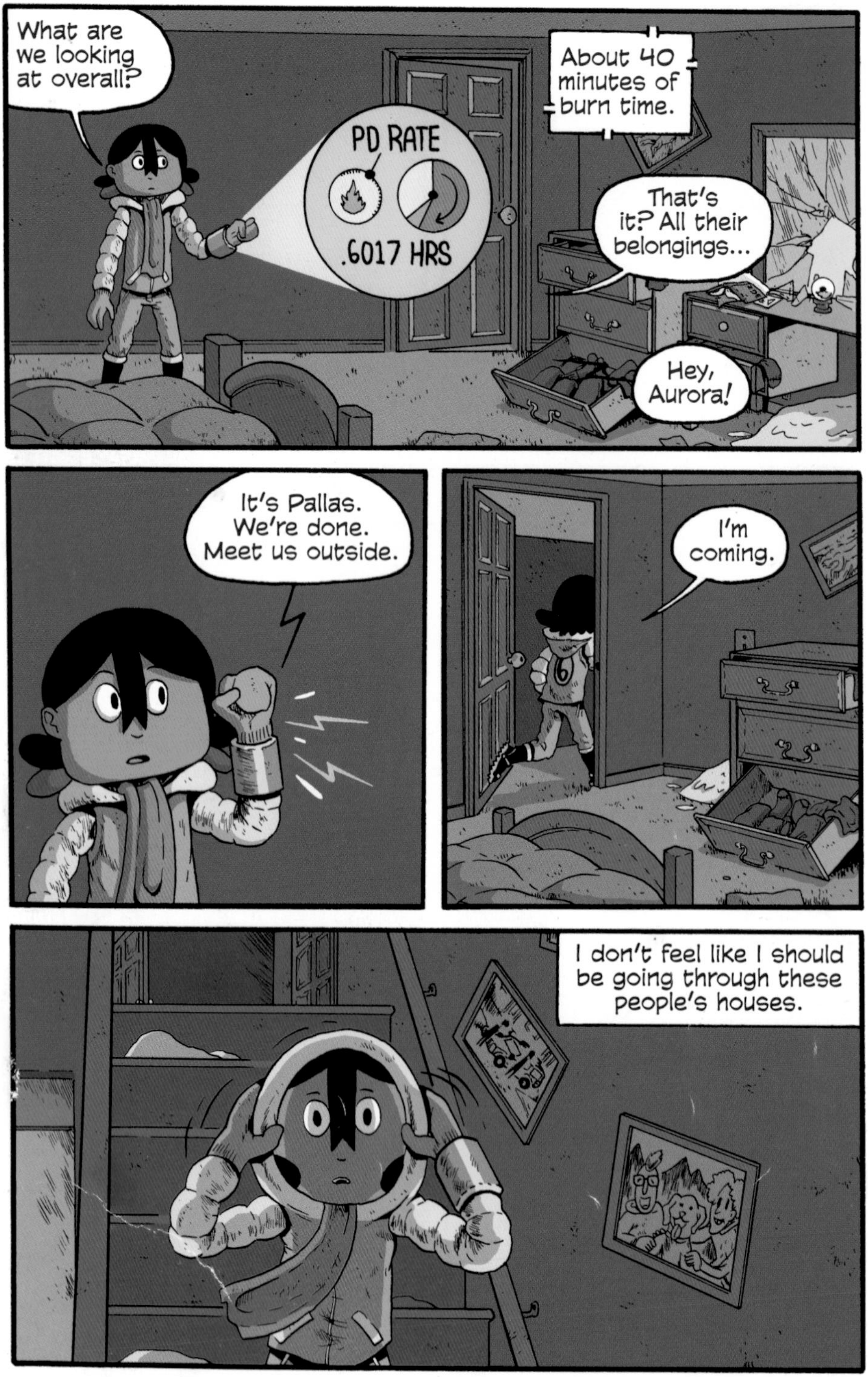
What are we looking at overall?
PD RATE
.6017 HRS
About 40 minutes of burn time.
That's it? All their belongings...
Hey, Aurora!
It's Pallas. We're done. Meet us outside.
I'm coming.
I don't feel like I should be going through these people's houses.

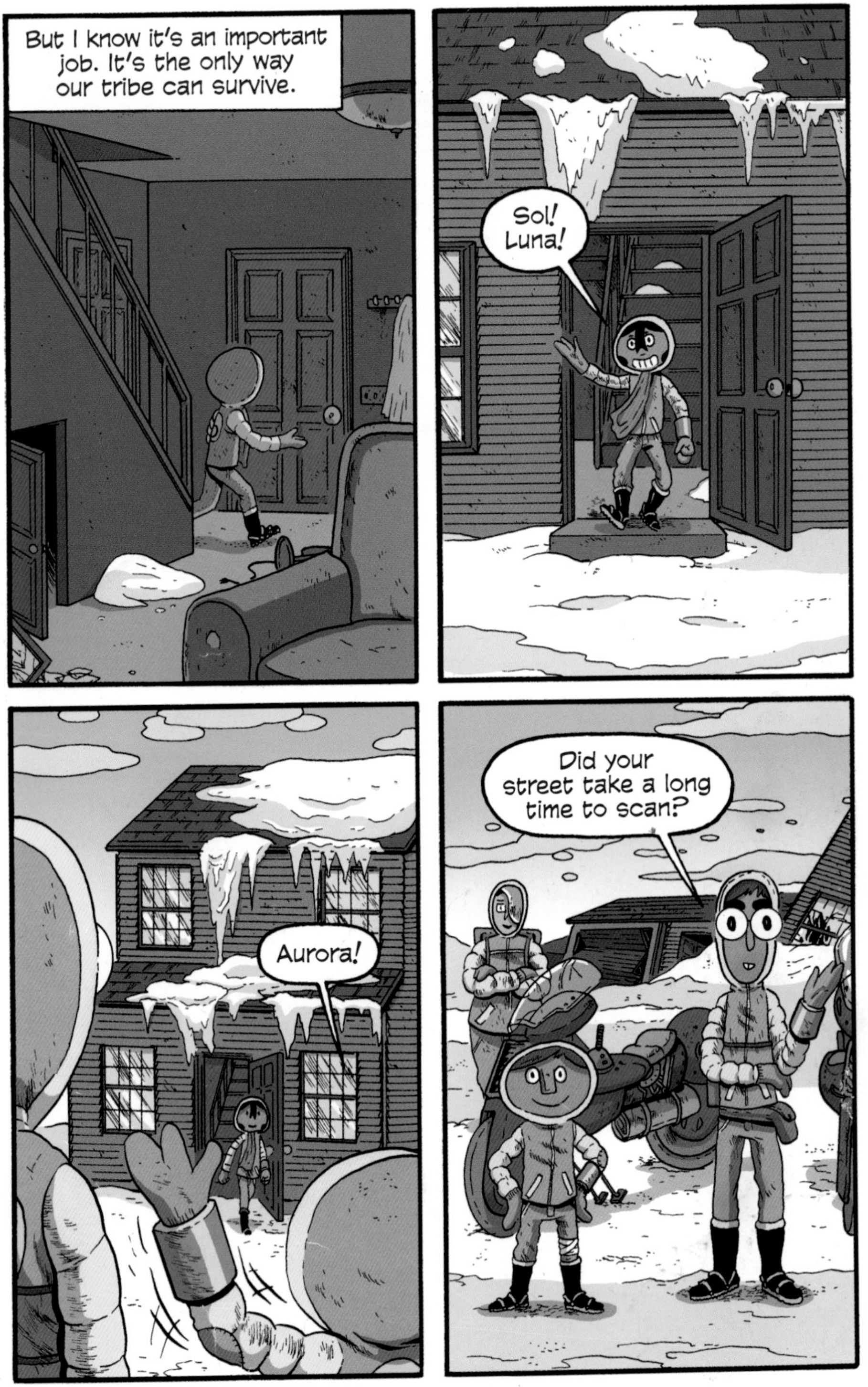
But I know it's an important job. It's the only way our tribe can survive.
Sol! Luna!
Aurora!
Did your street take a long time to scan?

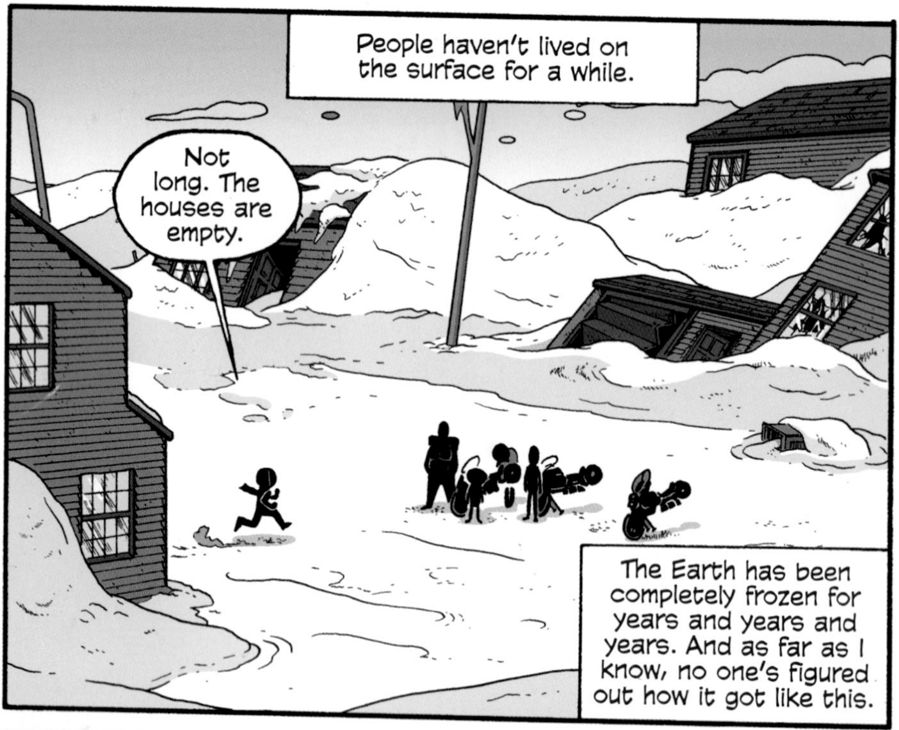
People haven't lived on the surface for a while.
Not long. The houses are empty.
The Earth has been completely frozen for years and years and years. And as far as I know, no one's figured out how it got like this.

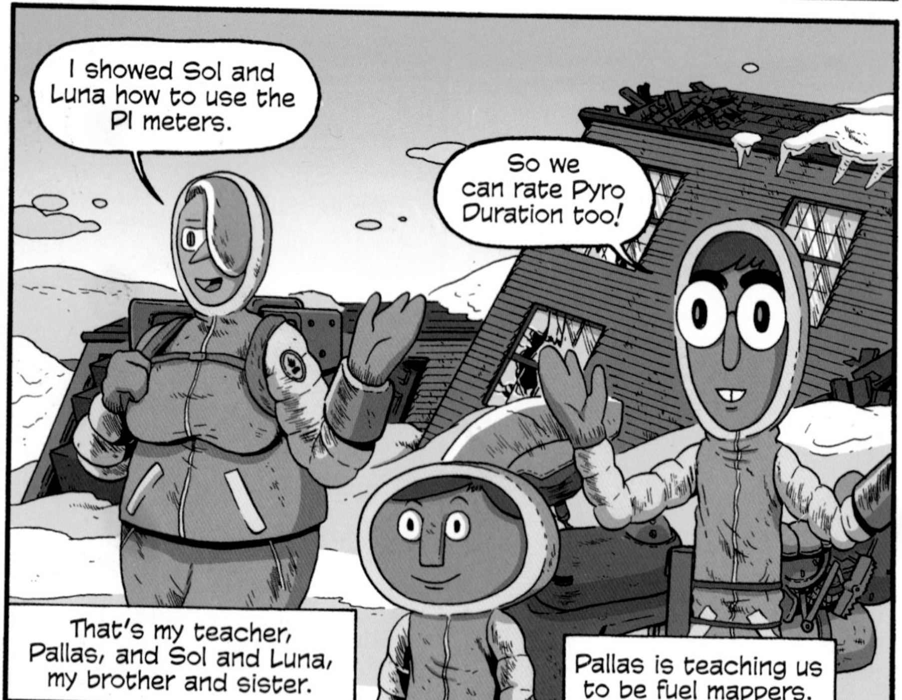
I showed Sol and Luna how to use the PI meters.
So we can rate Pyro Duration too!
That's my teacher, Pallas, and Sol and Luna, my brother and sister.
Pallas is teaching us to be fuel mappers.

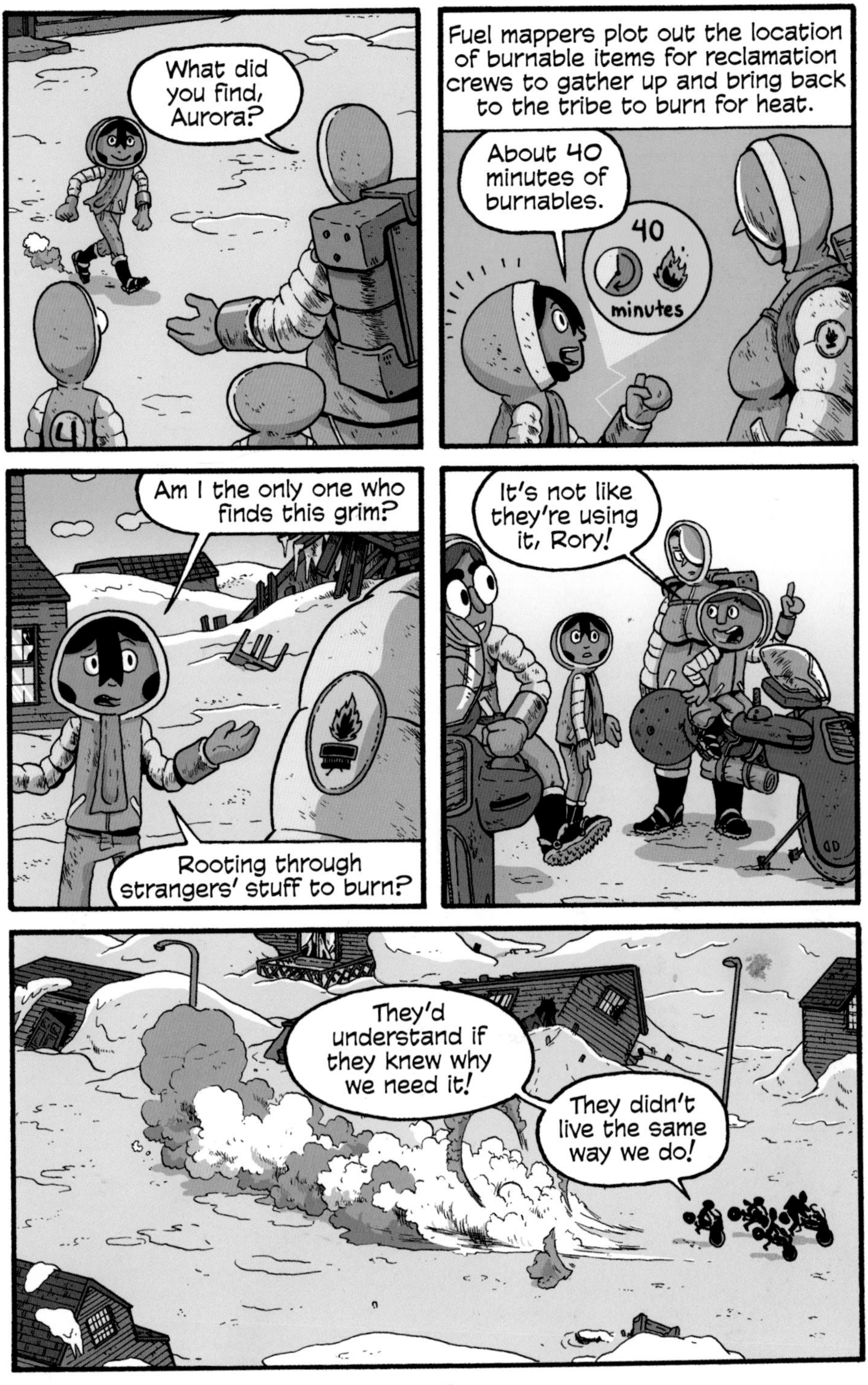

What did you find, Aurora?
Fuel mappers plot out the location of burnable items for reclamation crews to gather up and bring back to the tribe to burn for heat.
About 40 minutes of burnables.
40
minutes
Am I the only one who finds this grim?
Rooting through strangers' stuff to burn?
It's not like they're using it, Rory!
They'd understand if they knew why we need it!
They didn't live the same way we do!

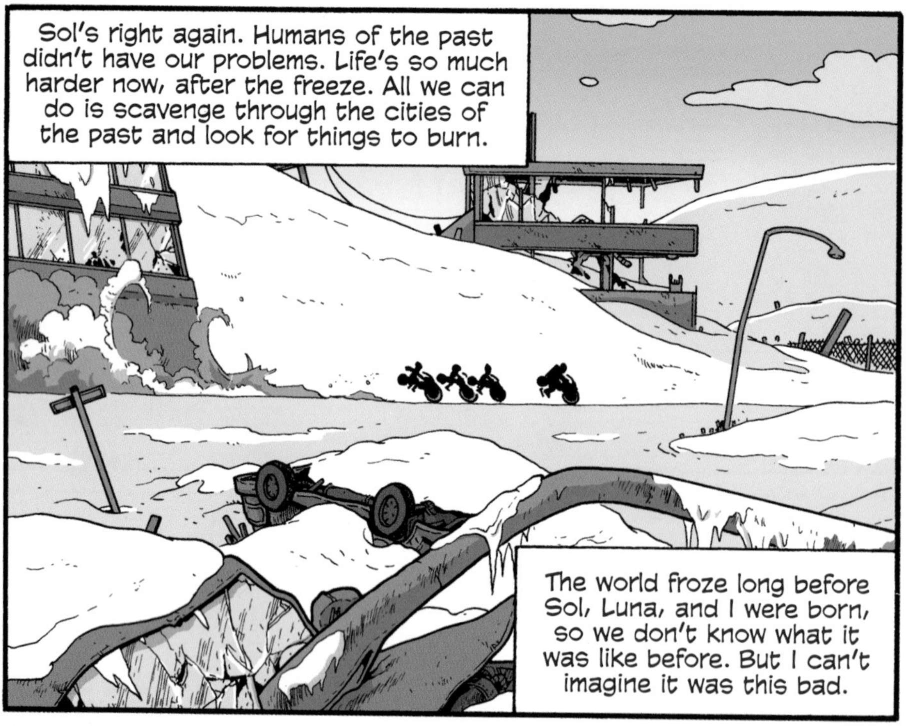
Sol's right again. Humans of the past didn't have our problems. Life's so much harder now, after the freeze. All we can do is scavenge through the cities of the past and look for things to burn.
The world froze long before Sol, Luna, and I were born, so we don't know what it was like before. But I can't imagine it was this bad.

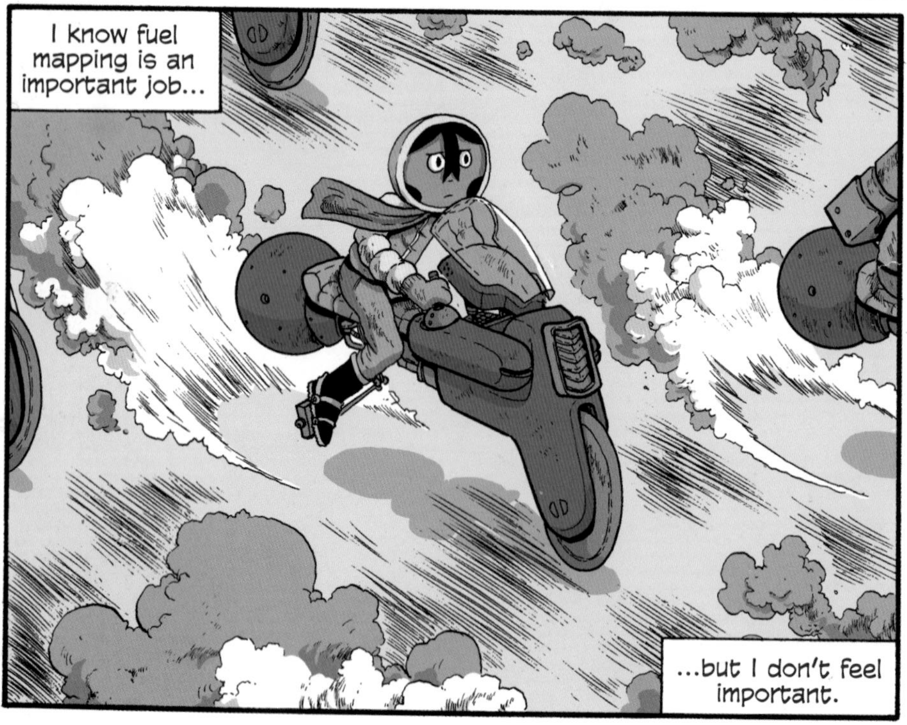
I know fuel mapping is an important job...
...but I don't feel important.

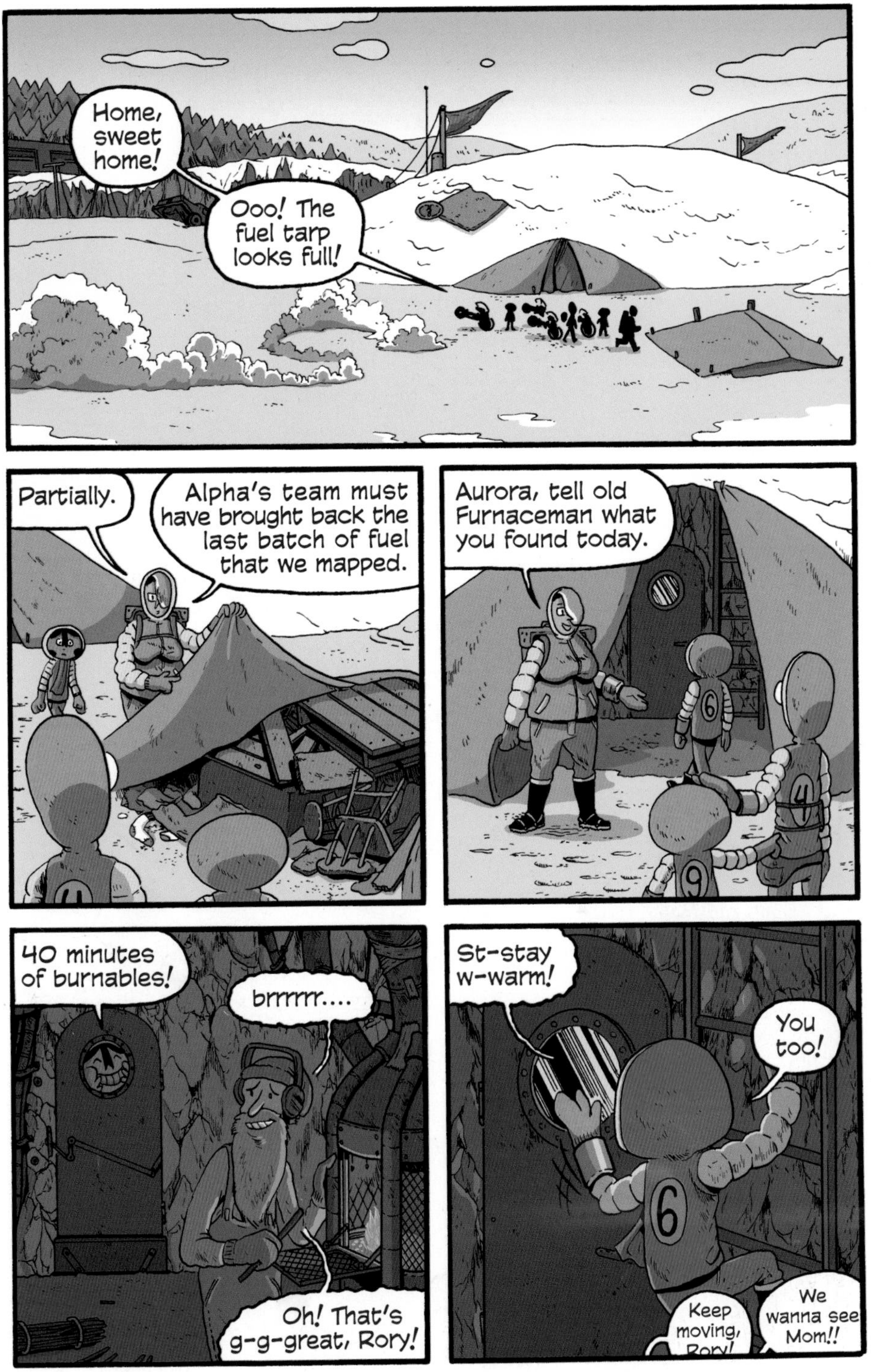
Home, sweet home!
Ooo! The fuel tarp looks full!
Partially.
Alpha's team must have brought back the last batch of fuel that we mapped.
Aurora, tell old Furnaceman what you found today.
40 minutes of burnables!
brrrrrr....
Oh! That's g-g-great, Rory!
St-stay w-warm!
You too!
Keep moving,
We wanna see Mom!!

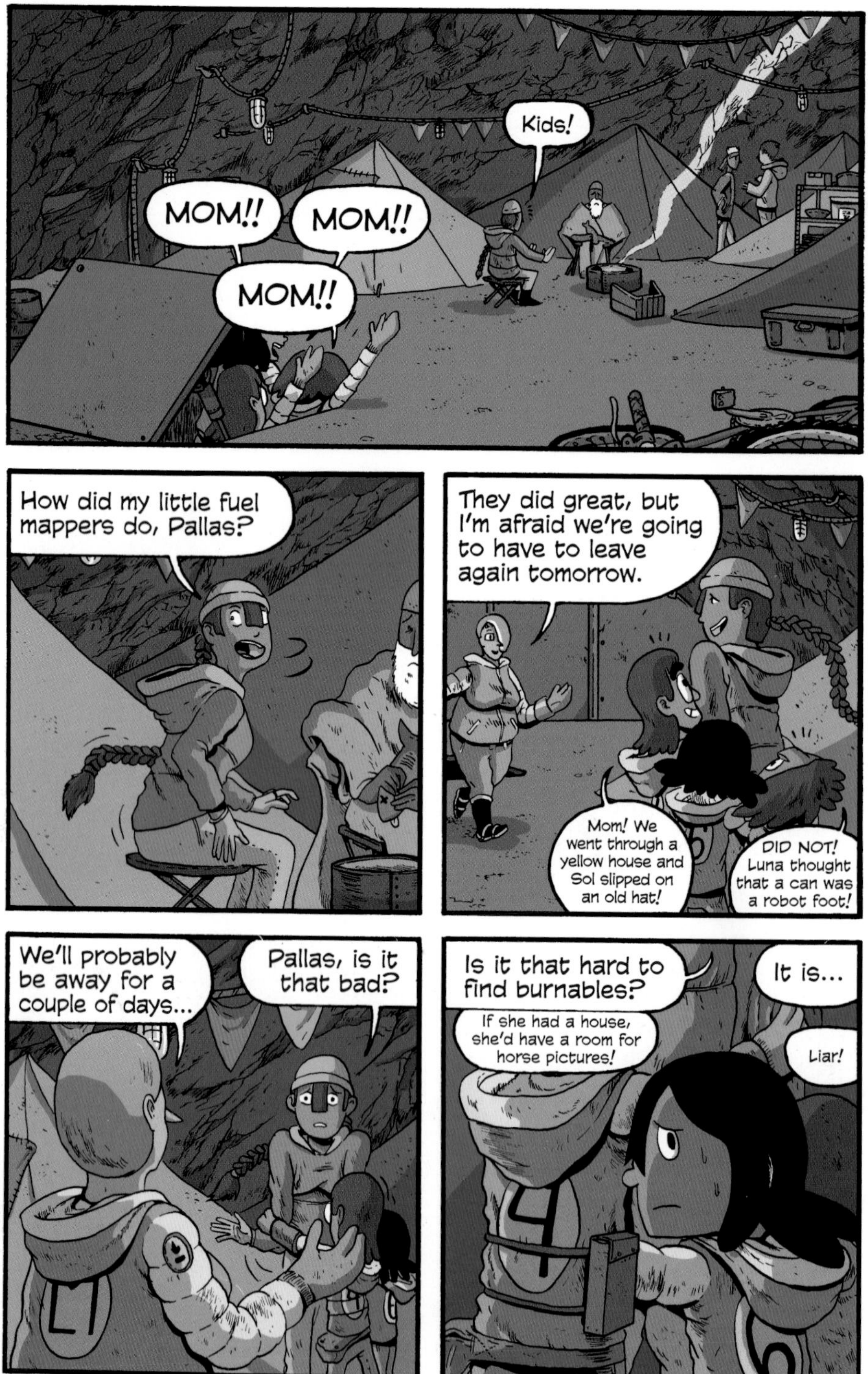
Kids!
MOM!!
MOM!!
MOM!!
How did my little fuel mappers do, Pallas?
They did great, but I'm afraid we're going to have to leave again tomorrow.
Mom! We went through a yellow house and Sol slipped on an old hat!
DID NOT! Luna thought that a can was a robot foot!
We'll probably be away for a couple of days...
Pallas, is it that bad?
Is it that hard to find burnables?
It is...
If she had a house, she'd have a room for horse pictures!
Liar!

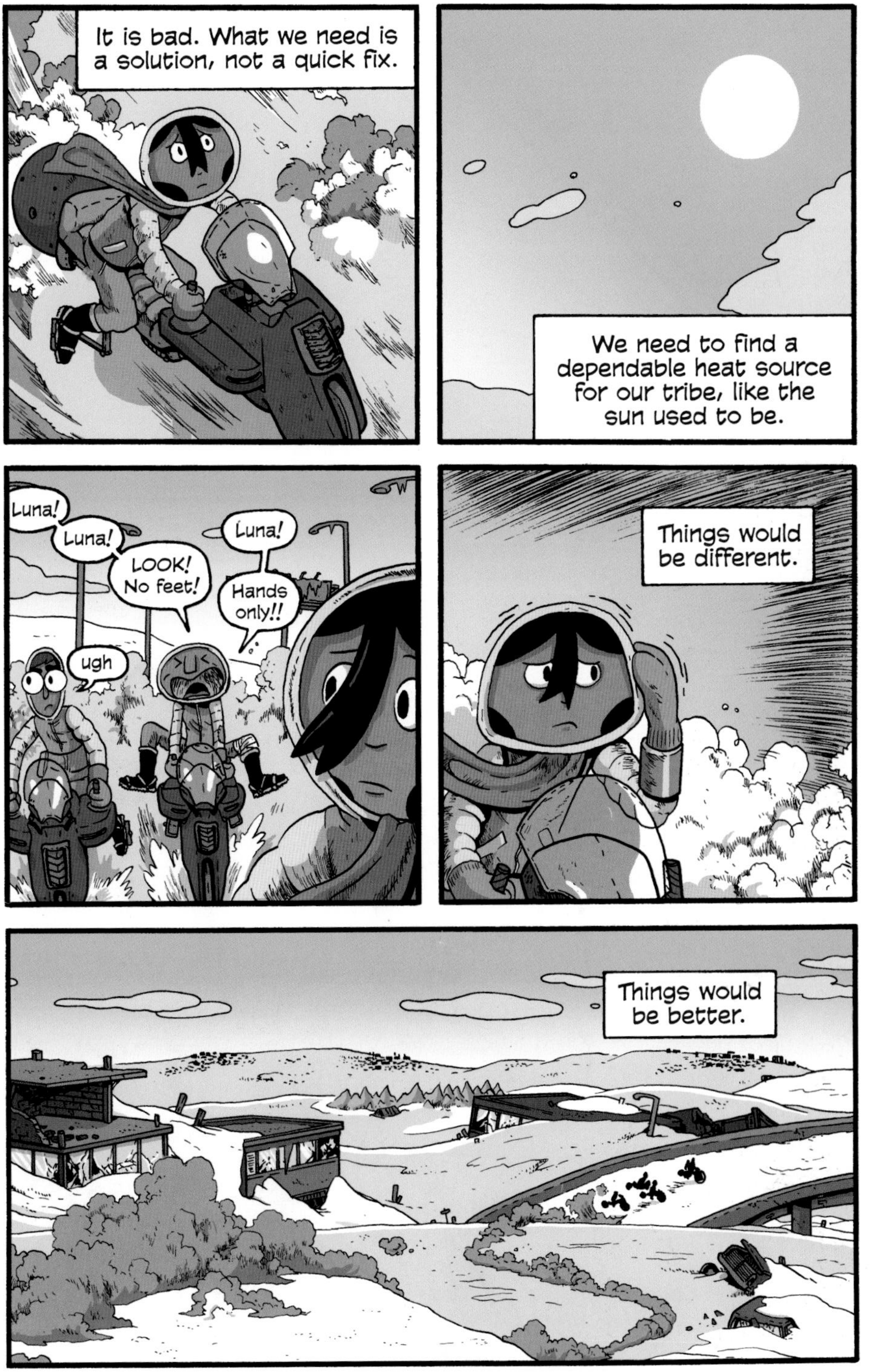
It is bad. What we need is a solution, not a quick fix.
We need to find a dependable heat source for our tribe, like the sun used to be.
Luna!
Luna!
LOOK! No feet!
ugh
Luna!
Hands only!!
Things would be different.
Things would be better.

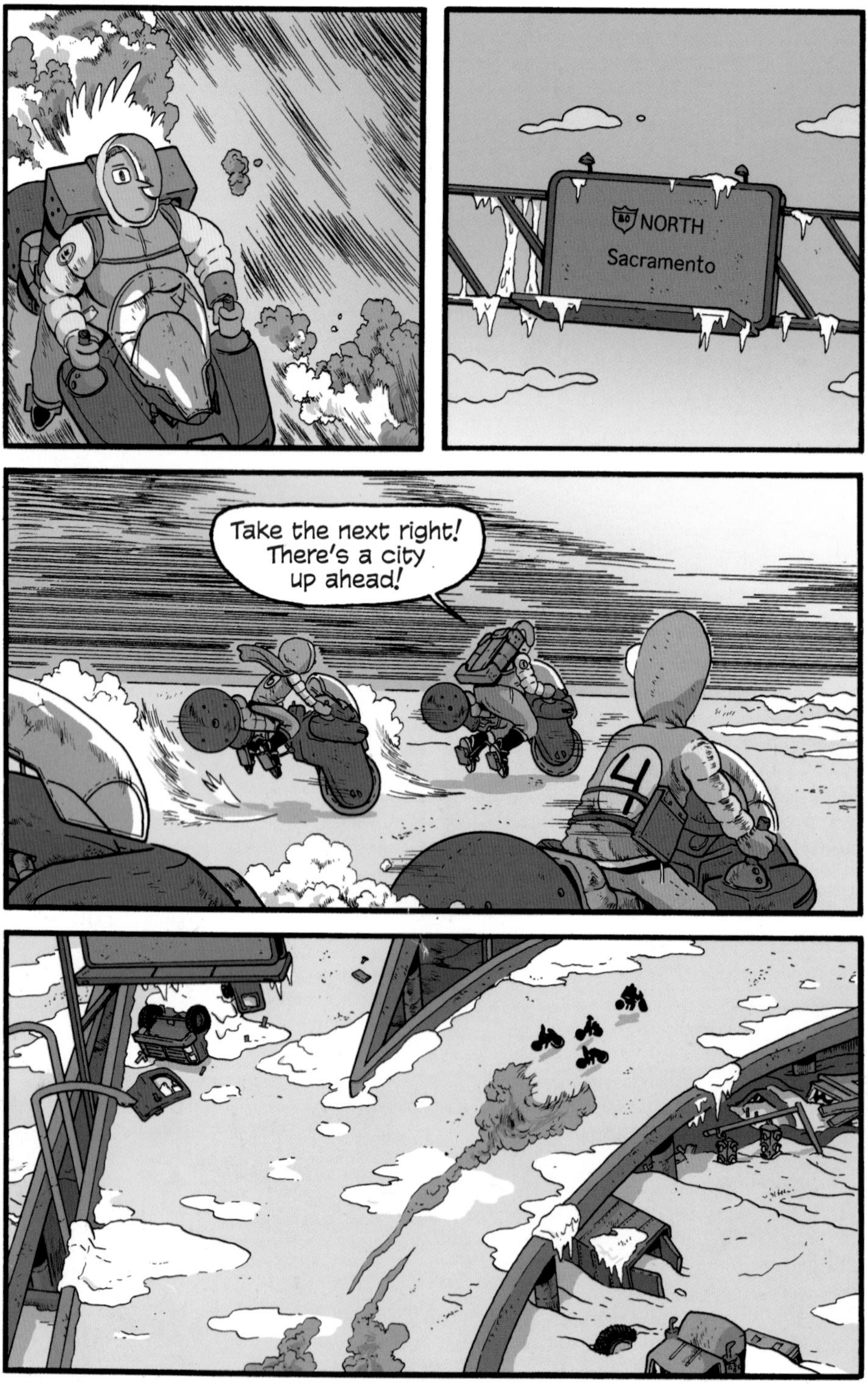
NORTH
Sacramento
Take the next right! There's a city up ahead!

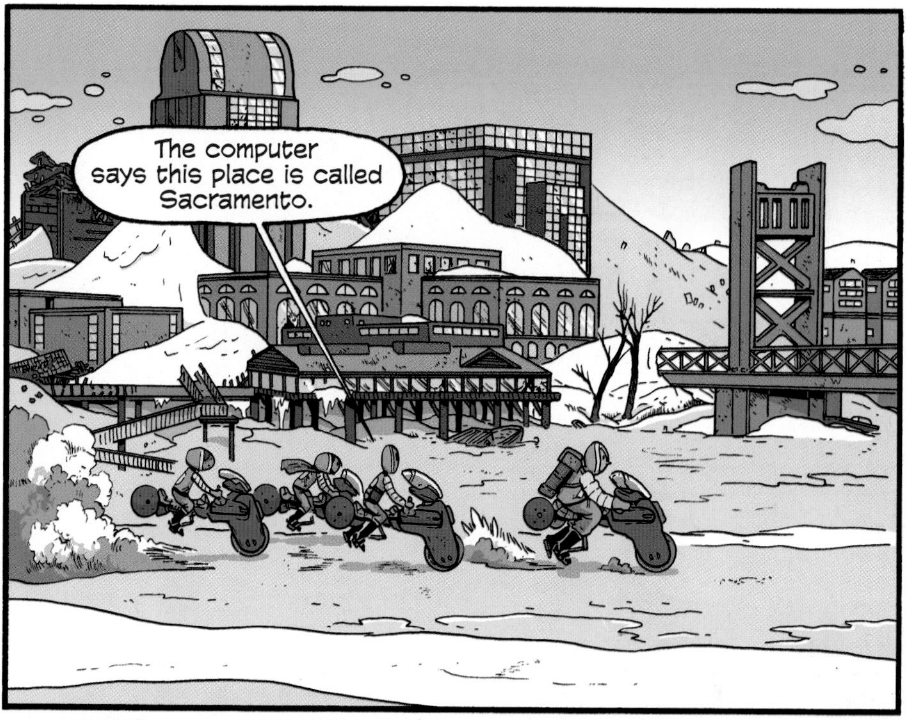
The computer says this place is called Sacramento.

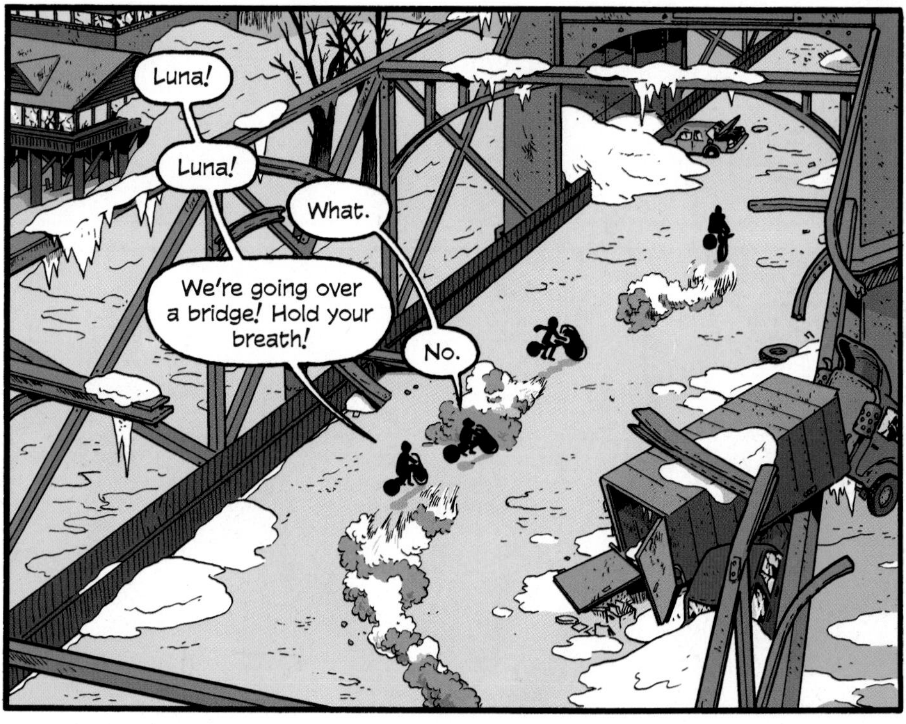
Luna!
Luna!
What.
We're going over a bridge! Hold your breath!
No.

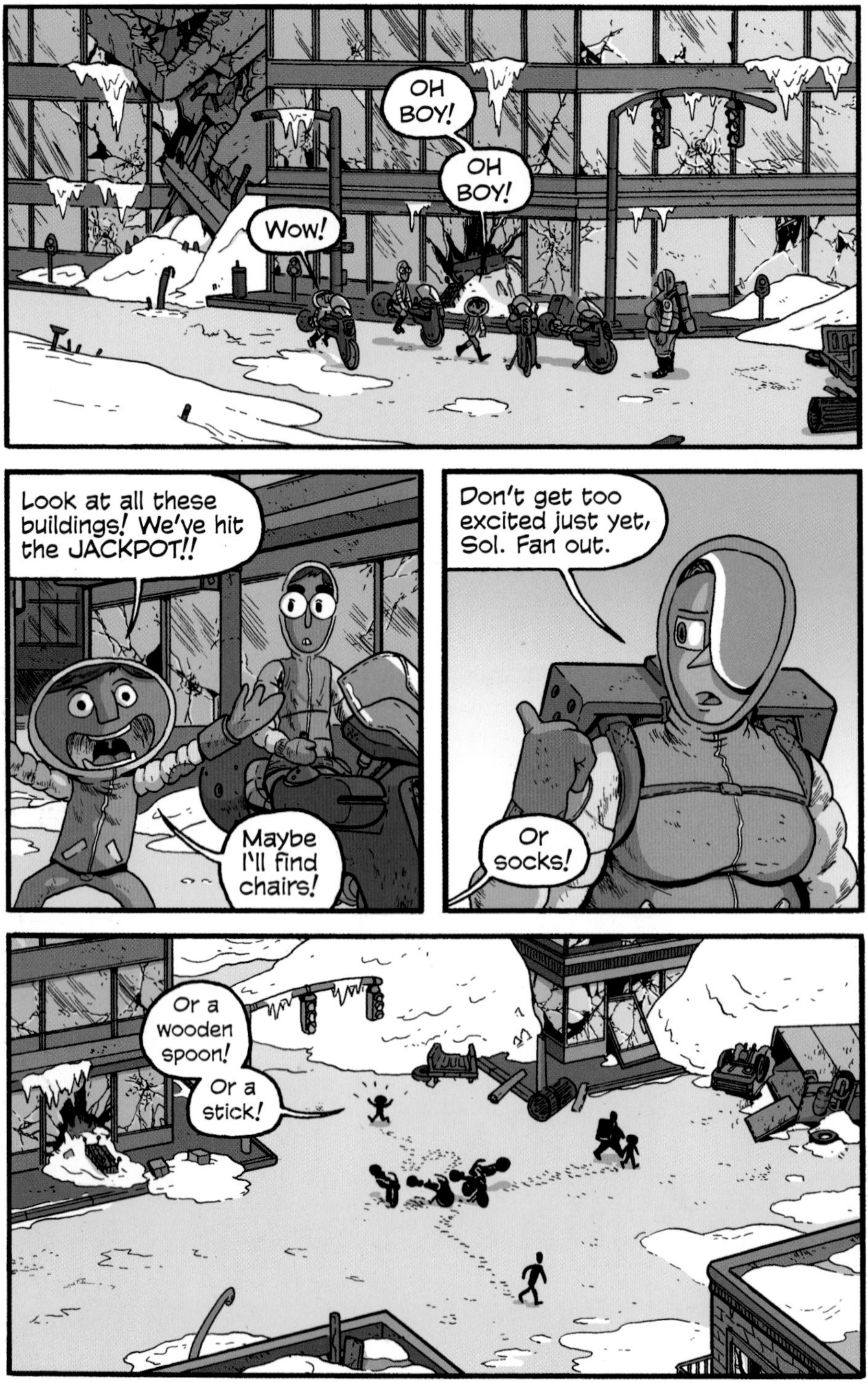
OH BOY!
OH BOY!
Wow!
Look at all these buildings! We've hit the JACKPOT!!
Maybe I'll find chairs!
Don't get too excited just yet, Sol. Fan out.
Or socks!
Or a wooden spoon!
Or a stick!

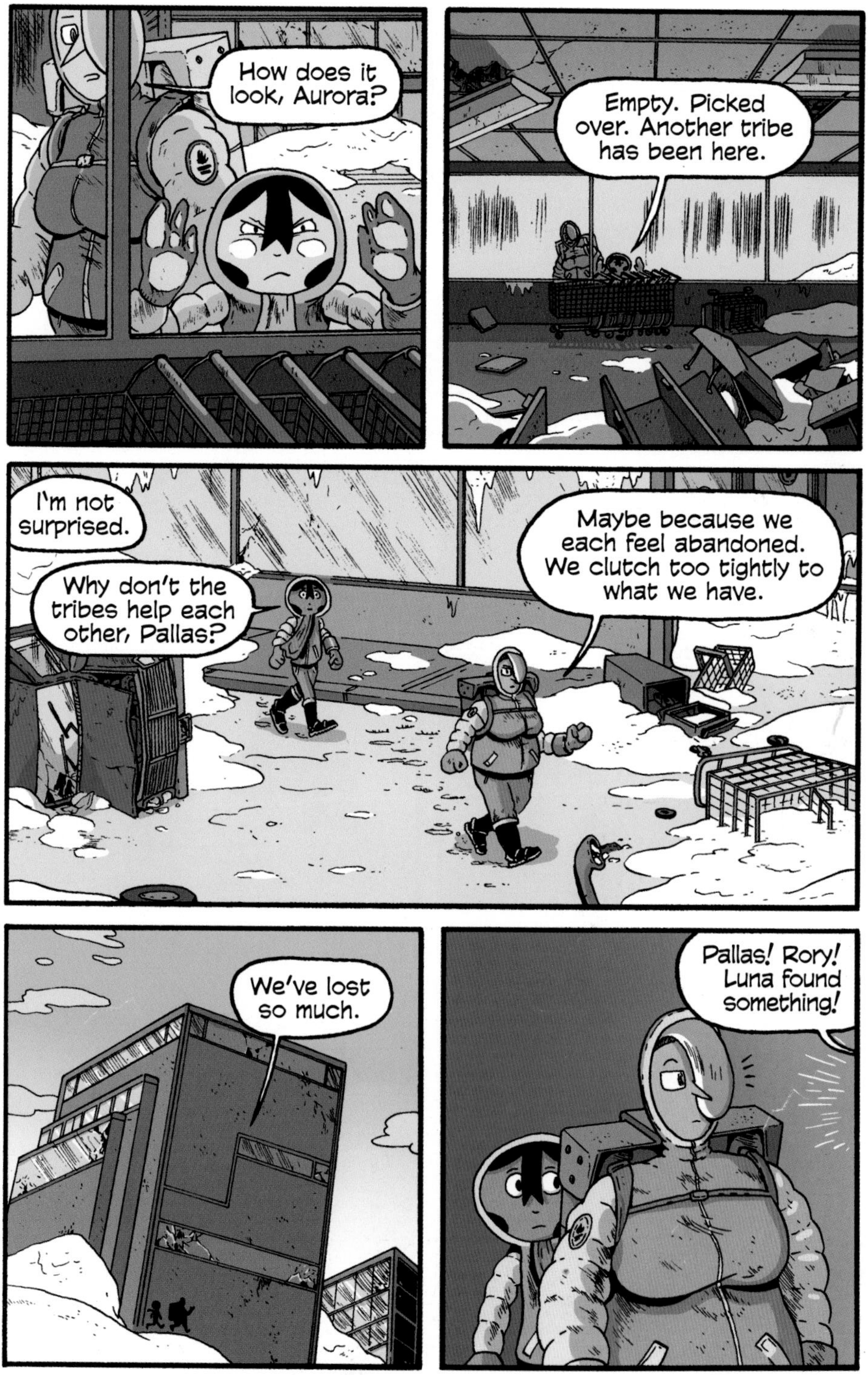
How does it look, Aurora?
Empty. Picked over. Another tribe has been here.
I'm not surprised.
Why don't the tribes help each other, Pallas?
Maybe because we each feel abandoned. We clutch too tightly to what we have.
We've lost so much.
Pallas! Rory! Luna found something!

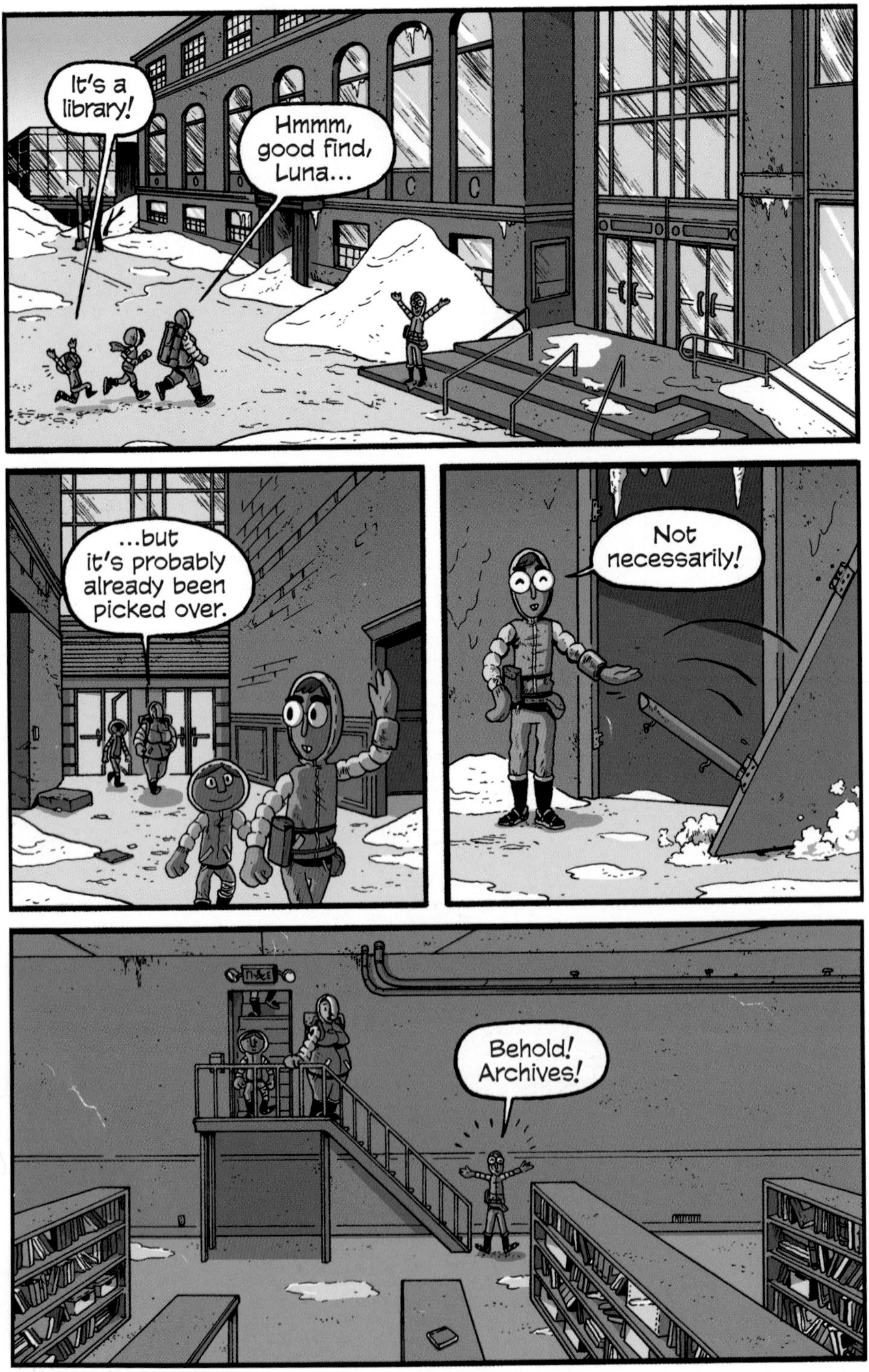
It's a library!
Hmmm, good find, Luna...
...but it's probably already been picked over.
Not necessarily!
Behold! Archives!

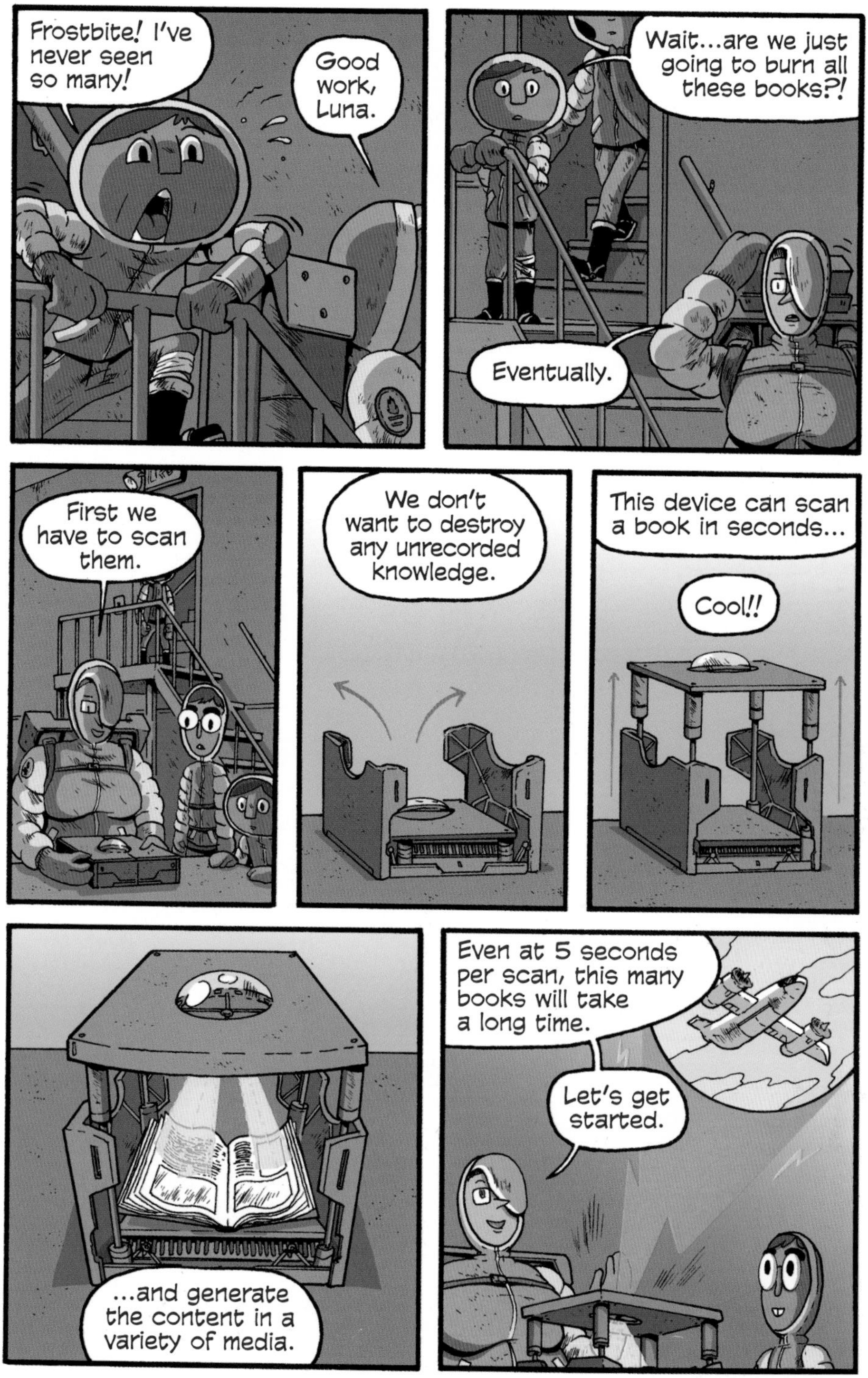

Frostbite! I've never seen so many!
Good work, Luna.
Wait...are we just going to burn all these books?!
Eventually.
First we have to scan them.
We don't want to destroy any unrecorded knowledge.
This device can scan a book in seconds...
Cool!!
...and generate the content in a variety of media.
Even at 5 seconds per scan, this many books will take a long time.
Let's get started.

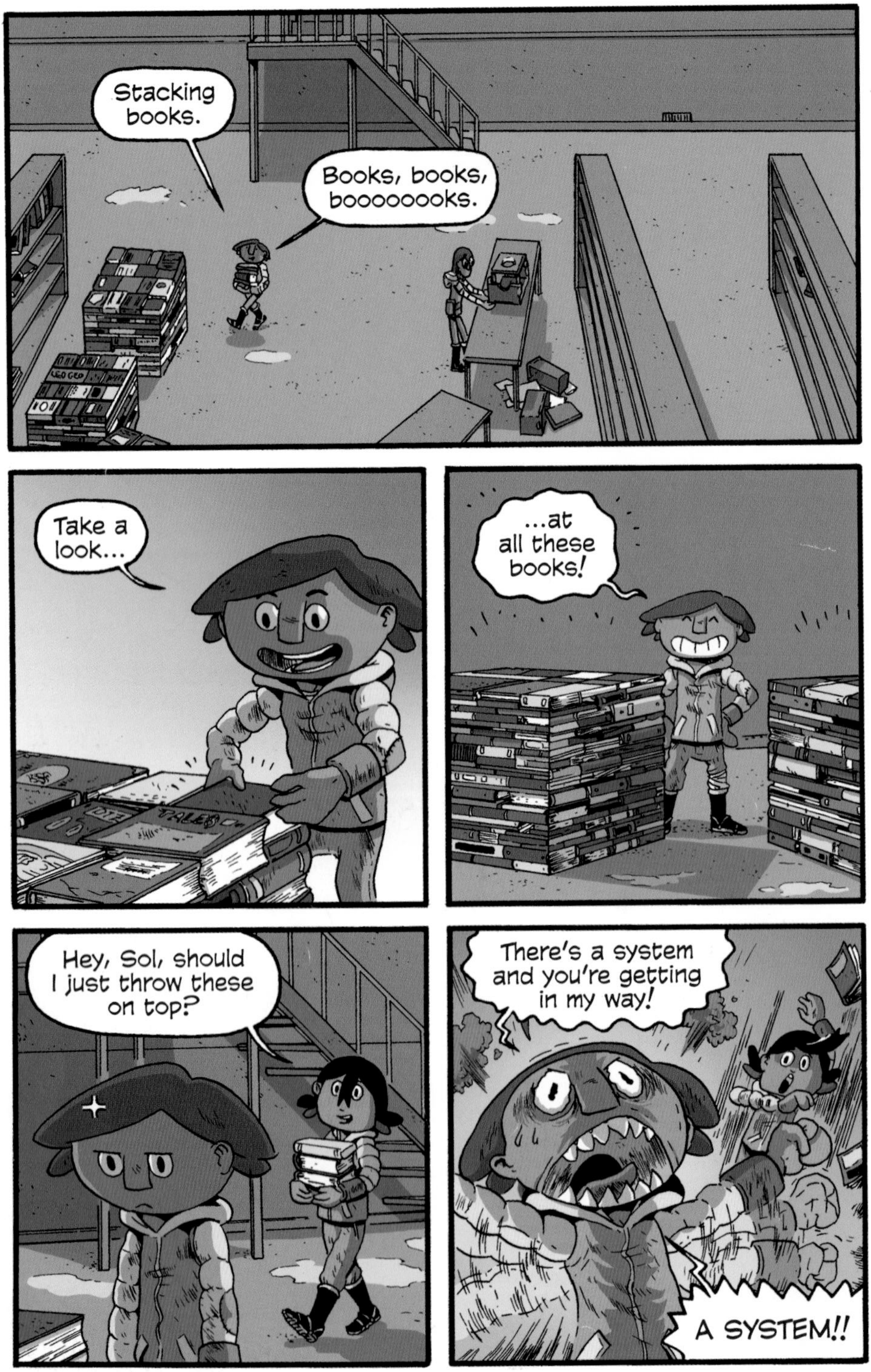
Stacking books.
Books, books, boooooooks.
Take a look...
...at all these books!
Hey, Sol, should I just throw these on top?
There's a system and you're getting in my way!
A SYSTEM!!

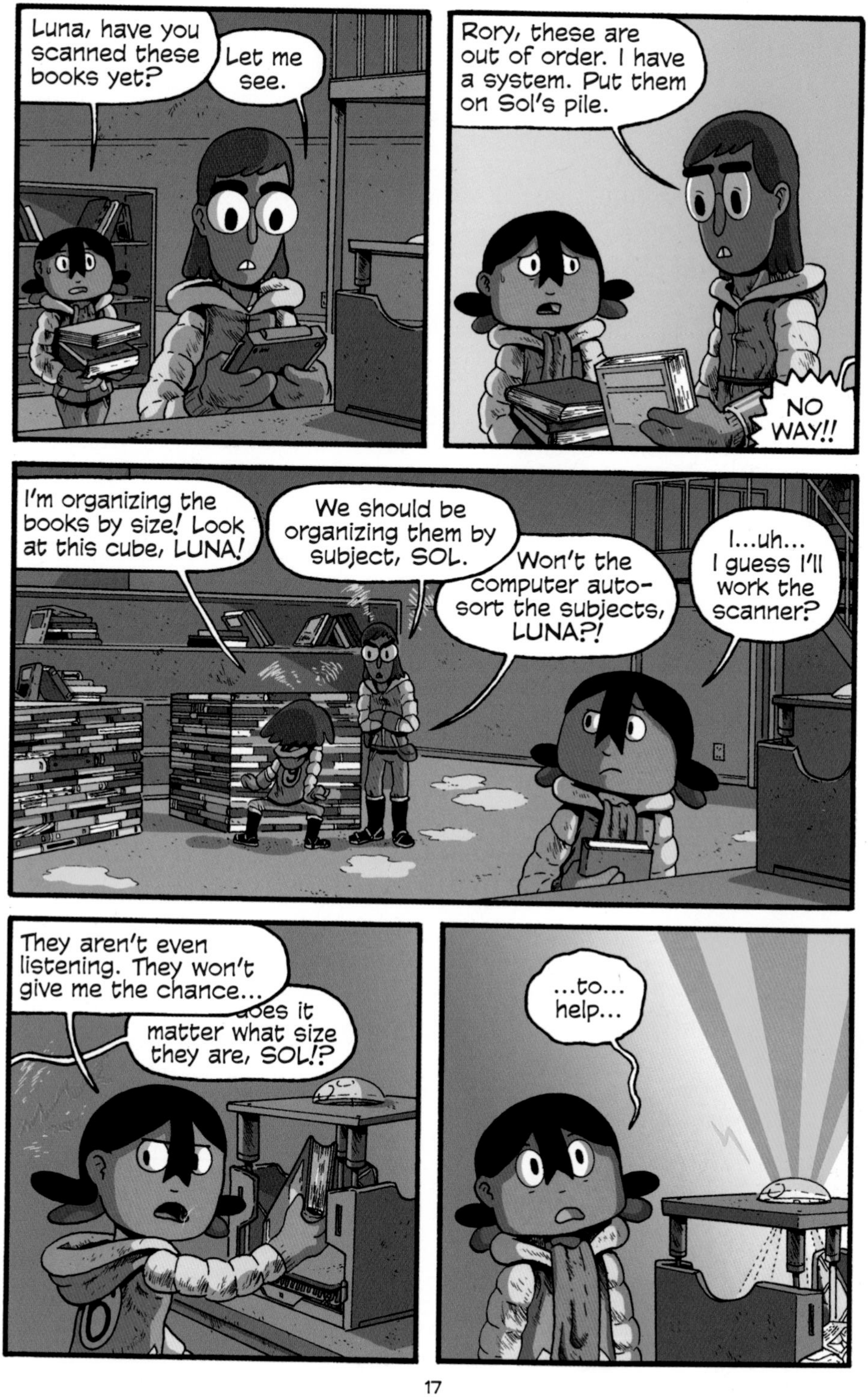
Luna, have you scanned these books yet?
Let me see.
Rory, these are out of order. I have a system. Put them on Sol's pile.
NO WAY!!
I'm organizing the books by size! Look at this cube, LUNA!
We should be organizing them by subject, SOL.
Won't the computer auto-sort the subjects, LUNA?!
I...uh... I guess I'll work the scanner?
They aren't even listening. They won't give me the chance...
...does it matter what size they are, SOL!?
...to... help...

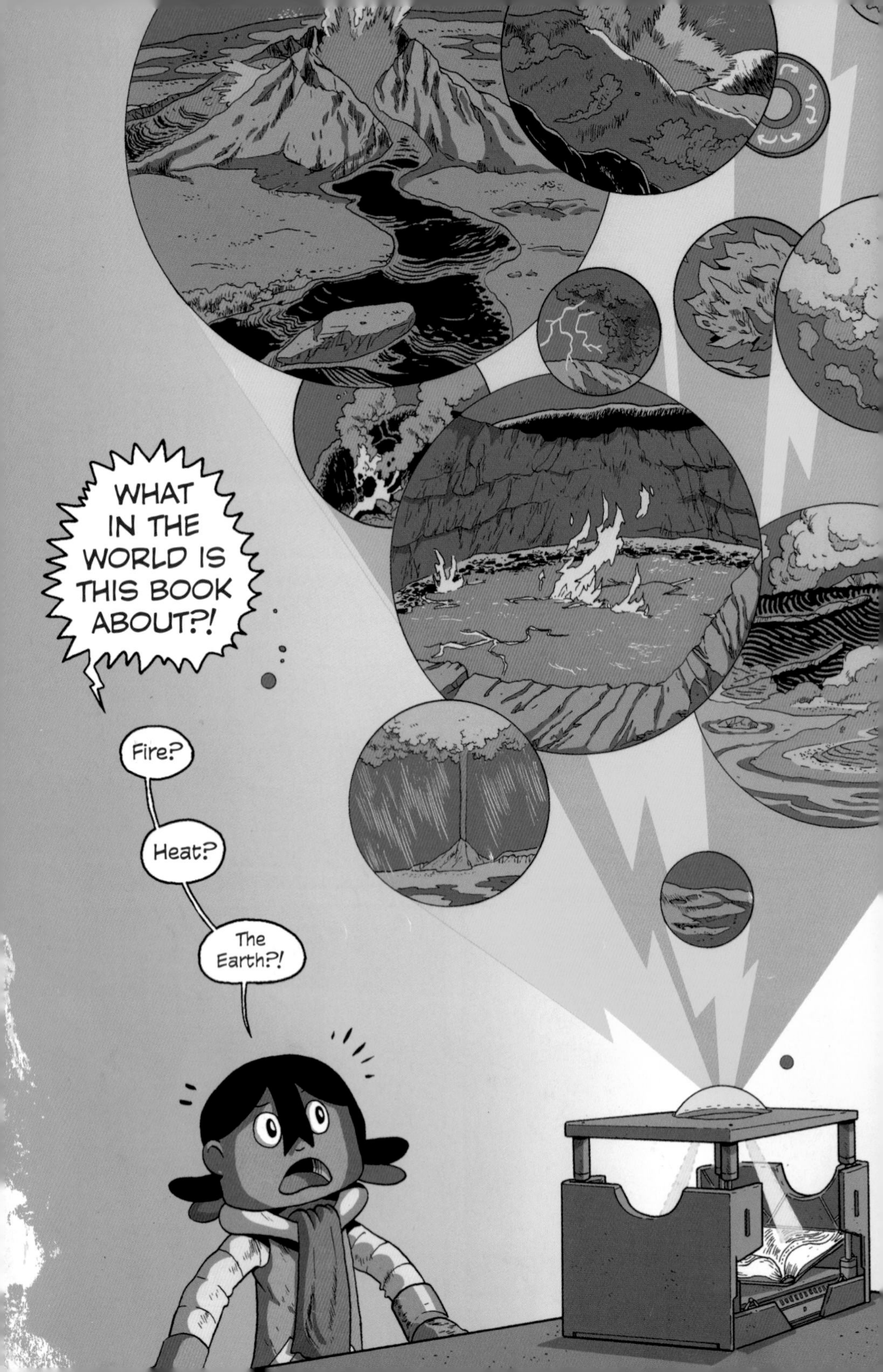
WHAT IN THE WORLD IS THIS BOOK ABOUT?!
Fire?
Heat?
The Earth?!

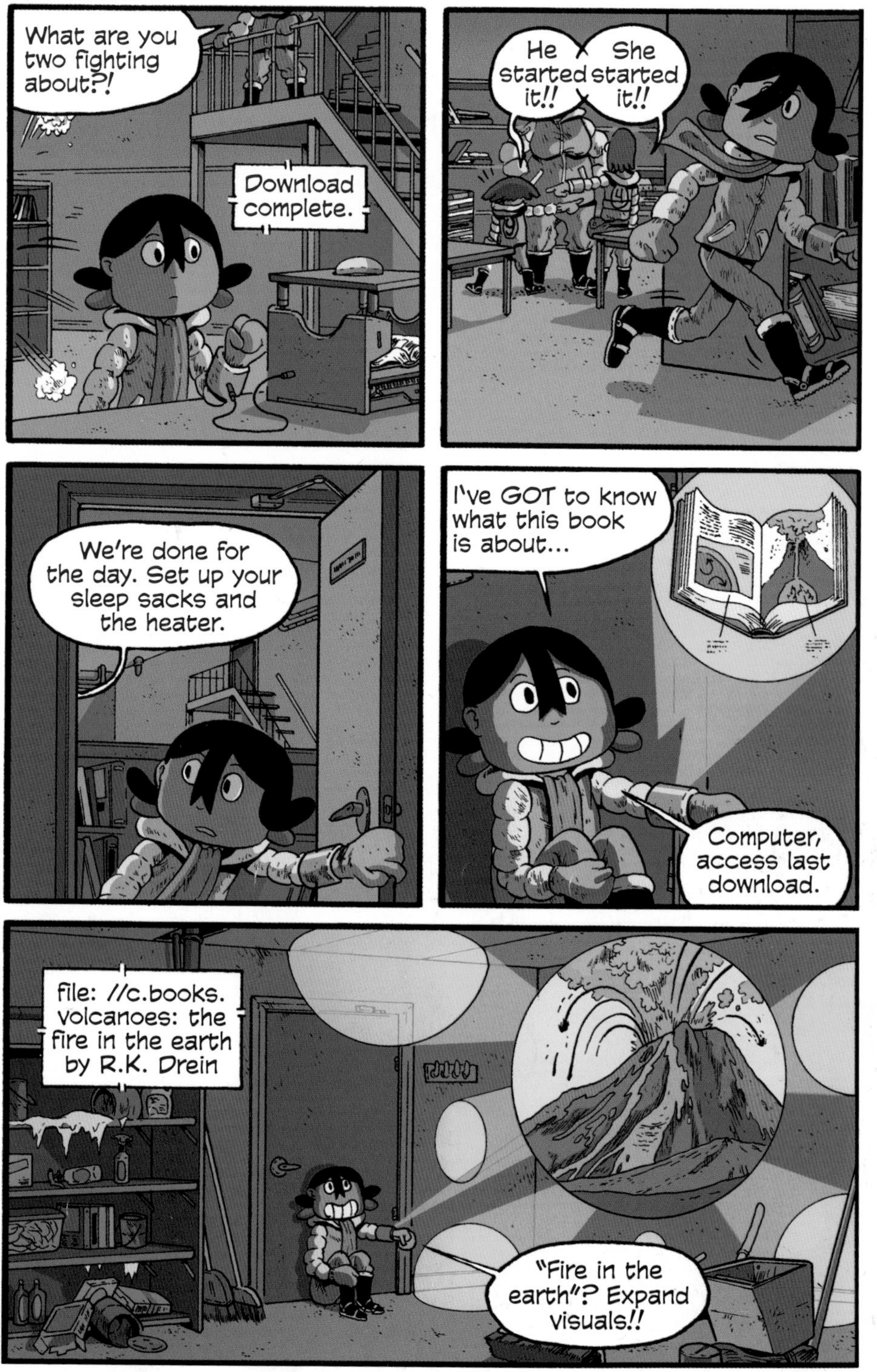
What are you two fighting about?!
Download complete.
He started it!!
She started it!!
We're done for the day. Set up your sleep sacks and the heater.
I've GOT to know what this book is about...
Computer, access last download.
file: //c.books. volcanoes: the fire in the earth by R.K. Drein
"Fire in the earth"? Expand visuals!!

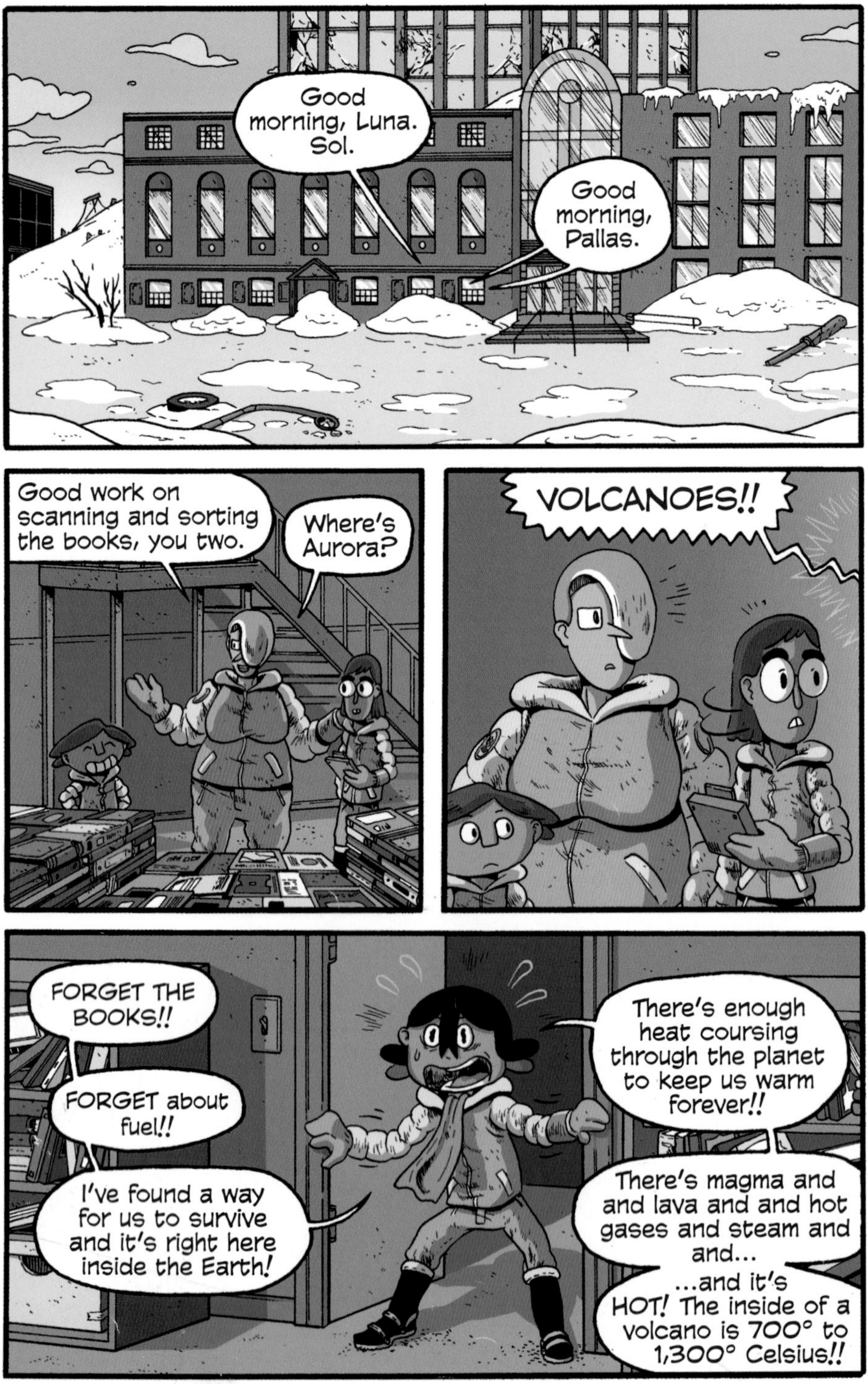
Good morning, Luna. Sol.
Good morning, Pallas.
Good work on scanning and sorting the books, you two.
Where's Aurora?
VOLCANOES!!
FORGET THE BOOKS!!
FORGET about fuel!!
I've found a way for us to survive and it's right here inside the Earth!
There's enough heat coursing through the planet to keep us warm forever!!
There's magma and and lava and and hot gases and steam and and...
...and it's HOT! The inside of a volcano is 700° to 1,300° Celsius!!

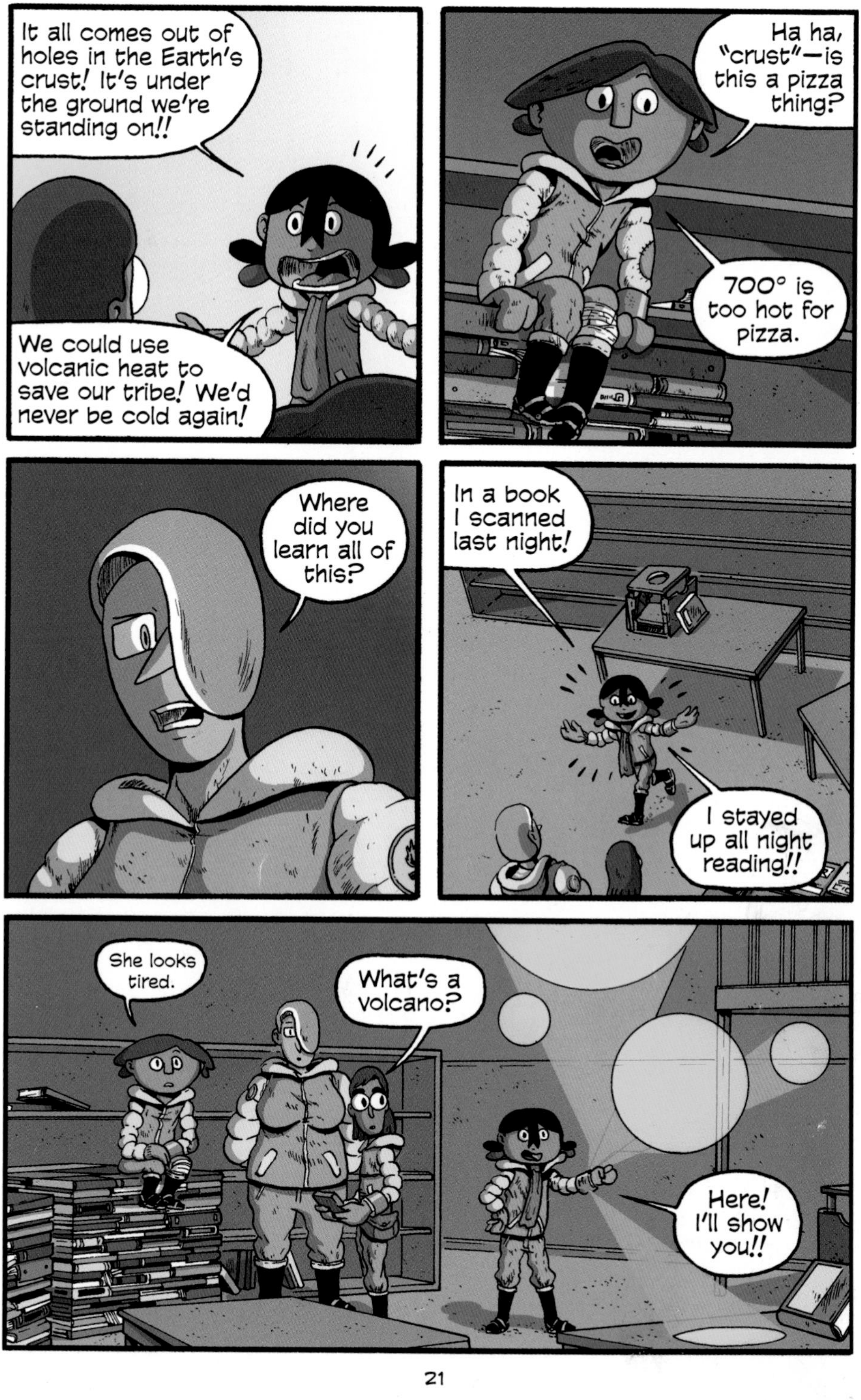
It all comes out of holes in the Earth's crust! It's under the ground we're standing on!!
We could use volcanic heat to save our tribe! We'd never be cold again!
Ha ha, "crust"—is this a pizza thing?
700° is too hot for pizza.
Where did you learn all of this?
In a book I scanned last night!
I stayed up all night reading!!
She looks tired.
What's a volcano?
Here! I'll show you!!

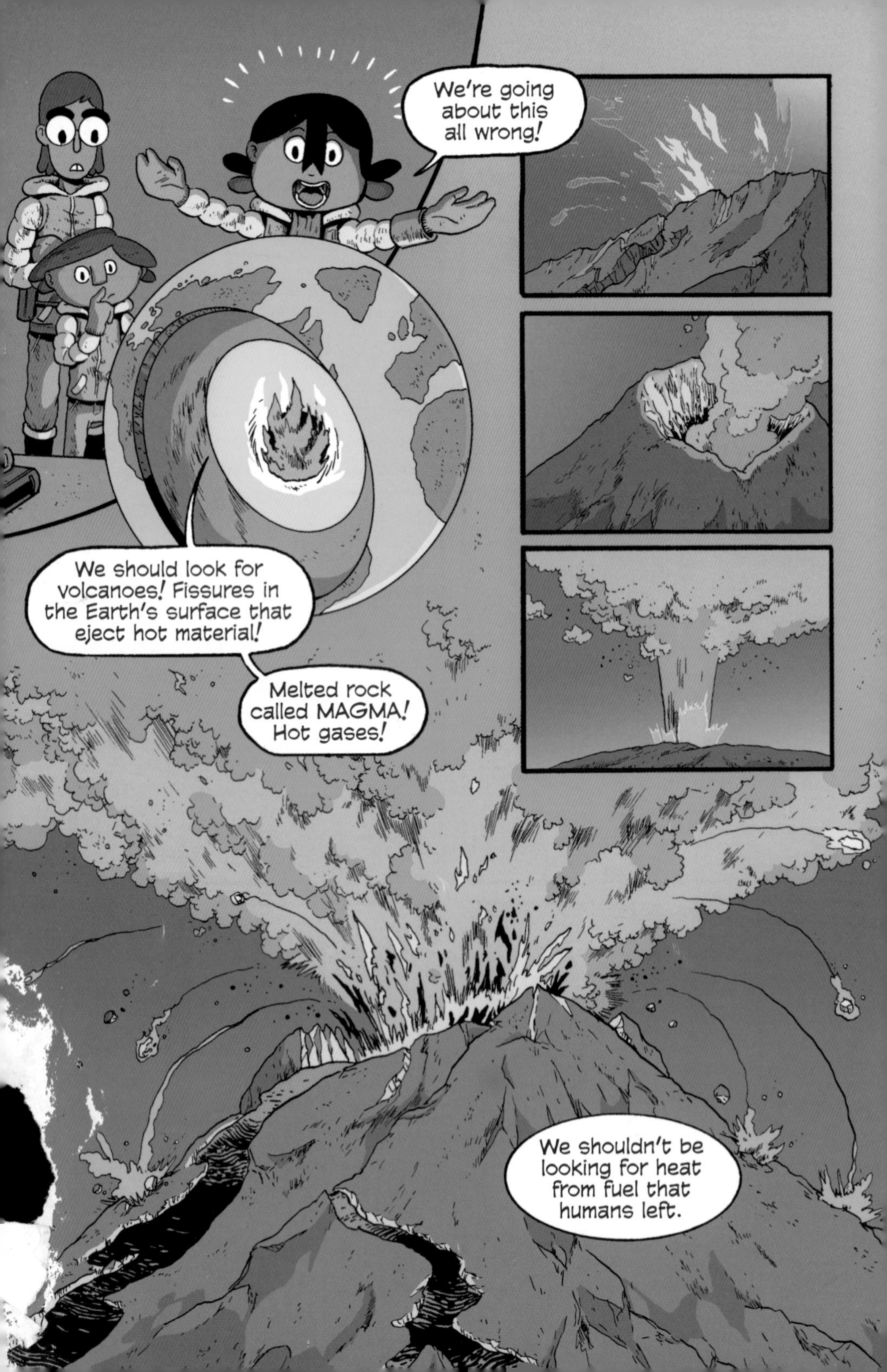
We're going about this all wrong!
We should look for volcanoes! Fissures in the Earth's surface that eject hot material!
Melted rock called MAGMA! Hot gases!
We shouldn't be looking for heat from fuel that humans left.

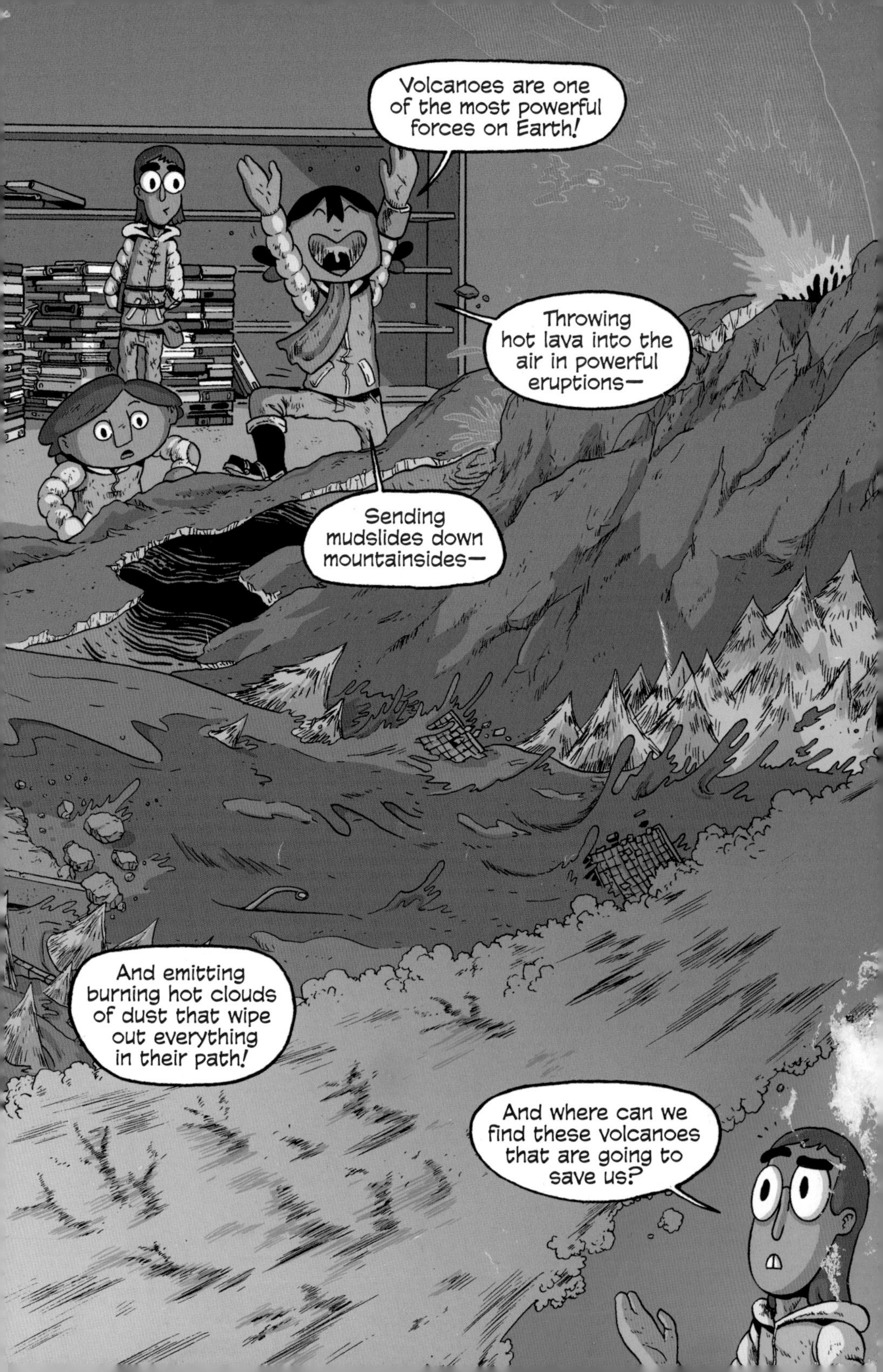
Volcanoes are one of the most powerful forces on Earth!
Throwing hot lava into the air in powerful eruptions—
Sending mudslides down mountainsides—
And emitting burning hot clouds of dust that wipe out everything in their path!
And where can we find these volcanoes that are going to save us?

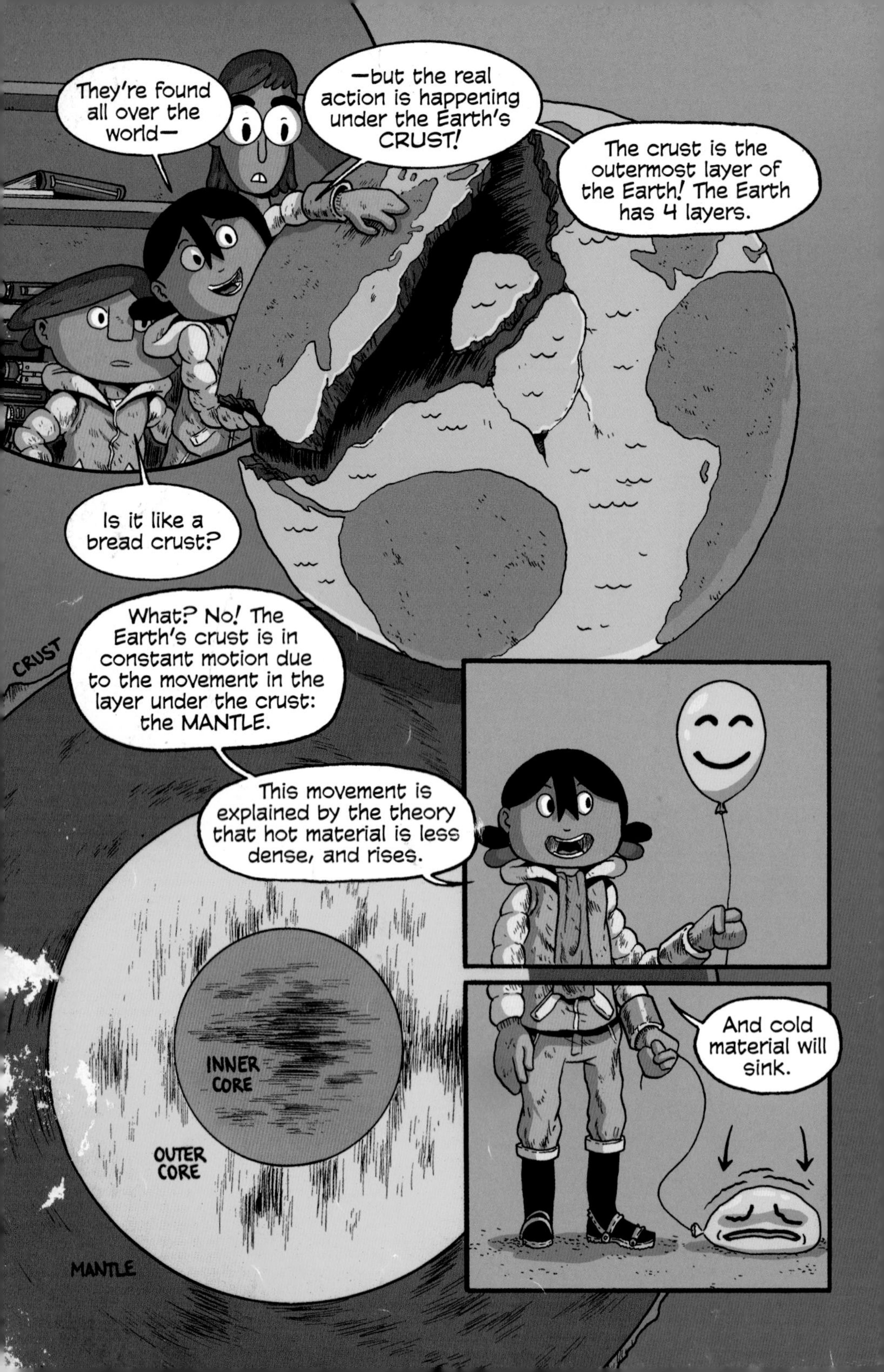
They're found all over the world—
—but the real action is happening under the Earth's CRUST!
The crust is the outermost layer of the Earth! The Earth has 4 layers.
Is it like a bread crust?
What? No! The Earth's crust is in constant motion due to the movement in the layer under the crust: the MANTLE.
CRUST
This movement is explained by the theory that hot material is less dense, and rises.
INNER CORE
OUTER CORE
MANTLE
And cold material will sink.

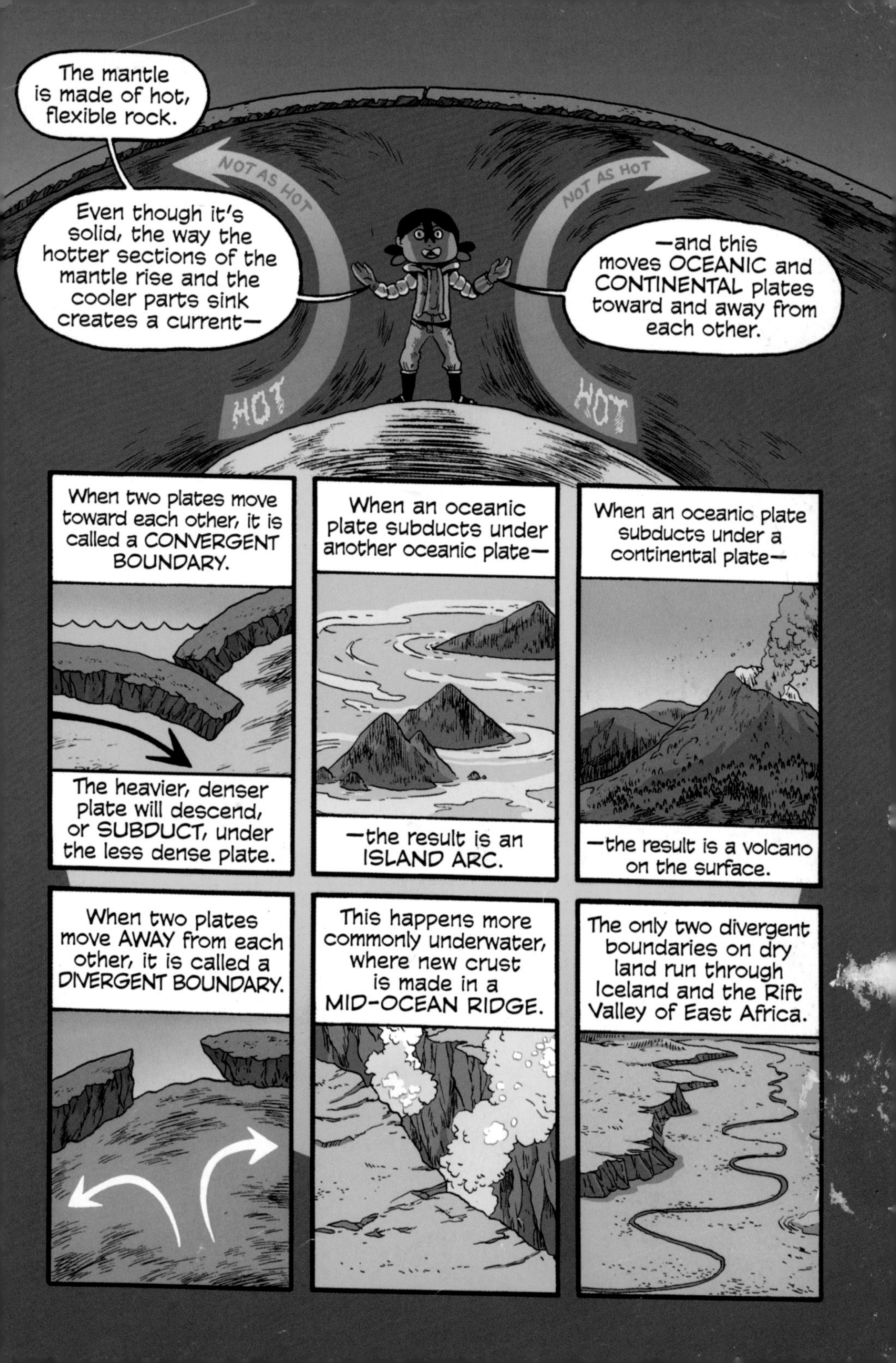
The mantle is made of hot, flexible rock.
NOT AS HOT
NOT AS HOT
Even though it's solid, the way the hotter sections of the mantle rise and the cooler parts sink creates a current—
—and this moves OCEANIC and CONTINENTAL plates toward and away from each other.
HOT
HOT
When two plates move toward each other, it is called a CONVERGENT BOUNDARY.
The heavier, denser plate will descend, or SUBDUCT, under the less dense plate.
When an oceanic plate subducts under another oceanic plate—
—the result is an ISLAND ARC.
When an oceanic plate subducts under a continental plate—
—the result is a volcano on the surface.
When two plates move AWAY from each other, it is called a DIVERGENT BOUNDARY.
This happens more commonly underwater, where new crust is made in a MID-OCEAN RIDGE.
The only two divergent boundaries on dry land run through Iceland and the Rift Valley of East Africa.

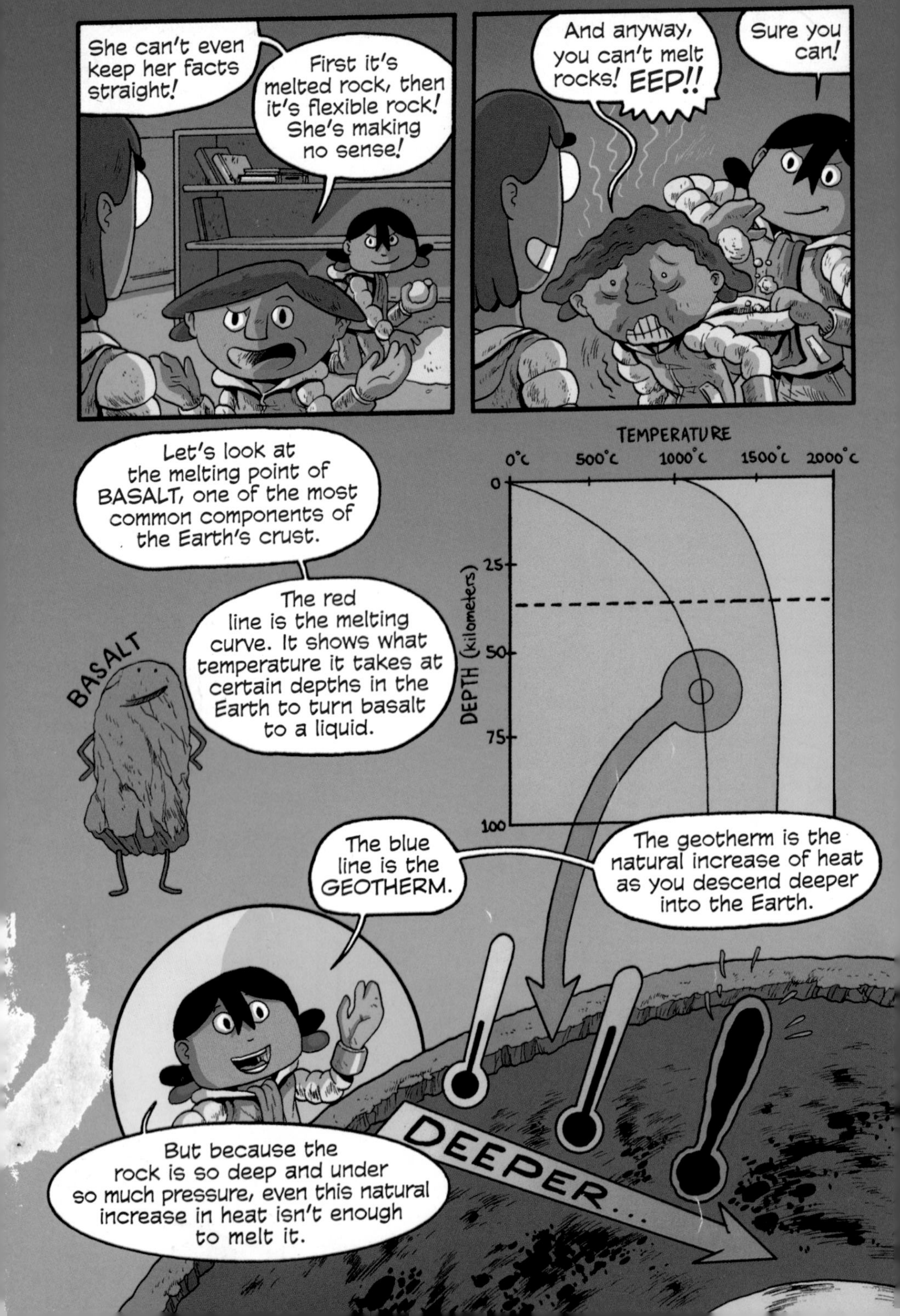

She can't even keep her facts straight!
First it's melted rock, then it's flexible rock! She's making no sense!
And anyway, you can't melt rocks! EEP!!
Sure you can!
Let's look at the melting point of BASALT, one of the most common components of the Earth's crust.
TEMPERATURE
0°C
500°C
1000°C
1500°C
2000°C
DEPTH (kilometers)
0
25
50
75
100
BASALT
The red line is the melting curve. It shows what temperature it takes at certain depths in the Earth to turn basalt to a liquid.
The blue line is the GEOTHERM.
The geotherm is the natural increase of heat as you descend deeper into the Earth.
DEEPER...
But because the rock is so deep and under so much pressure, even this natural increase in heat isn't enough to melt it.

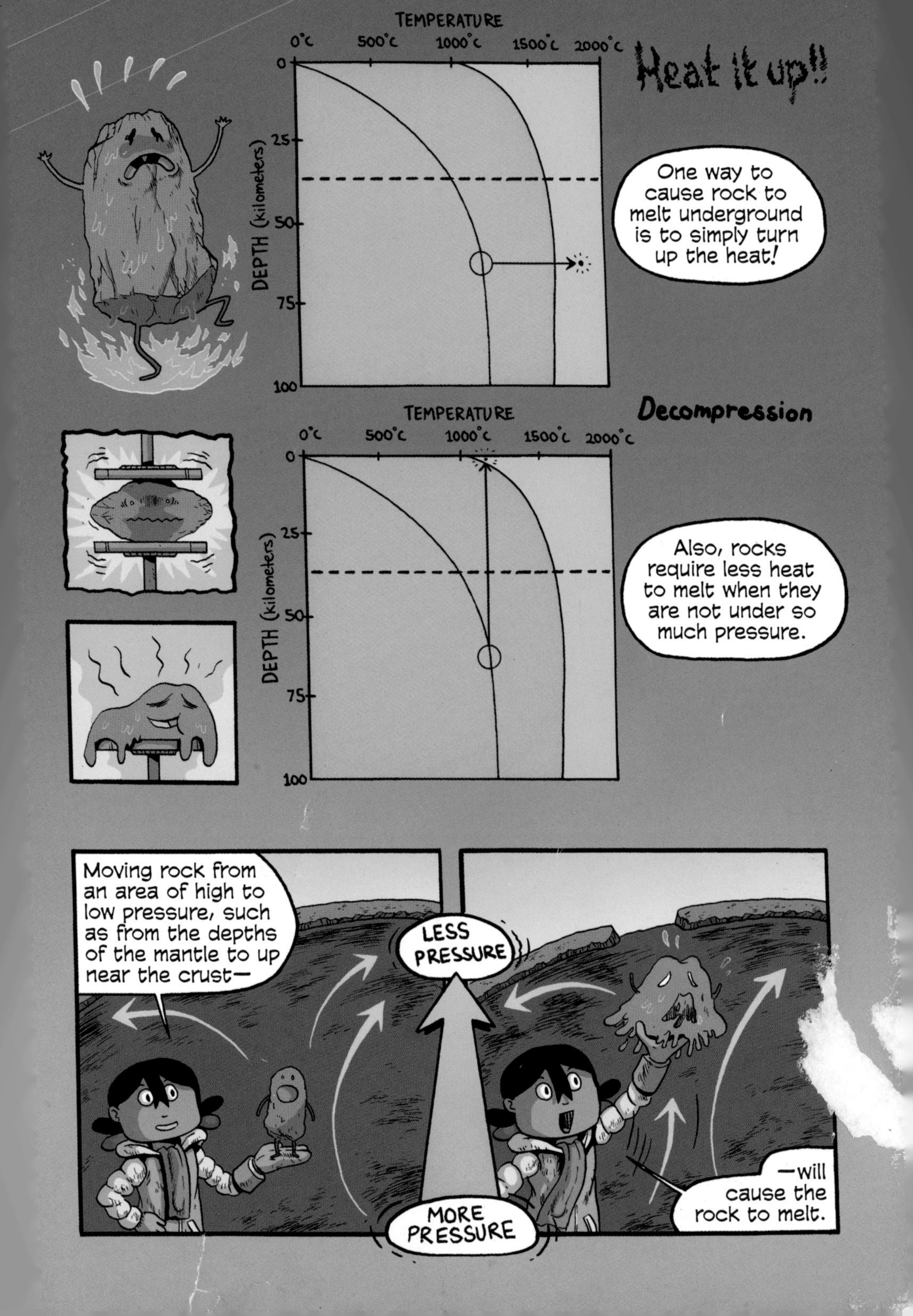

Heat it up!!
TEMPERATURE
0°C 500°C 1000°C 1500°C 2000°C
DEPTH (kilometers)
0 25 50 75 100
One way to cause rock to melt underground is to simply turn up the heat!
Decompression
TEMPERATURE
0°C 500°C 1000°C 1500°C 2000°C
DEPTH (kilometers)
0 25 50 75 100
Also, rocks require less heat to melt when they are not under so much pressure.
Moving rock from an area of high to low pressure, such as from the depths of the mantle to up near the crust—
LESS PRESSURE
MORE PRESSURE
—will cause the rock to melt.

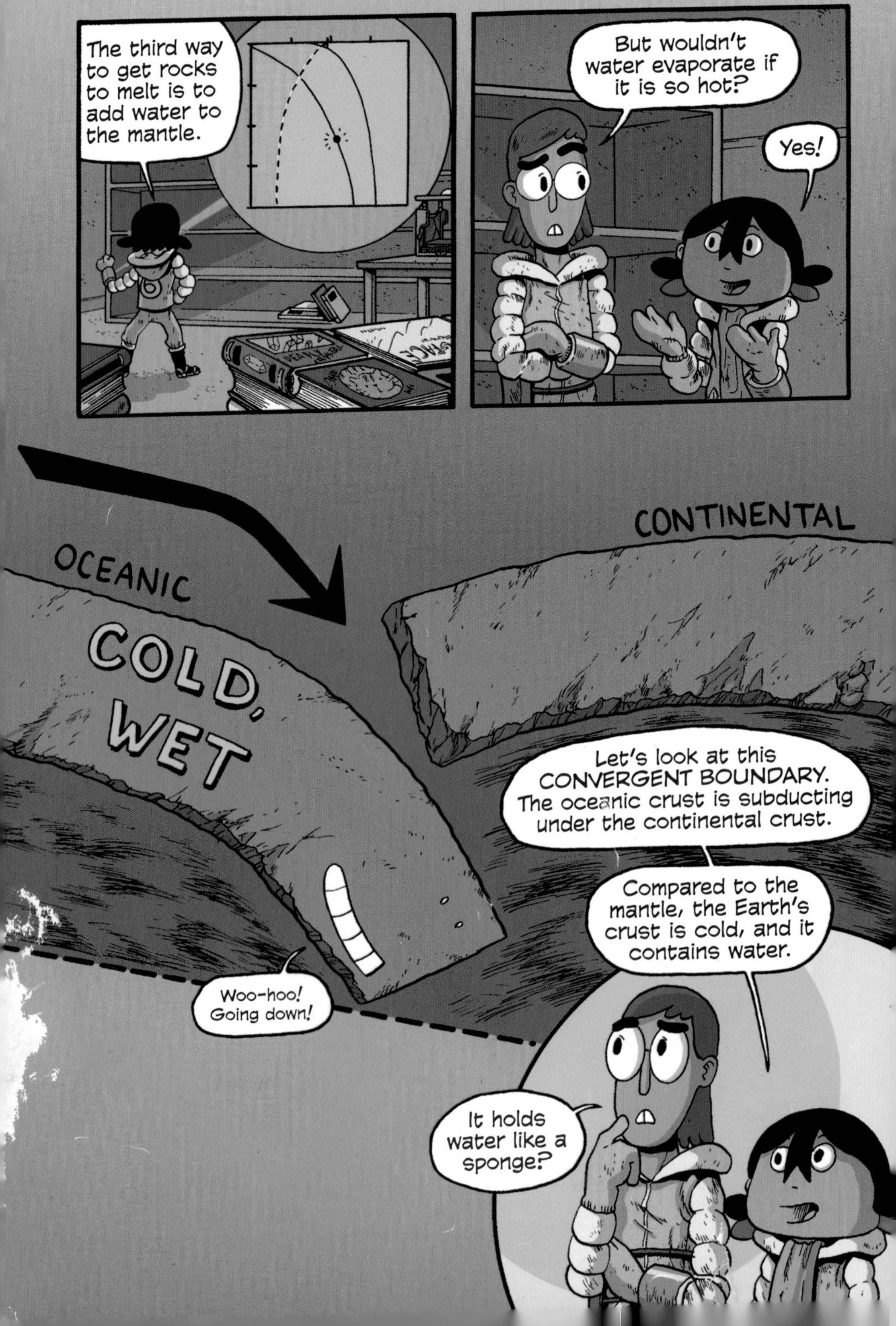
The third way to get rocks to melt is to add water to the mantle.
But wouldn't water evaporate if it is so hot?
Yes!
OCEANIC
CONTINENTAL
COLD, WET
Let's look at this CONVERGENT BOUNDARY. The oceanic crust is subducting under the continental crust.
Compared to the mantle, the Earth's crust is cold, and it contains water.
Woo-hoo! Going down!
It holds water like a sponge?

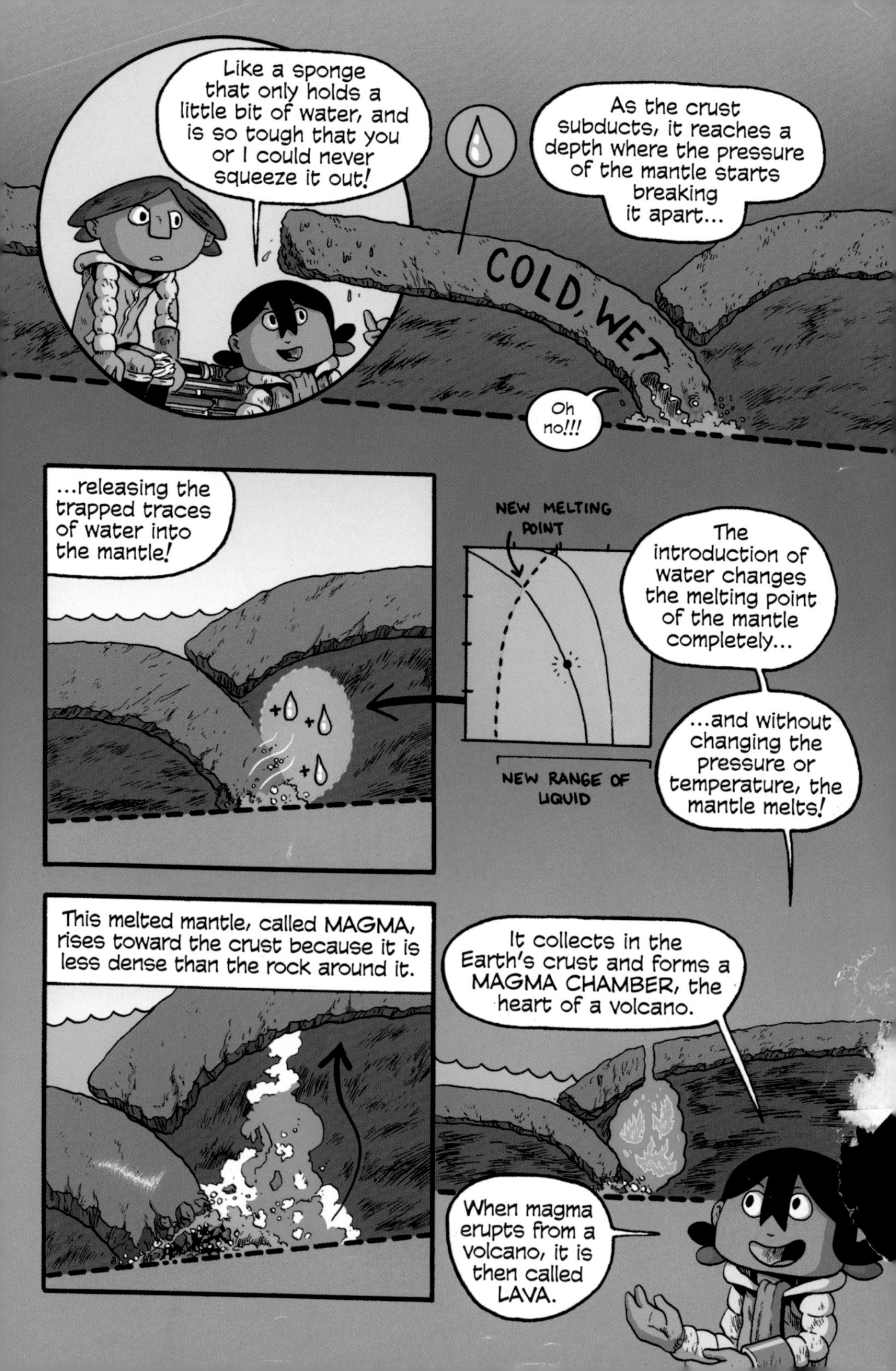
Like a sponge that only holds a little bit of water, and is so tough that you or I could never squeeze it out!
As the crust subducts, it reaches a depth where the pressure of the mantle starts breaking it apart...
COLD, WET
Oh no!!!
...releasing the trapped traces of water into the mantle!
NEW MELTING POINT
NEW RANGE OF LIQUID
The introduction of water changes the melting point of the mantle completely...
...and without changing the pressure or temperature, the mantle melts!
This melted mantle, called MAGMA, rises toward the crust because it is less dense than the rock around it.
It collects in the Earth's crust and forms a MAGMA CHAMBER, the heart of a volcano.
When magma erupts from a volcano, it is then called LAVA.

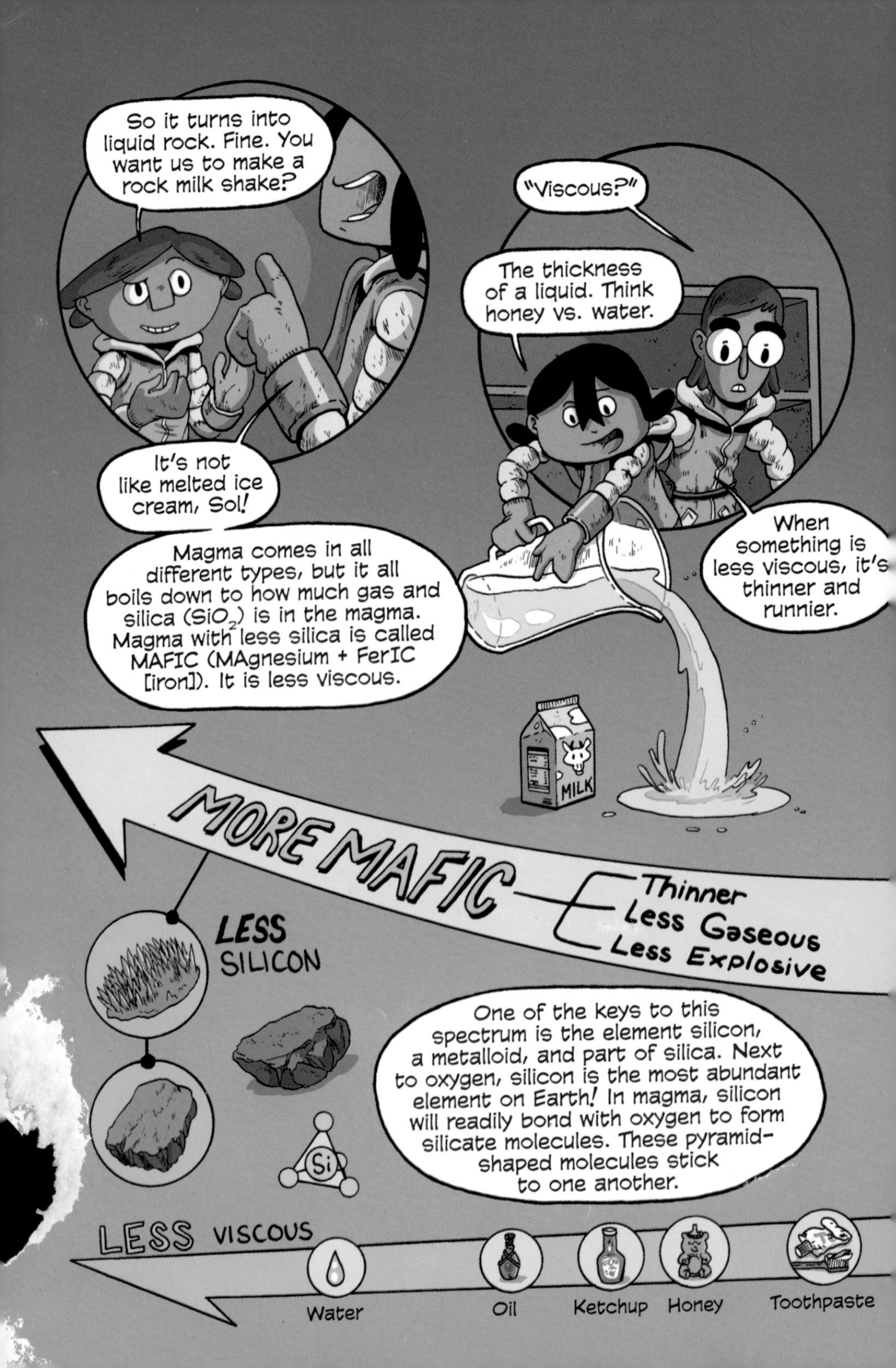

So it turns into liquid rock. Fine. You want us to make a rock milk shake?
It's not like melted ice cream, Sol!
"Viscous?"
The thickness of a liquid. Think honey vs. water.
Magma comes in all different types, but it all boils down to how much gas and silica (SiO_2) is in the magma. Magma with less silica is called MAFIC (MAgnesium + FerIC [iron]). It is less viscous.
When something is less viscous, it's thinner and runnier.
MILK
MORE MAFIC
Thinner
Less Gaseous
Less Explosive
LESS SILICON
Si
One of the keys to this spectrum is the element silicon, a metalloid, and part of silica. Next to oxygen, silicon is the most abundant element on Earth! In magma, silicon will readily bond with oxygen to form silicate molecules. These pyramid-shaped molecules stick to one another.
LESS VISCOUS
Water
Oil
Ketchup
Honey
Toothpaste

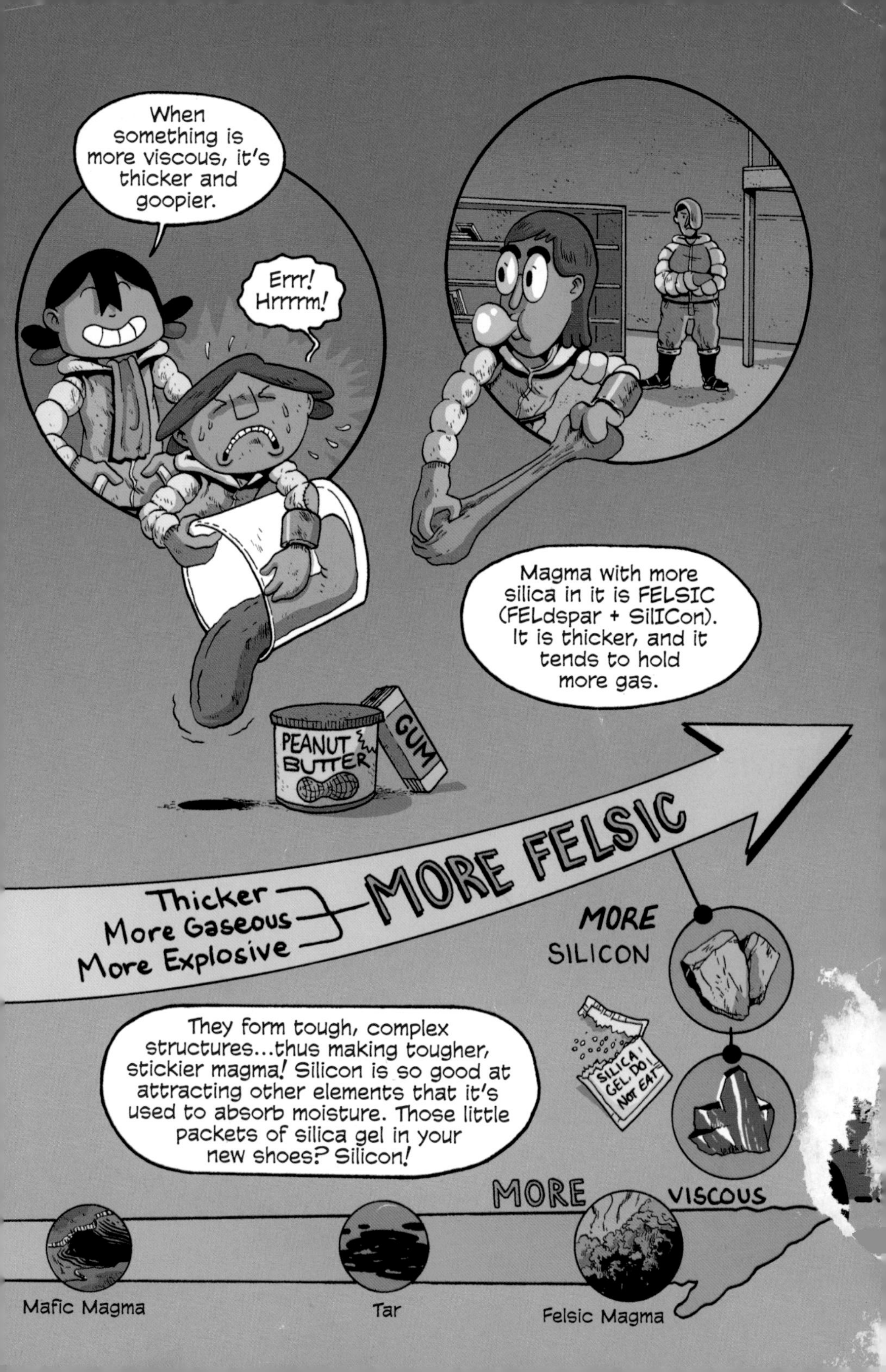

When something is more viscous, it's thicker and goopier.
Errr! Hrrrrm!
Magma with more silica in it is FELSIC (FELdspar + SilICon). It is thicker, and it tends to hold more gas.
PEANUT BUTTER
GUM
MORE FELSIC
Thicker
More Gaseous
More Explosive
MORE SILICON
They form tough, complex structures...thus making tougher, stickier magma! Silicon is so good at attracting other elements that it's used to absorb moisture. Those little packets of silica gel in your new shoes? Silicon!
SILICA GEL, DO NOT EAT
MORE VISCOUS
Mafic Magma
Tar
Felsic Magma

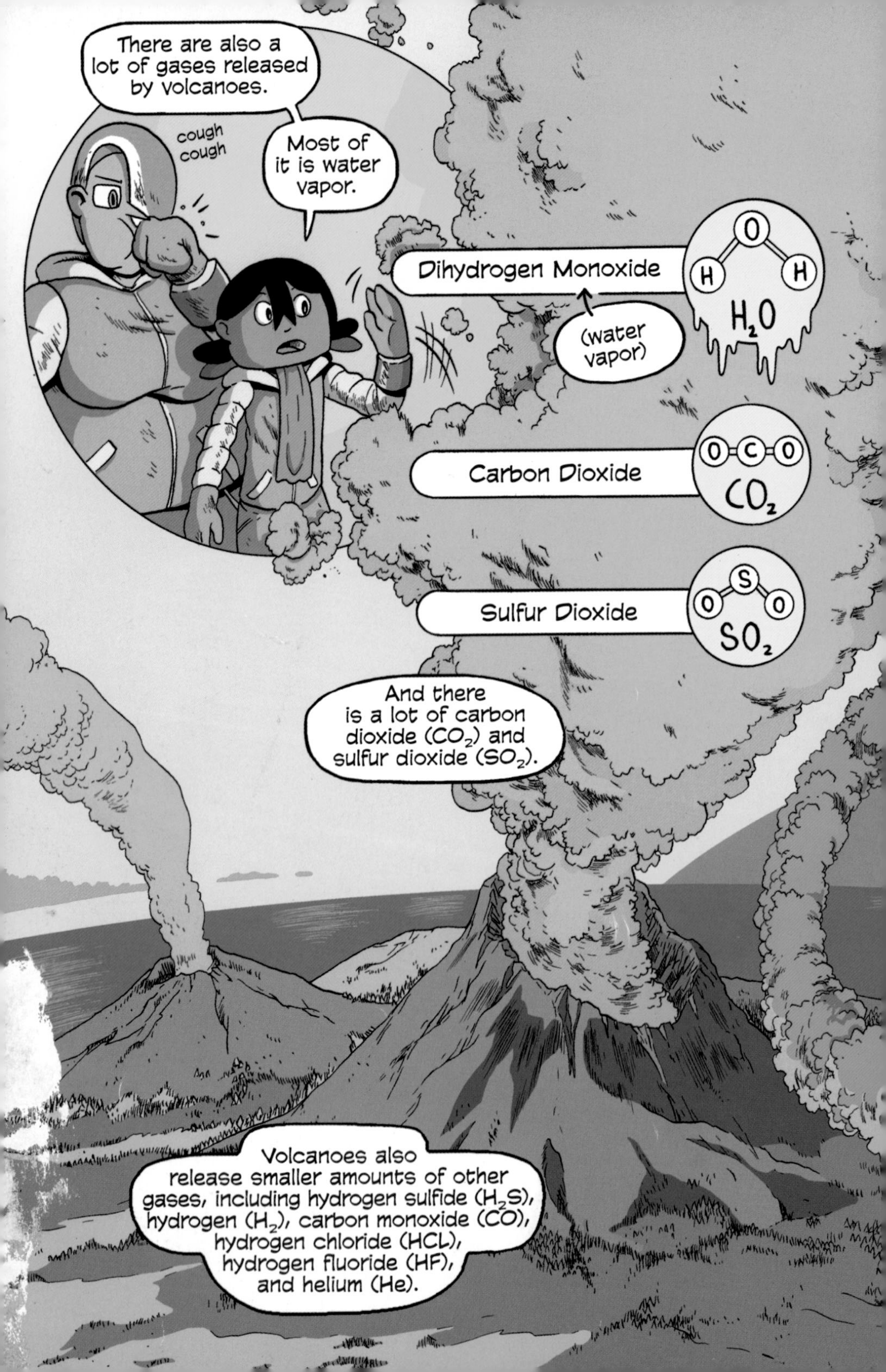
There are also a lot of gases released by volcanoes.
cough cough
Most of it is water vapor.
Dihydrogen Monoxide
(water vapor)
H_2O
Carbon Dioxide
CO_2
Sulfur Dioxide
SO_2
And there is a lot of carbon dioxide (CO_2) and sulfur dioxide (SO_2).
Volcanoes also release smaller amounts of other gases, including hydrogen sulfide (H_2S), hydrogen (H_2), carbon monoxide (CO), hydrogen chloride (HCL), hydrogen fluoride (HF), and helium (He).

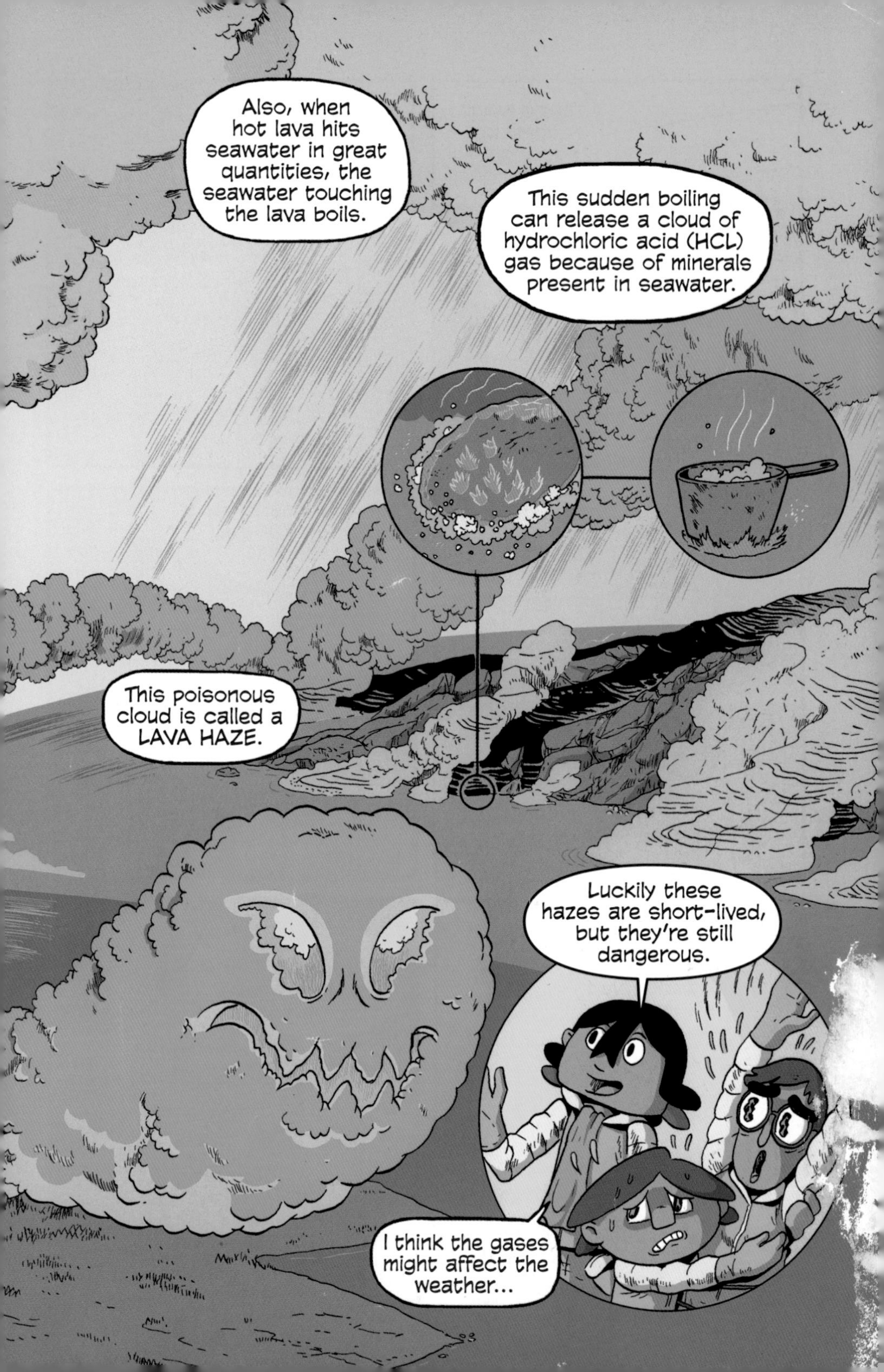
Also, when hot lava hits seawater in great quantities, the seawater touching the lava boils.
This sudden boiling can release a cloud of hydrochloric acid (HCL) gas because of minerals present in seawater.
This poisonous cloud is called a LAVA HAZE.
Luckily these hazes are short-lived, but they're still dangerous.
I think the gases might affect the weather...

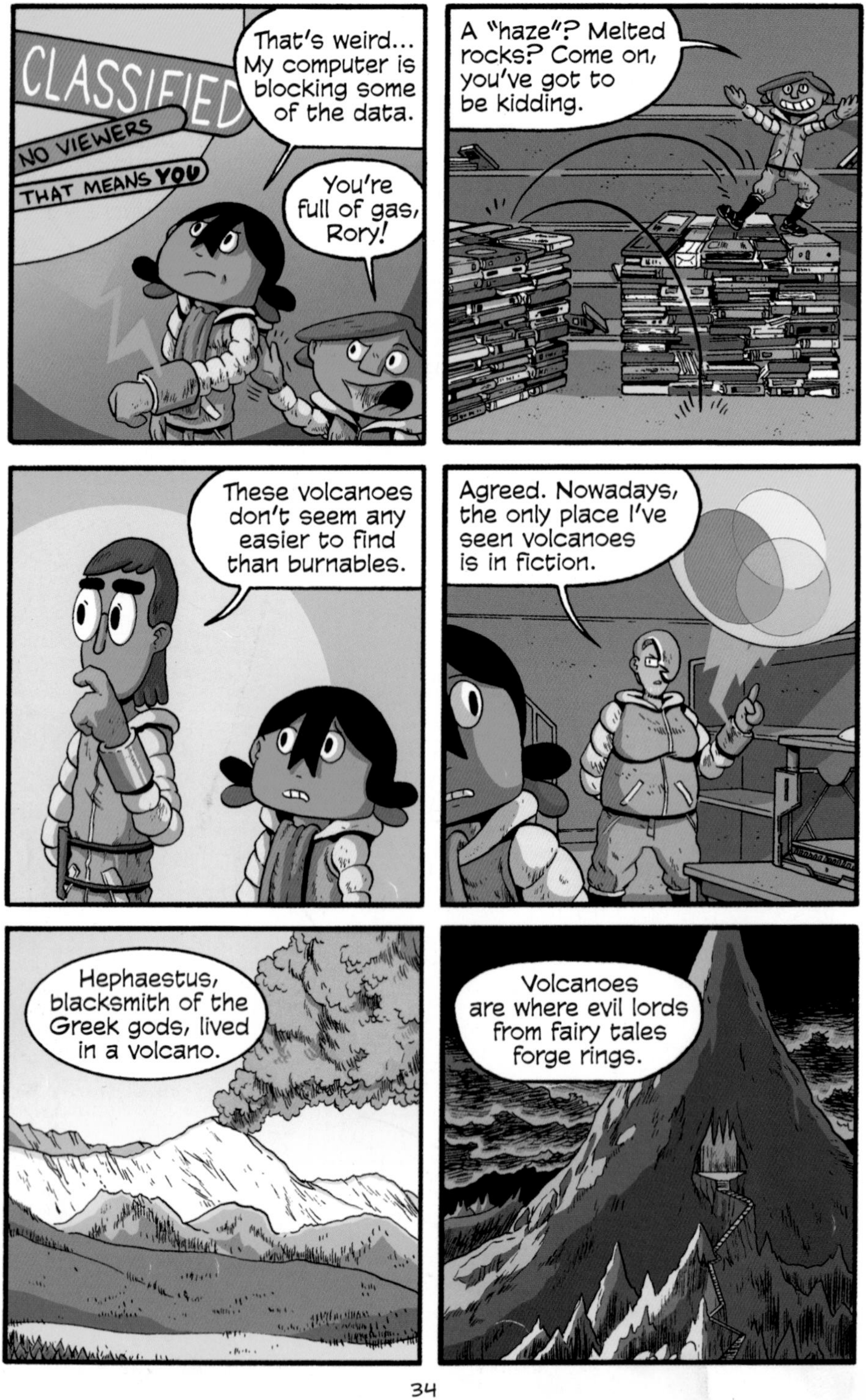
CLASSIFIED
NO VIEWERS
THAT MEANS YOU
That's weird... My computer is blocking some of the data.
You're full of gas, Rory!
A "haze"? Melted rocks? Come on, you've got to be kidding.
These volcanoes don't seem any easier to find than burnables.
Agreed. Nowadays, the only place I've seen volcanoes is in fiction.
Hephaestus, blacksmith of the Greek gods, lived in a volcano.
Volcanoes are where evil lords from fairy tales forge rings.

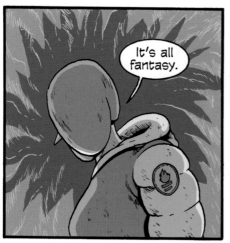

It's all fantasy.

Looking for volcanoes would be a waste of our time.

I find something that shows that the Earth might not be a frozen ball of mud...

...an alternative to scraping the bottom of the barrel of how humans used to live...

...and you say it's fantasy?

If there's anyone who's serious about wanting to find ways to stay warm—

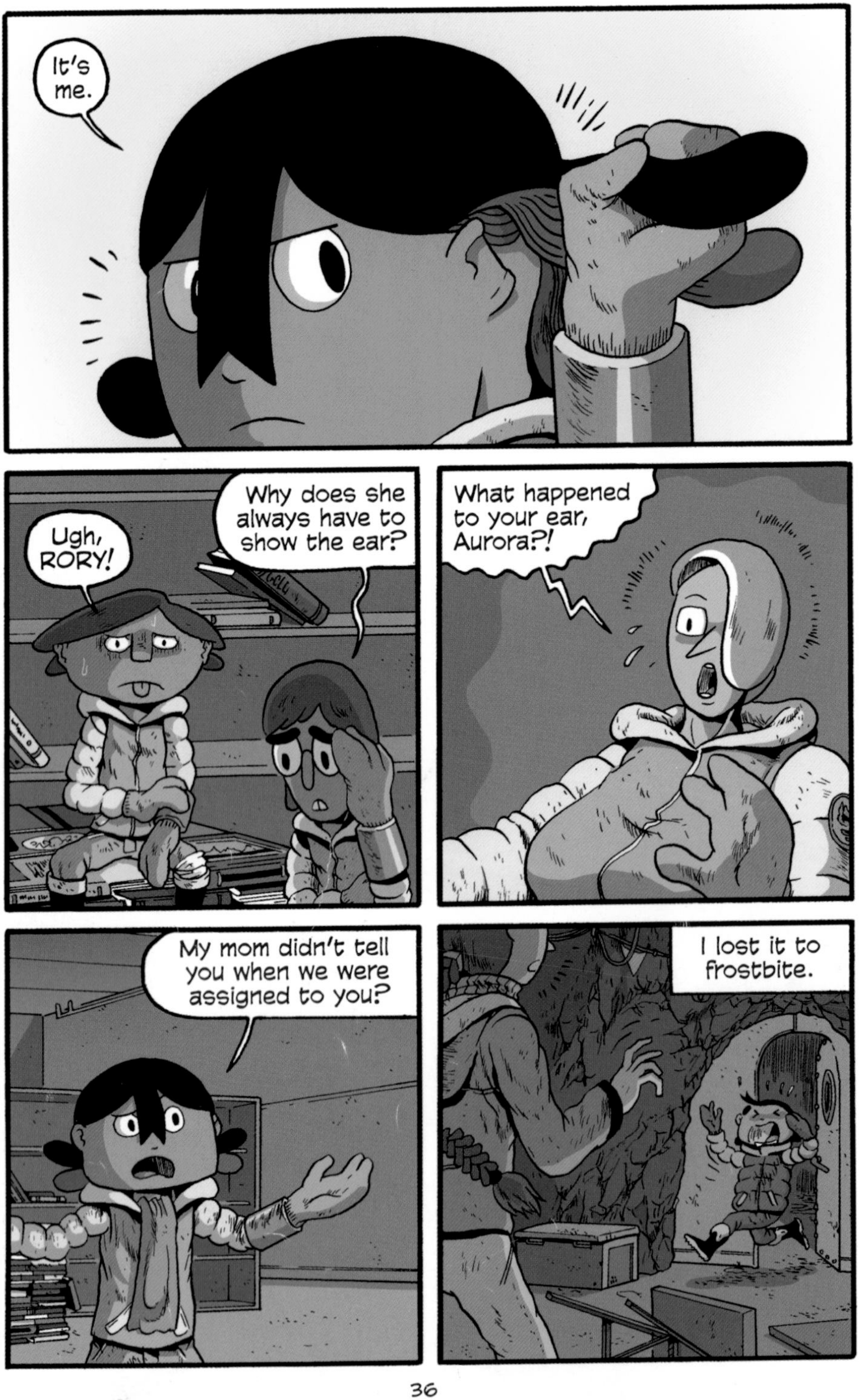
It's me.
Ugh, RORY!
Why does she always have to show the ear?
What happened to your ear, Aurora?!
My mom didn't tell you when we were assigned to you?
I lost it to frostbite.

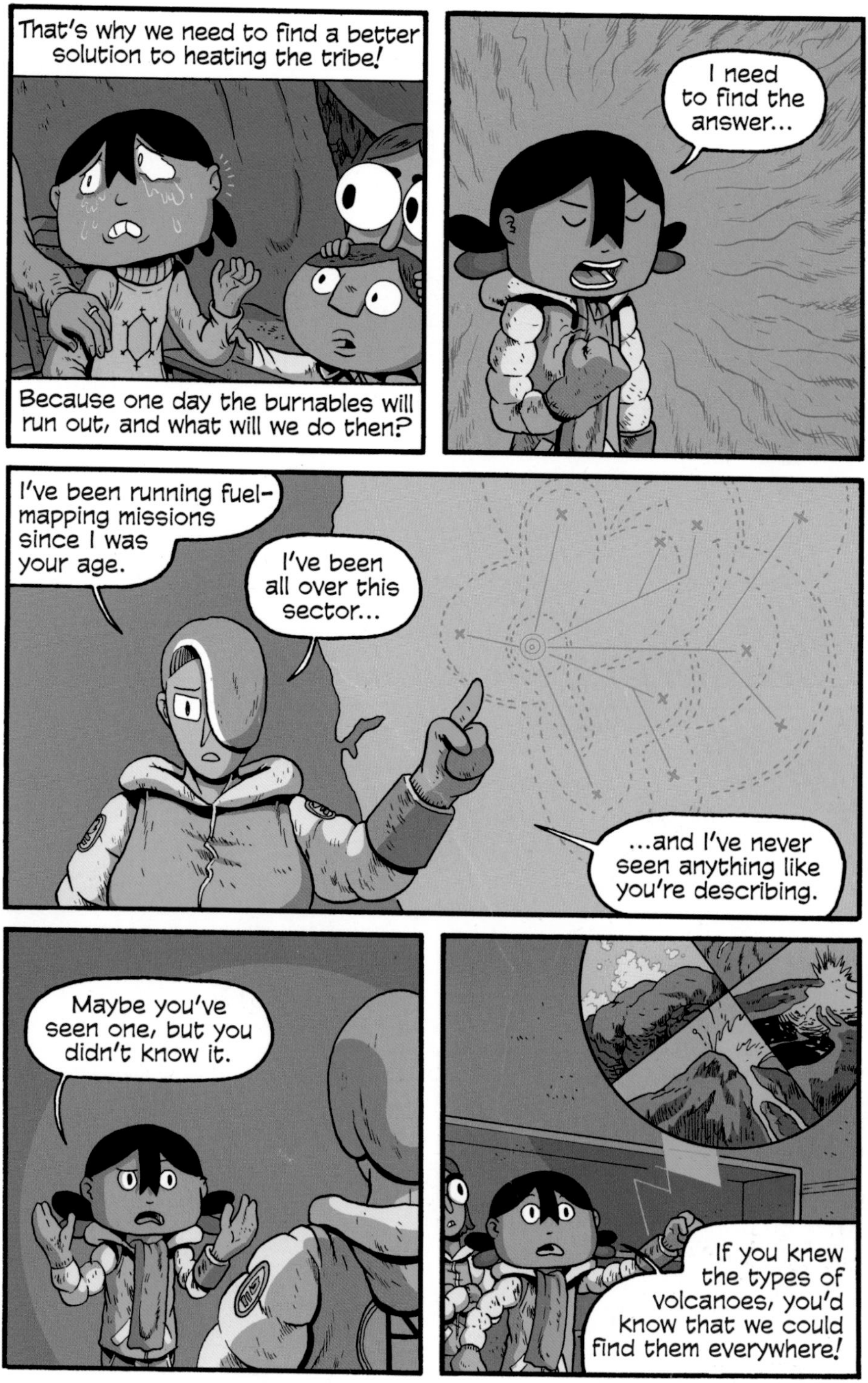
That's why we need to find a better solution to heating the tribe!
Because one day the burnables will run out, and what will we do then?
I need to find the answer...
I've been running fuel-mapping missions since I was your age.
I've been all over this sector...
...and I've never seen anything like you're describing.
Maybe you've seen one, but you didn't know it.
If you knew the types of volcanoes, you'd know that we could find them everywhere!

Volcanoes at divergent boundaries are the most common.

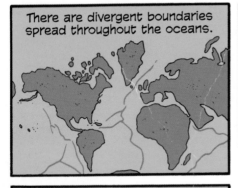

There are divergent boundaries spread throughout the oceans.

But only two on land.

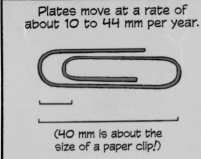

Plates move at a rate of about 10 to 44 mm per year.

(40 mm is about the size of a paper clip!)

As the plates spread, new crust is made.

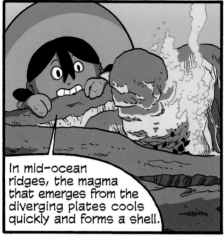

In mid-ocean ridges, the magma that emerges from the diverging plates cools quickly and forms a shell.

But then it will suddenly appear to grow! Weird!

Even though it looks like it's cooled and hardened, that's only on the outside.

Hot magma is still pushing up, trying to get out.

Eventually the shell will crack and the magma flow will continue.

BREAK

This process repeats itself; the lava hardens on the outside, only to have the outer shell break, and the flow continue to grow.

BREAK   BREAK

Because of the soft, rounded appearance of these lava flows, they are often referred to as PILLOW LAVA.

I wouldn't want to sleep on them, though!

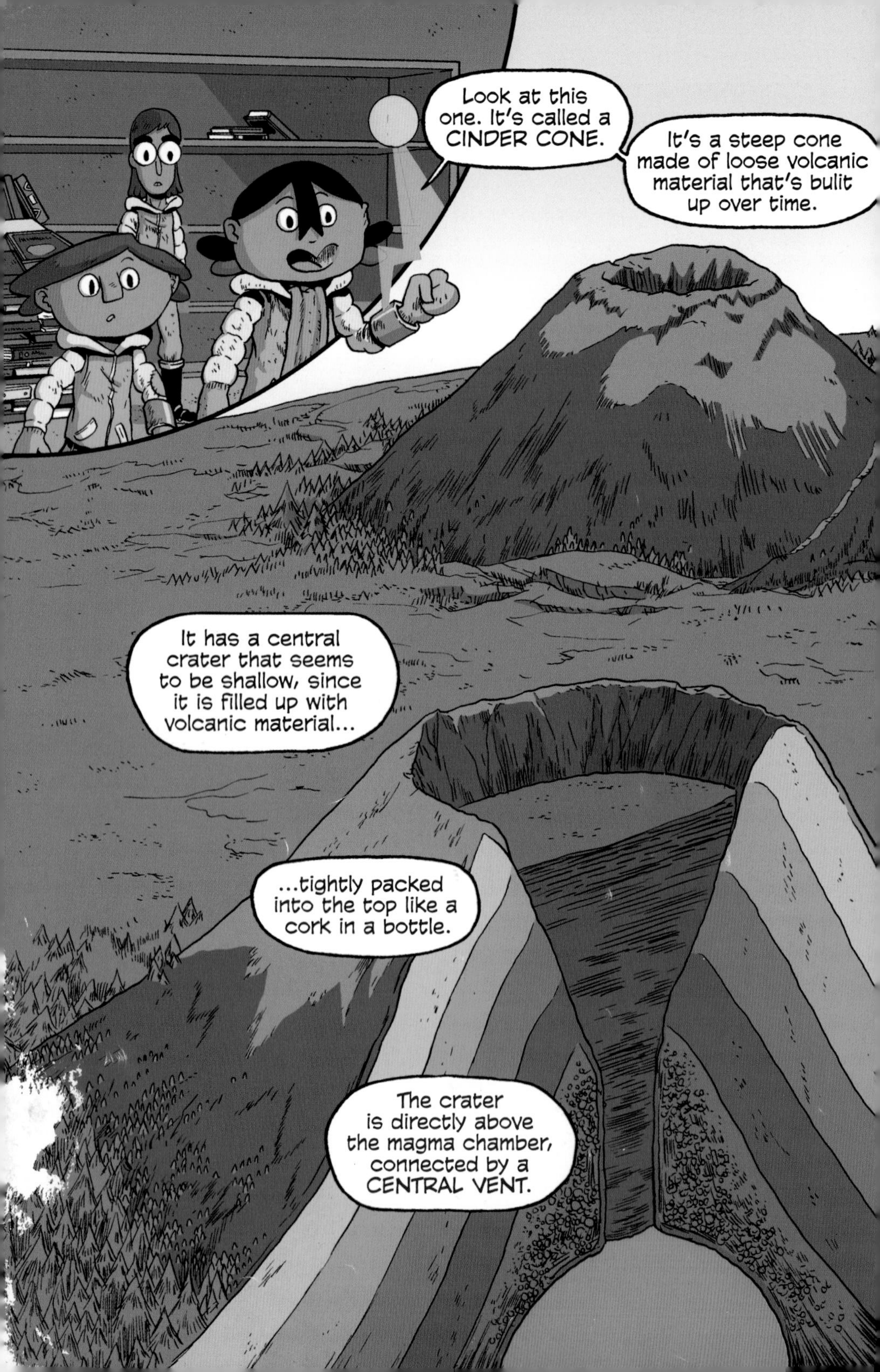
Look at this one. It's called a CINDER CONE.
It's a steep cone made of loose volcanic material that's bulit up over time.
It has a central crater that seems to be shallow, since it is filled up with volcanic material...
...tightly packed into the top like a cork in a bottle.
The crater is directly above the magma chamber, connected by a CENTRAL VENT.

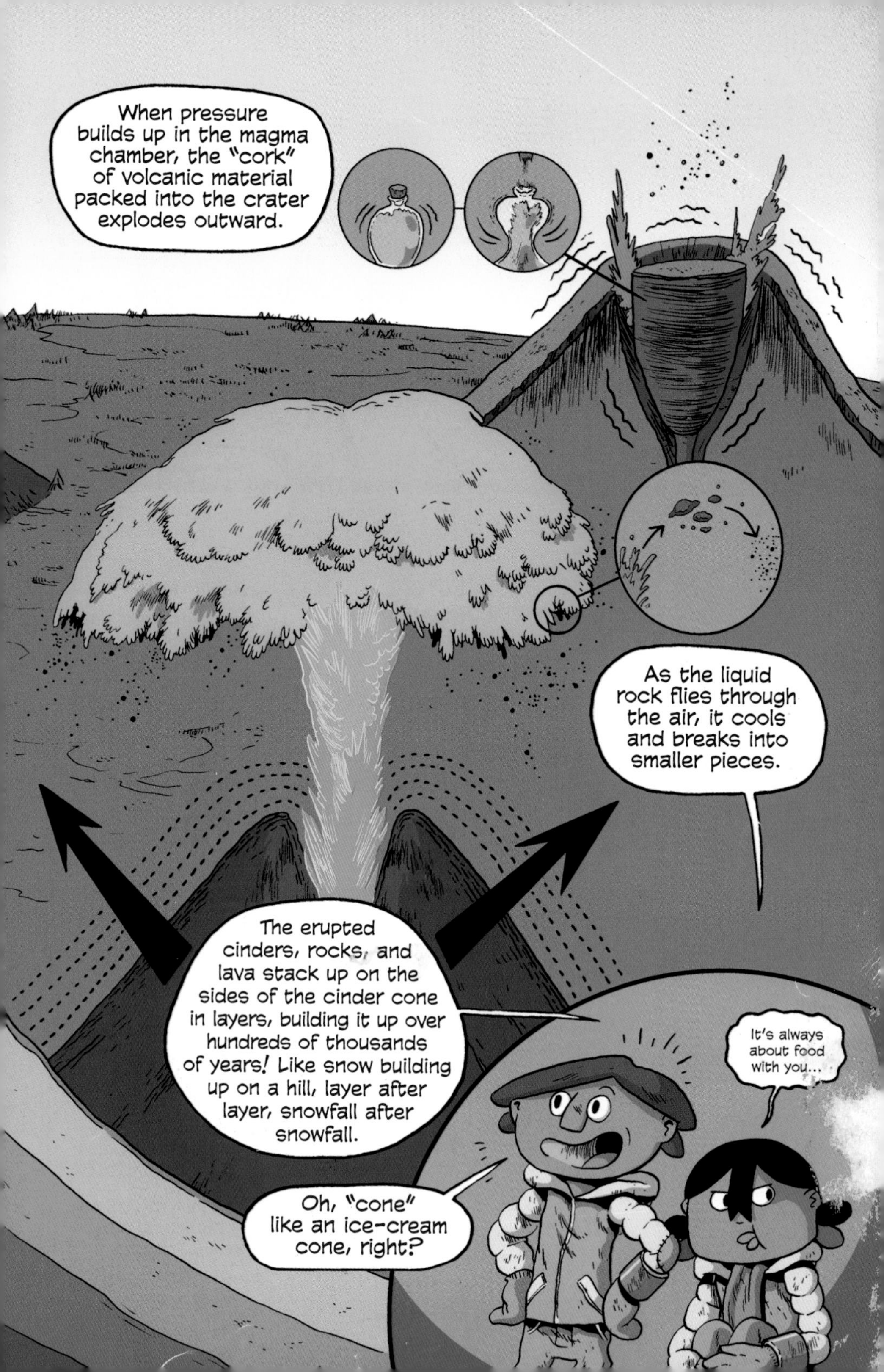
When pressure builds up in the magma chamber, the "cork" of volcanic material packed into the crater explodes outward.
As the liquid rock flies through the air, it cools and breaks into smaller pieces.
The erupted cinders, rocks, and lava stack up on the sides of the cinder cone in layers, building it up over hundreds of thousands of years! Like snow building up on a hill, layer after layer, snowfall after snowfall.
Oh, "cone" like an ice-cream cone, right?
It's always about food with you...

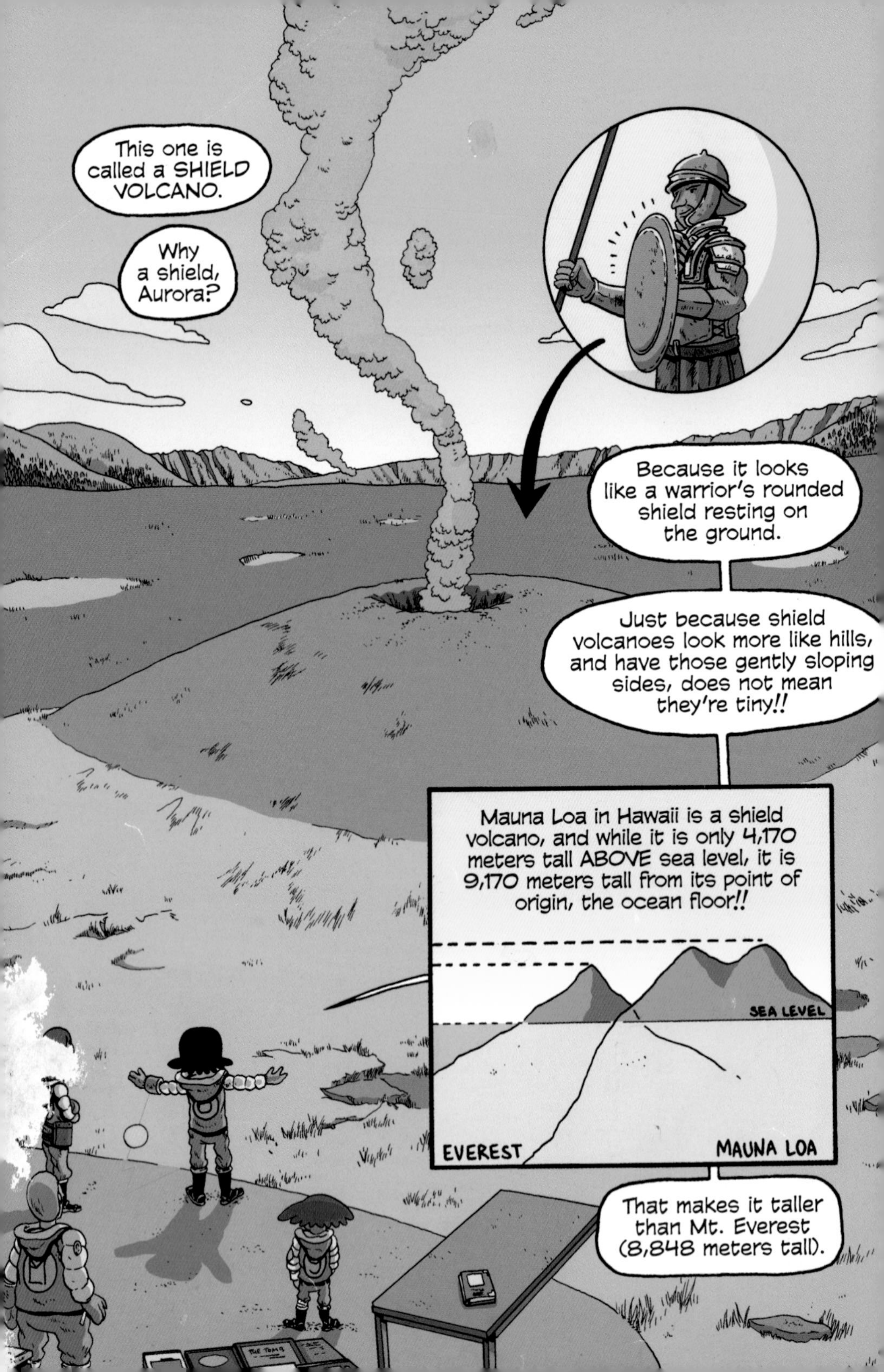
This one is called a SHIELD VOLCANO.
Why a shield, Aurora?
Because it looks like a warrior's rounded shield resting on the ground.
Just because shield volcanoes look more like hills, and have those gently sloping sides, does not mean they're tiny!!
Mauna Loa in Hawaii is a shield volcano, and while it is only 4,170 meters tall ABOVE sea level, it is 9,170 meters tall from its point of origin, the ocean floor!!
SEA LEVEL
EVEREST
MAUNA LOA
That makes it taller than Mt. Everest (8,848 meters tall).

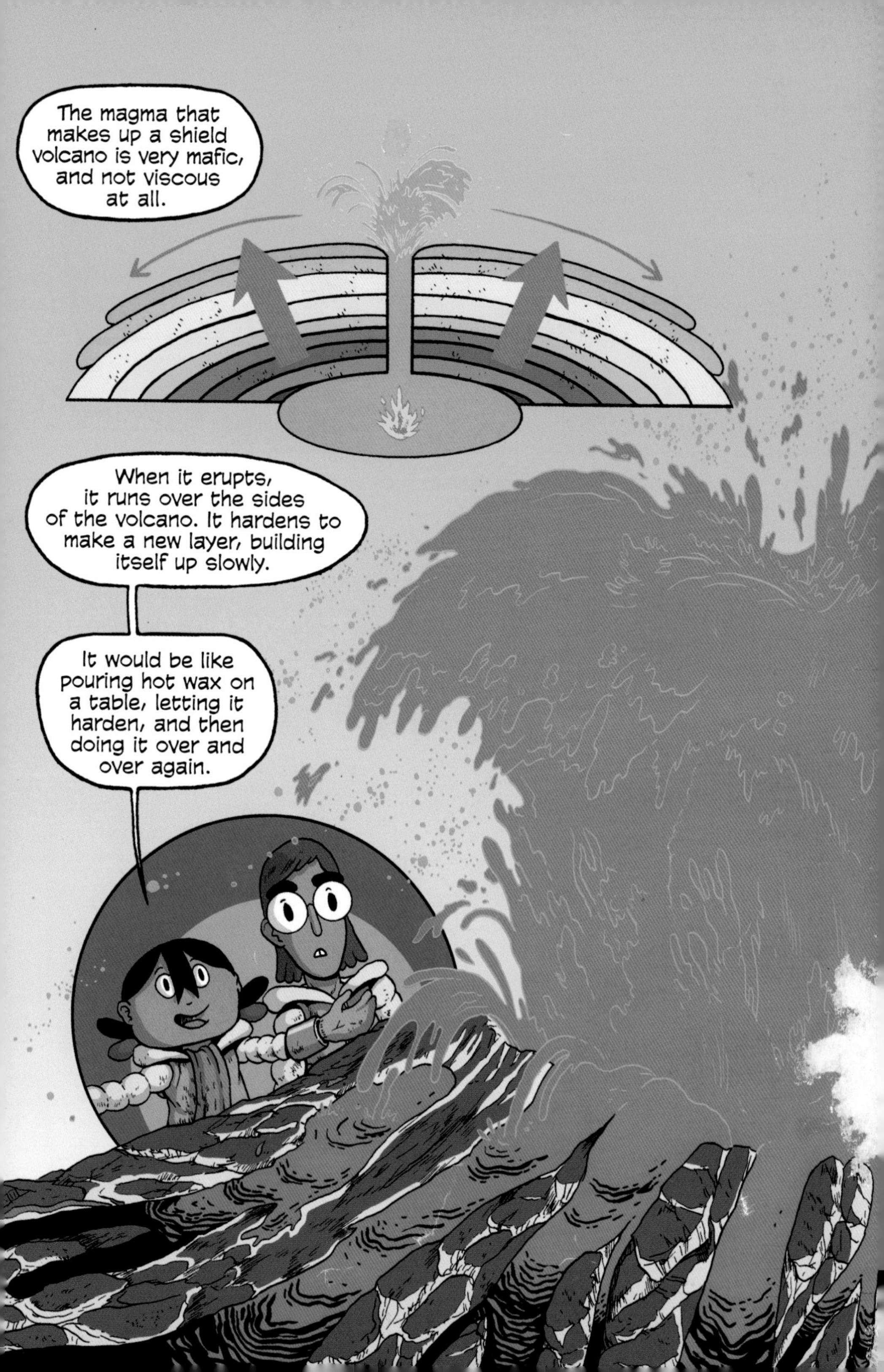
The magma that makes up a shield volcano is very mafic, and not viscous at all.
When it erupts, it runs over the sides of the volcano. It hardens to make a new layer, building itself up slowly.
It would be like pouring hot wax on a table, letting it harden, and then doing it over and over again.

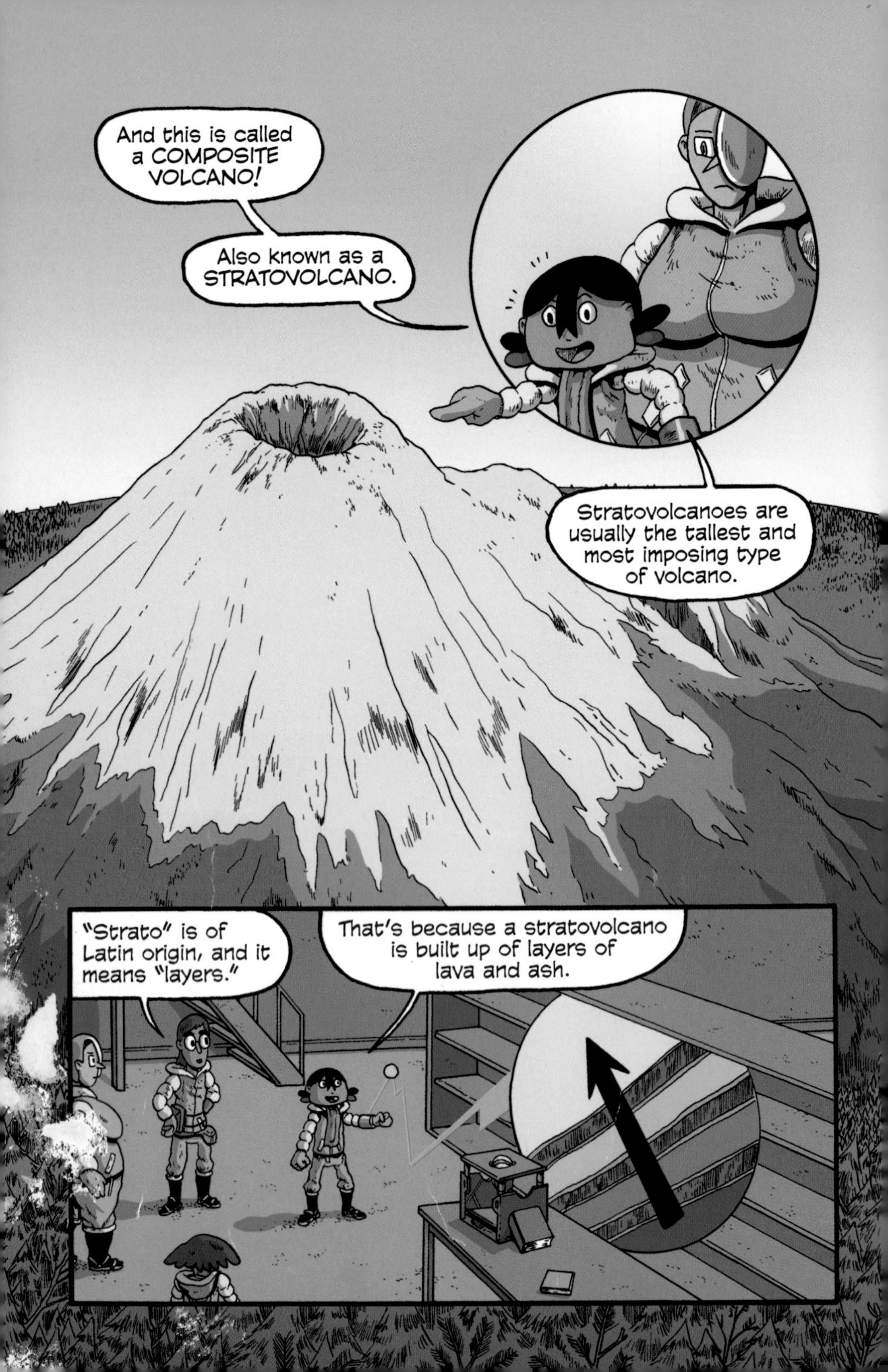

And this is called a COMPOSITE VOLCANO!
Also known as a STRATOVOLCANO.
Stratovolcanoes are usually the tallest and most imposing type of volcano.
"Strato" is of Latin origin, and it means "layers."
That's because a stratovolcano is built up of layers of lava and ash.

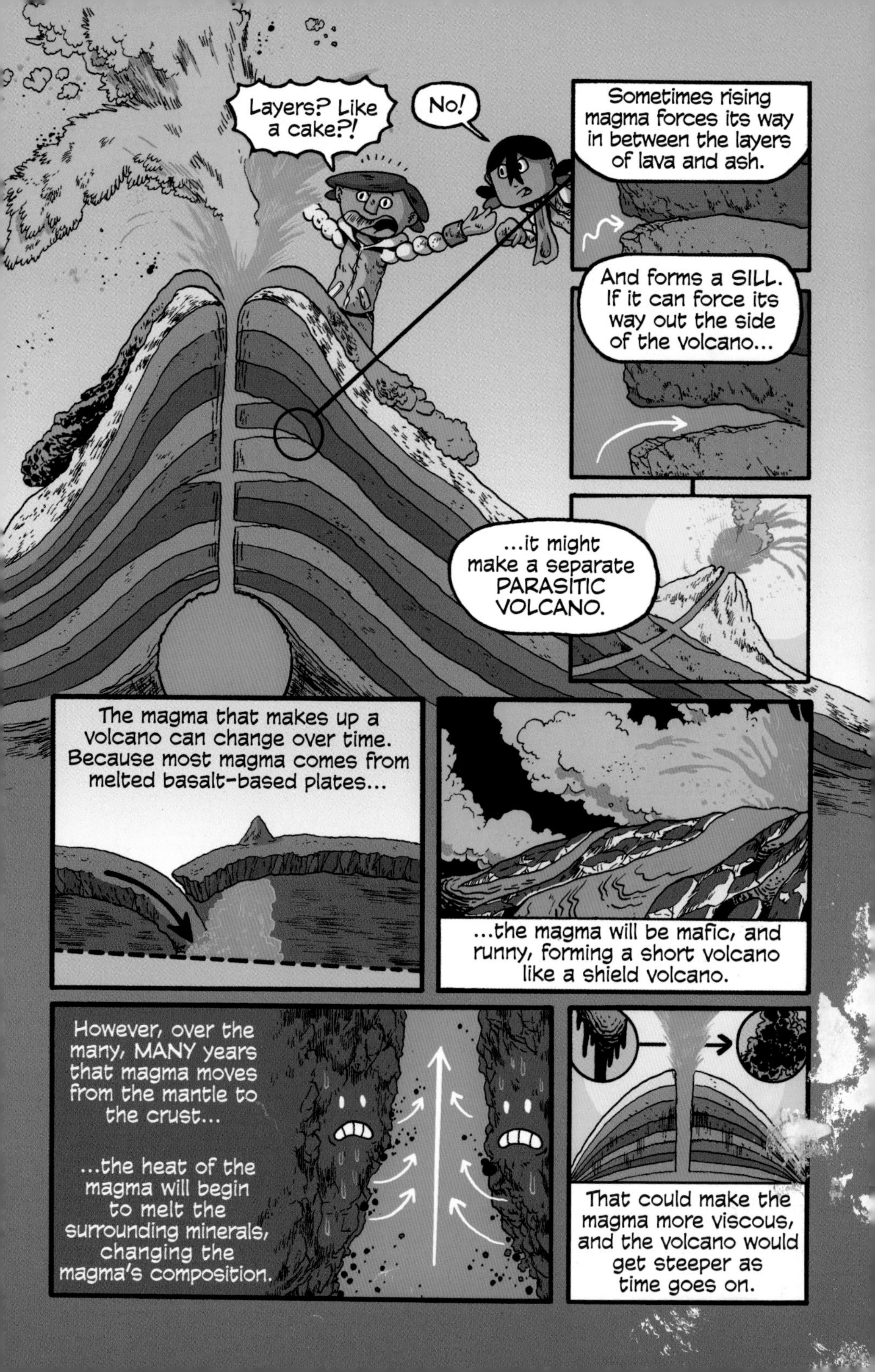
Layers? Like a cake?!
No!
Sometimes rising magma forces its way in between the layers of lava and ash.
And forms a SILL. If it can force its way out the side of the volcano...
...it might make a separate PARASITIC VOLCANO.
The magma that makes up a volcano can change over time. Because most magma comes from melted basalt-based plates...
...the magma will be mafic, and runny, forming a short volcano like a shield volcano.
However, over the many, MANY years that magma moves from the mantle to the crust...
...the heat of the magma will begin to melt the surrounding minerals, changing the magma's composition.
That could make the magma more viscous, and the volcano would get steeper as time goes on.

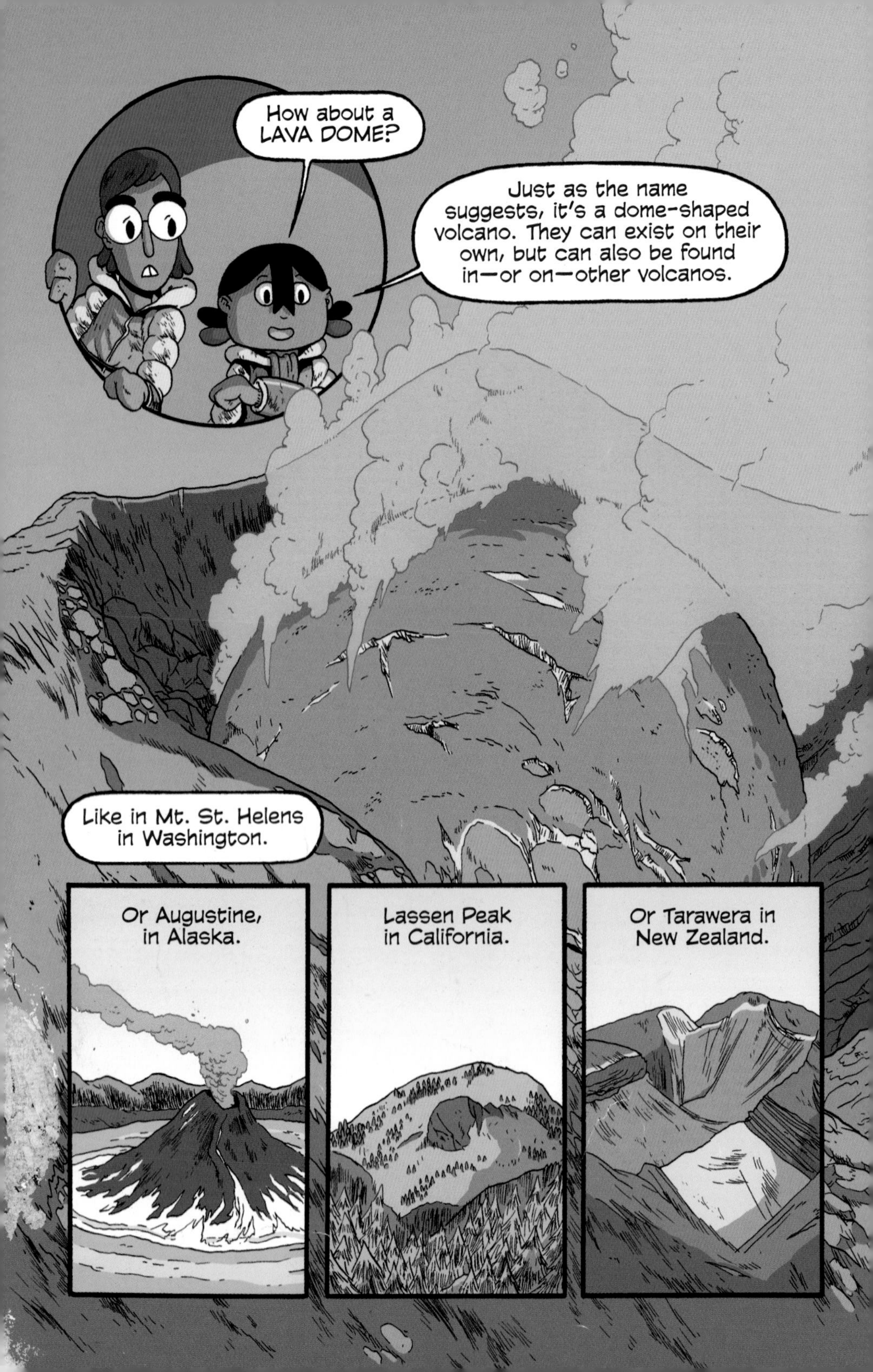
How about a LAVA DOME?
Just as the name suggests, it's a dome-shaped volcano. They can exist on their own, but can also be found in—or on—other volcanos.
Like in Mt. St. Helens in Washington.
Or Augustine, in Alaska.
Lassen Peak in California.
Or Tarawera in New Zealand.

1 Lava domes grow in one of two ways:

If the magma is thick and viscous, it will push on all sides of the dome, bursting it and expanding it outward.

2

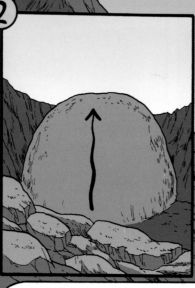 

If the magma is thinner and runny, it will only have enough pressure to break out of the top of the volcano and run down the sides, making another layer like a shield volcano.

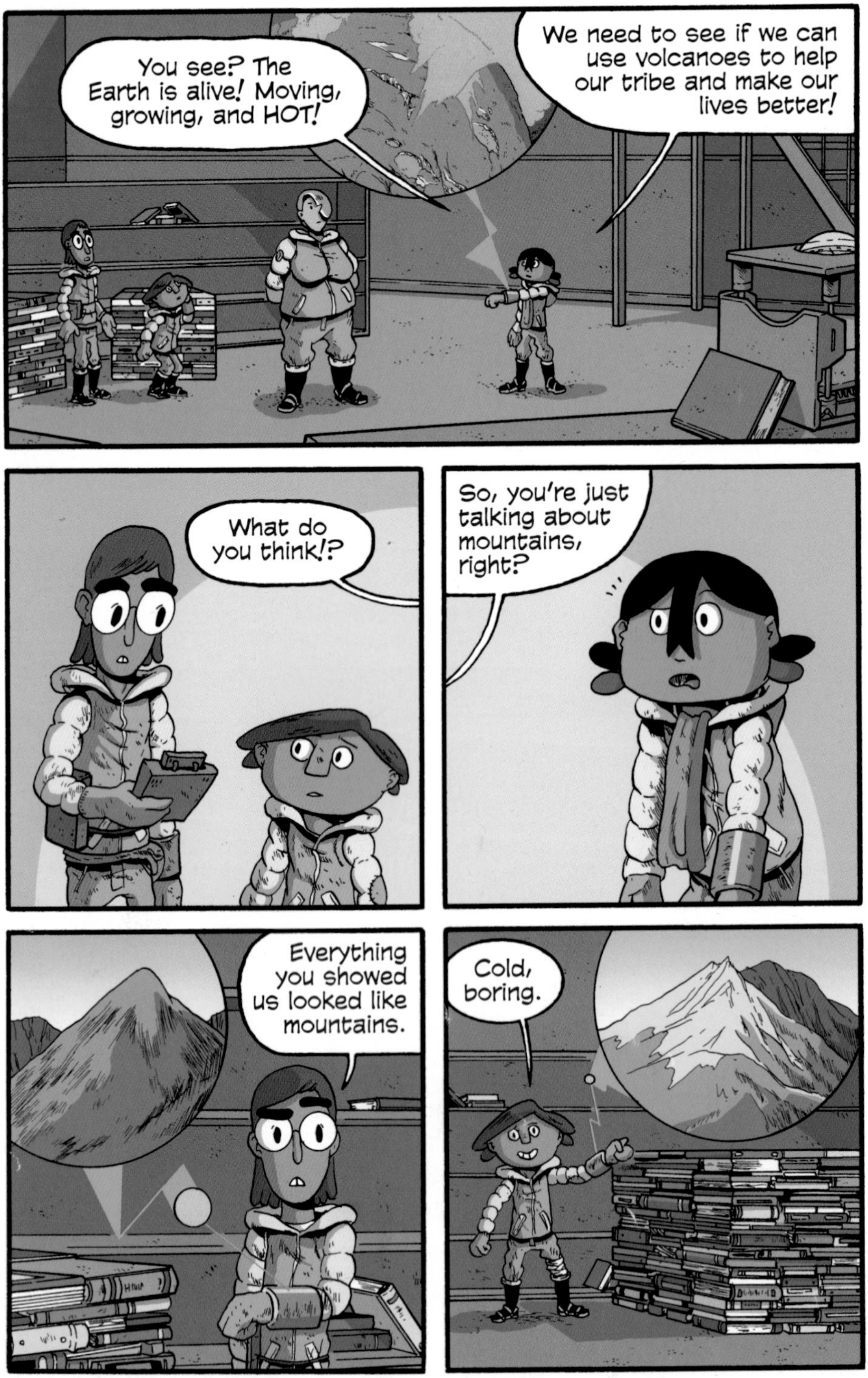
You see? The Earth is alive! Moving, growing, and HOT!
We need to see if we can use volcanoes to help our tribe and make our lives better!
What do you think!?
So, you're just talking about mountains, right?
Everything you showed us looked like mountains.
Cold, boring.

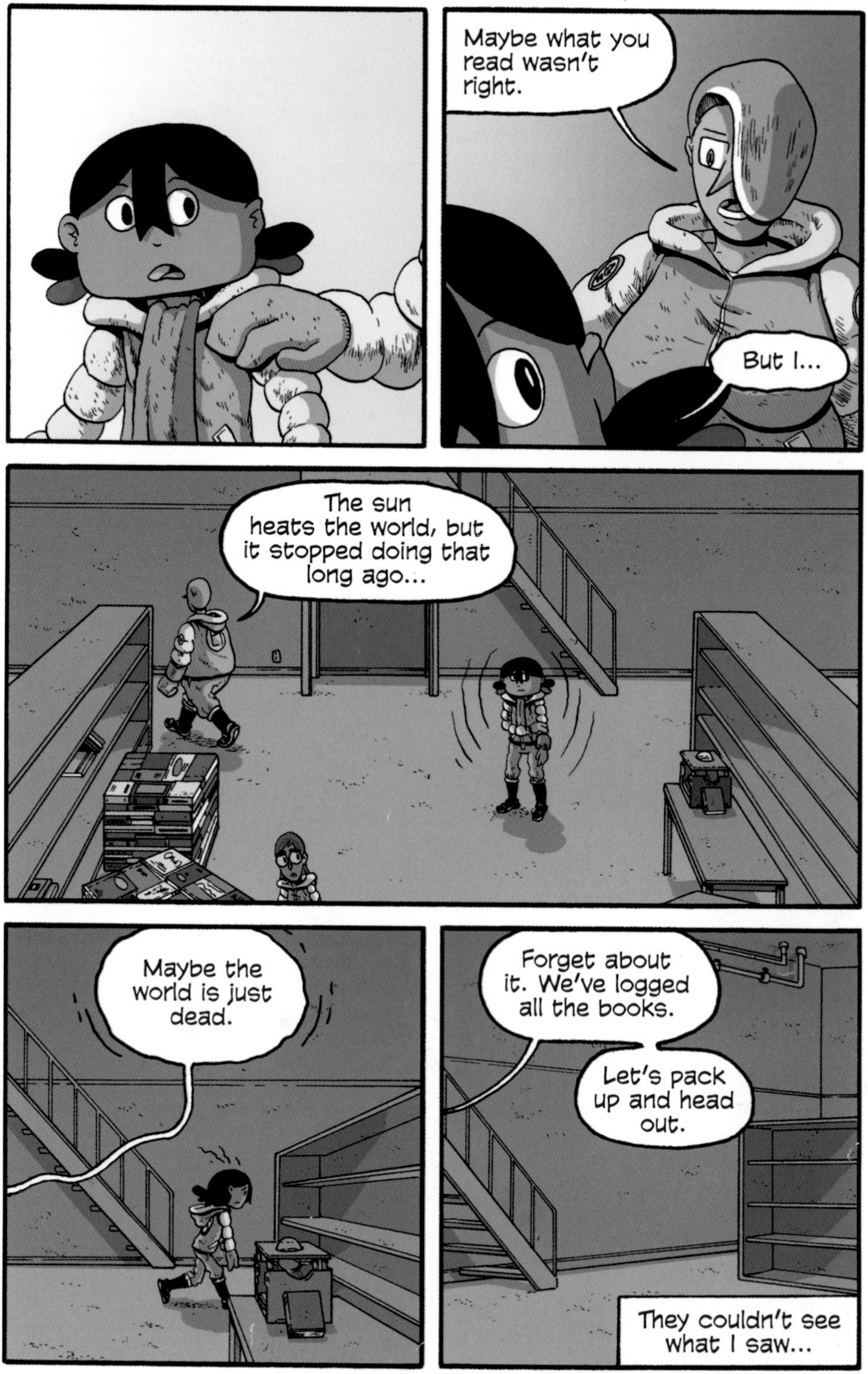
Maybe what you read wasn't right.
But I...
The sun heats the world, but it stopped doing that long ago...
Maybe the world is just dead.
Forget about it. We've logged all the books.
Let's pack up and head out.
They couldn't see what I saw...

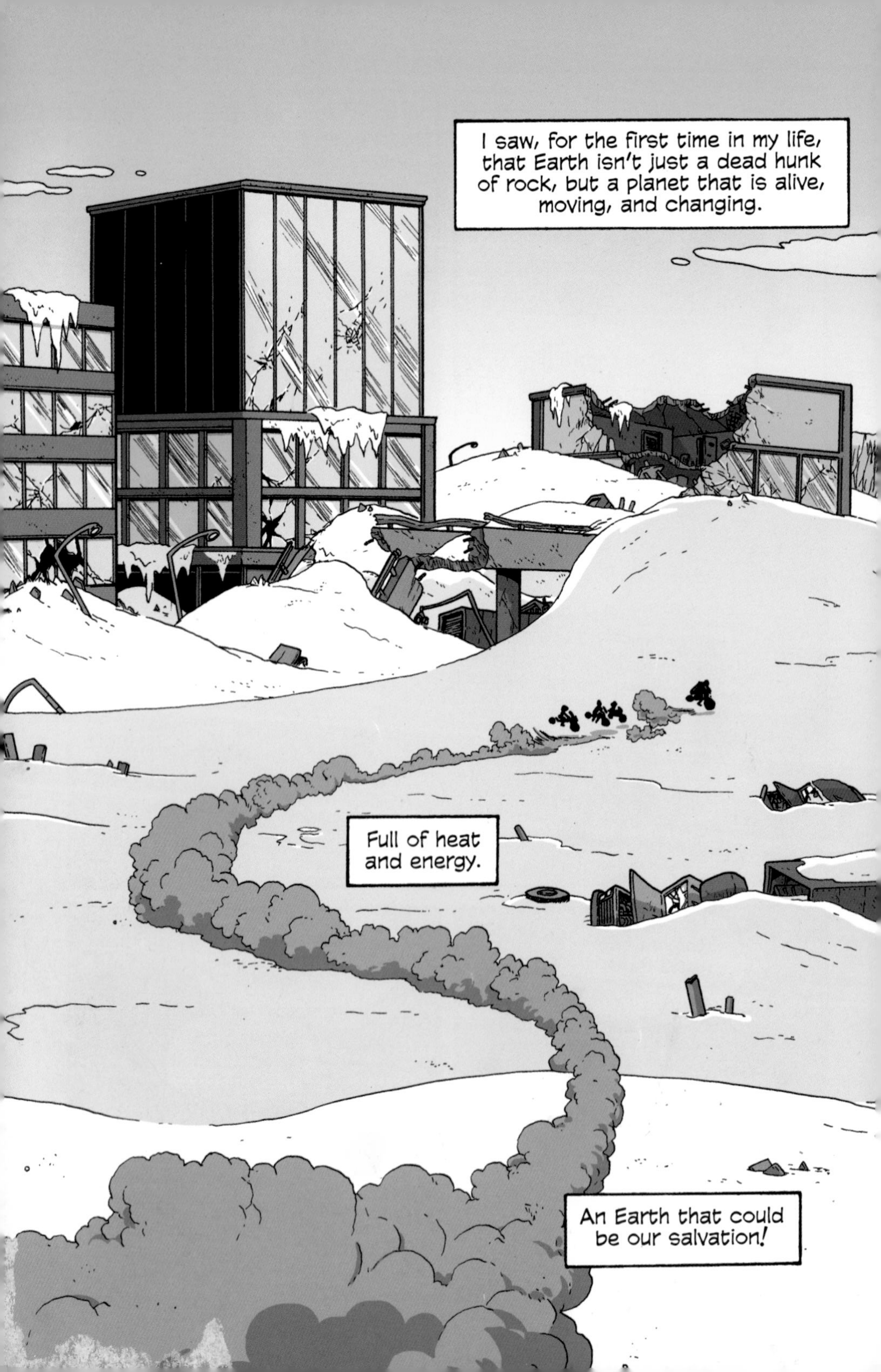
I saw, for the first time in my life, that Earth isn't just a dead hunk of rock, but a planet that is alive, moving, and changing.
Full of heat and energy.
An Earth that could be our salvation!

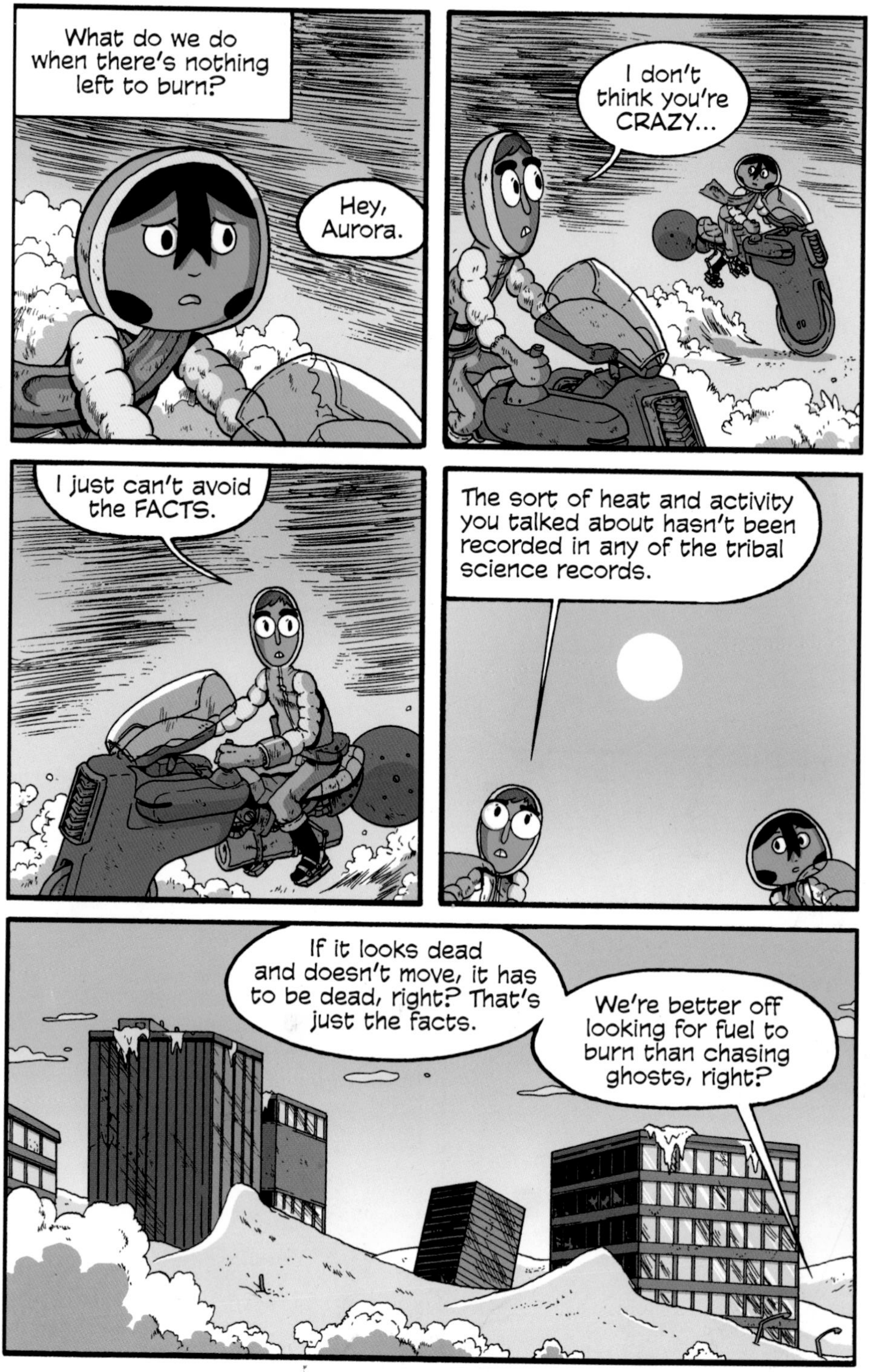
What do we do when there's nothing left to burn?
Hey, Aurora.
I don't think you're CRAZY...
I just can't avoid the FACTS.
The sort of heat and activity you talked about hasn't been recorded in any of the tribal science records.
If it looks dead and doesn't move, it has to be dead, right? That's just the facts.
We're better off looking for fuel to burn than chasing ghosts, right?

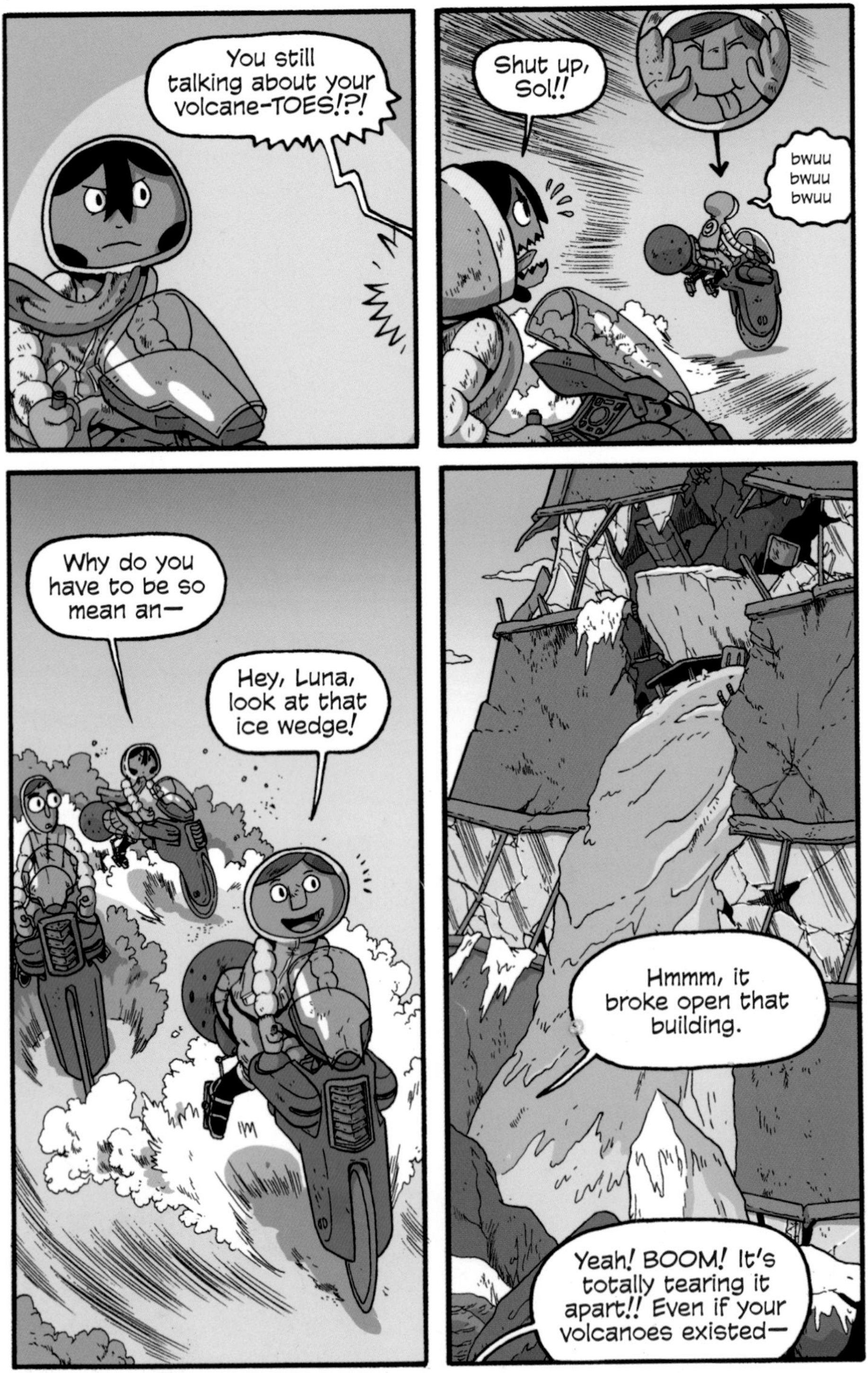
You still talking about your volcane-TOES!?!
Shut up, Sol!!
bwuu bwuu bwuu
Why do you have to be so mean an—
Hey, Luna, look at that ice wedge!
Hmmm, it broke open that building.
Yeah! BOOM! It's totally tearing it apart!! Even if your volcanoes existed—

—they would be trapped under the ice. They're too weak to bust ice!

They are not!

Yeah, right.

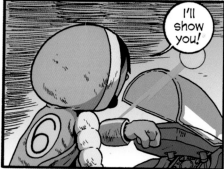

I'll show you!

Ohhh, look, Sol.

Ice cracking rock. COOL, right?

Whoa, yeah, that's what I'M talking about!

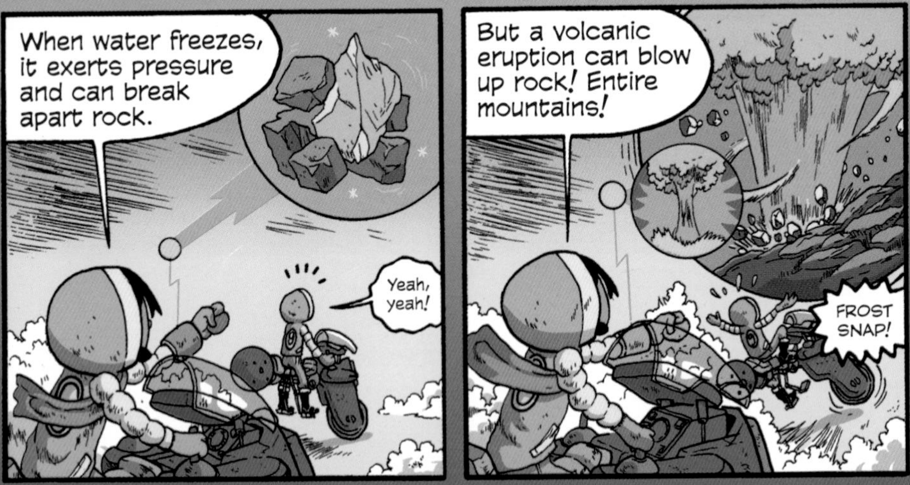
When water freezes, it exerts pressure and can break apart rock.
Yeah, yeah!
But a volcanic eruption can blow up rock! Entire mountains!
FROST SNAP!

The two main variables that will determine the strength and type of an eruption will be the viscosity of the magma...

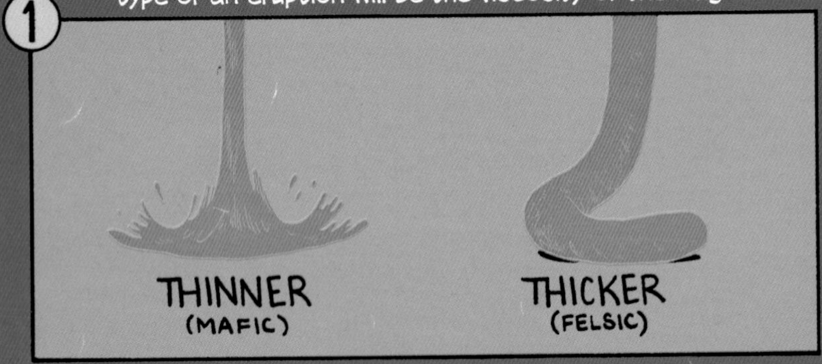
1
THINNER
(MAFIC)
THICKER
(FELSIC)

...and the amount of gas in the magma.

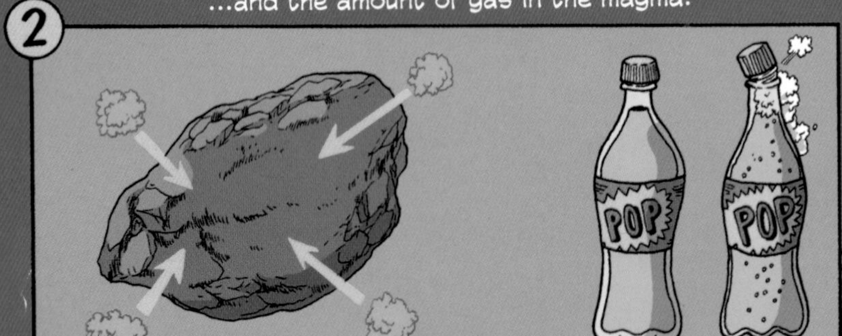
2
POP
POP

When the rock is molten, the pressure is so great that the gasses are dissolved completely into the rock. Think of a soda bottle before you open it. There is CO_2 in the soda, but the bubbles aren't visible because they're under pressure.

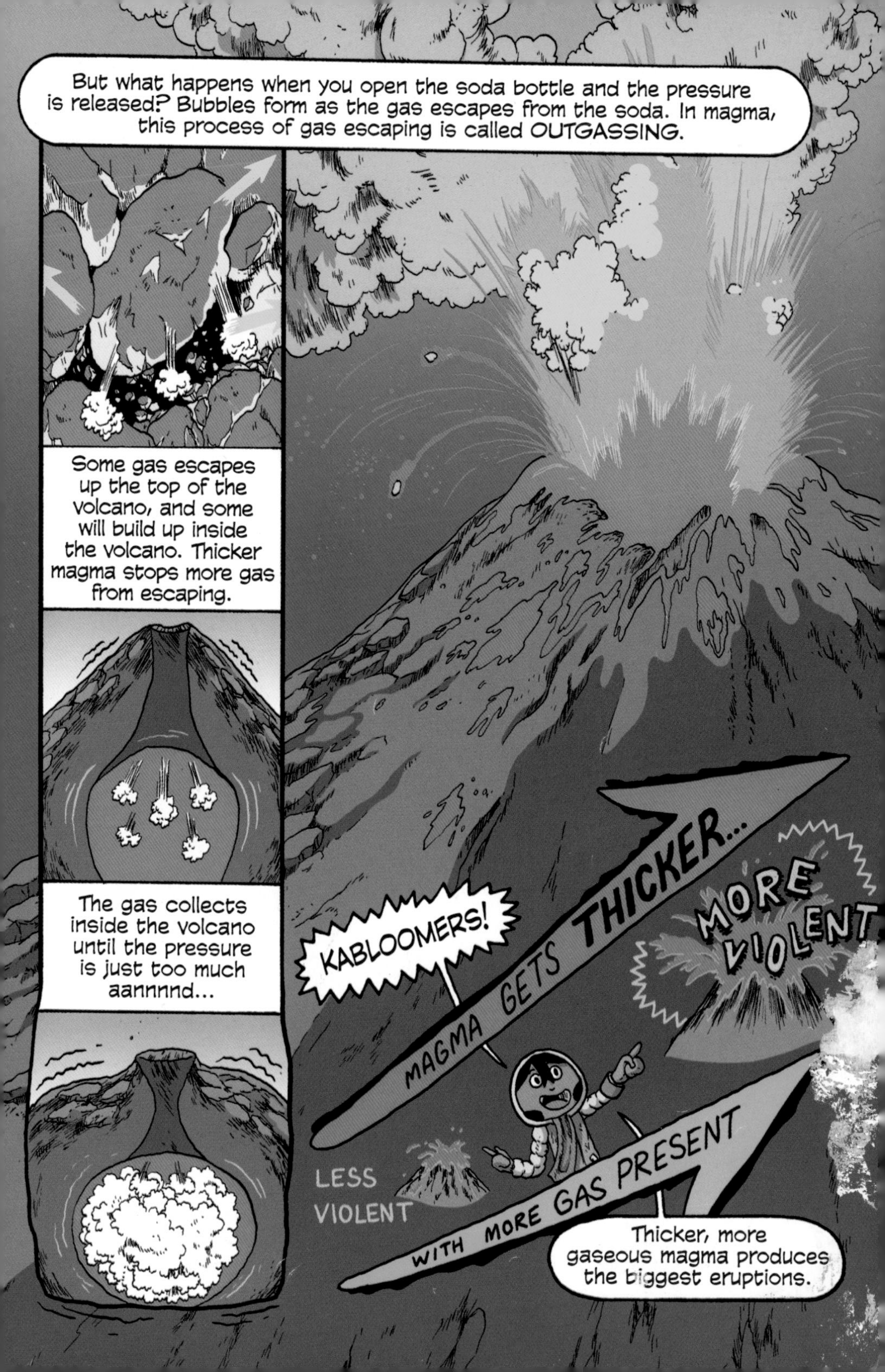

But what happens when you open the soda bottle and the pressure is released? Bubbles form as the gas escapes from the soda. In magma, this process of gas escaping is called OUTGASSING.
Some gas escapes up the top of the volcano, and some will build up inside the volcano. Thicker magma stops more gas from escaping.
The gas collects inside the volcano until the pressure is just too much aannnnd...
KABLOOMERS!
MAGMA GETS THICKER...
WITH MORE GAS PRESENT
LESS VIOLENT
MORE VIOLENT
Thicker, more gaseous magma produces the biggest eruptions.

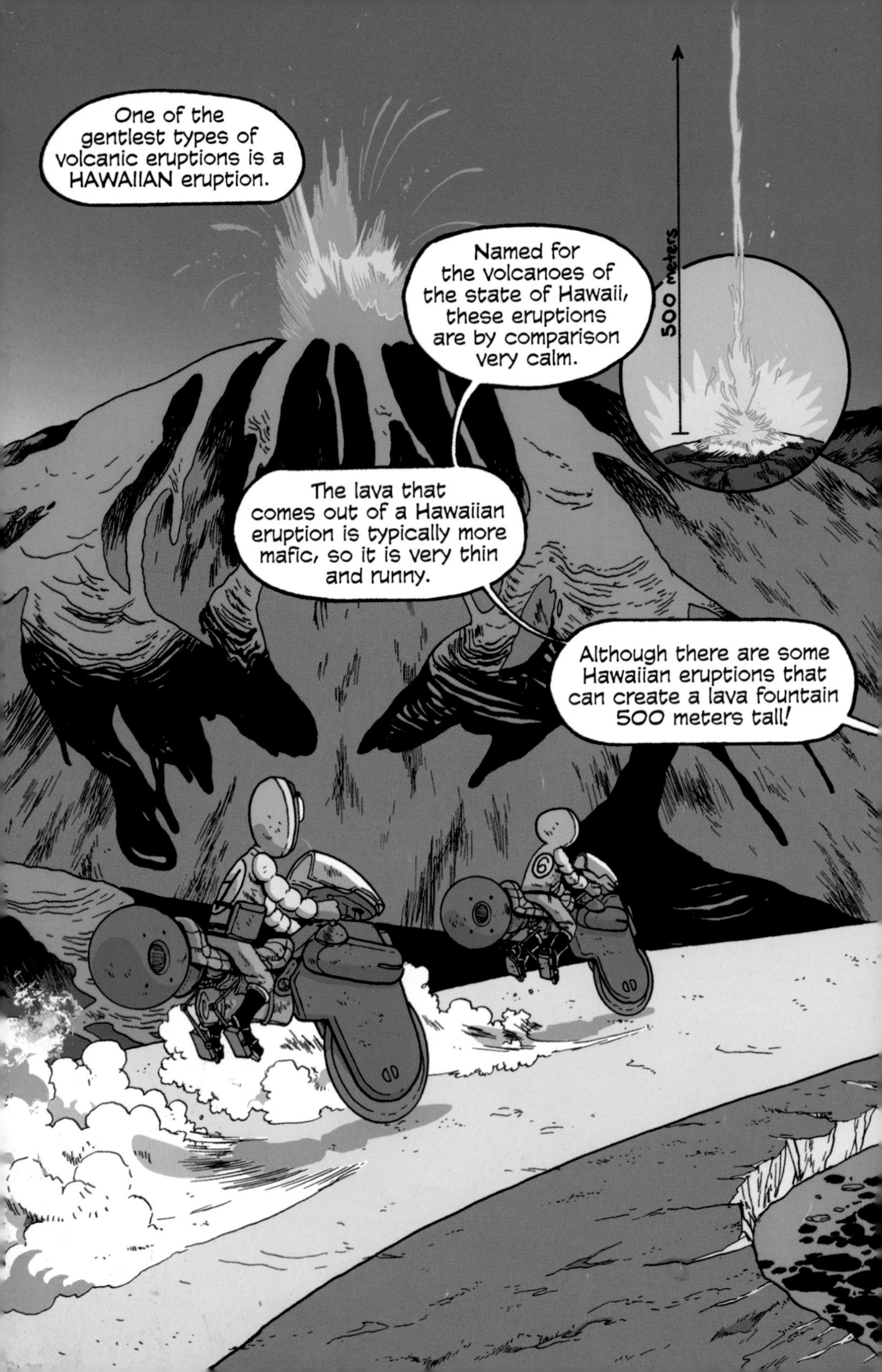

One of the gentlest types of volcanic eruptions is a HAWAIIAN eruption.
Named for the volcanoes of the state of Hawaii, these eruptions are by comparison very calm.
500 meters
The lava that comes out of a Hawaiian eruption is typically more mafic, so it is very thin and runny.
Although there are some Hawaiian eruptions that can create a lava fountain 500 meters tall!
6

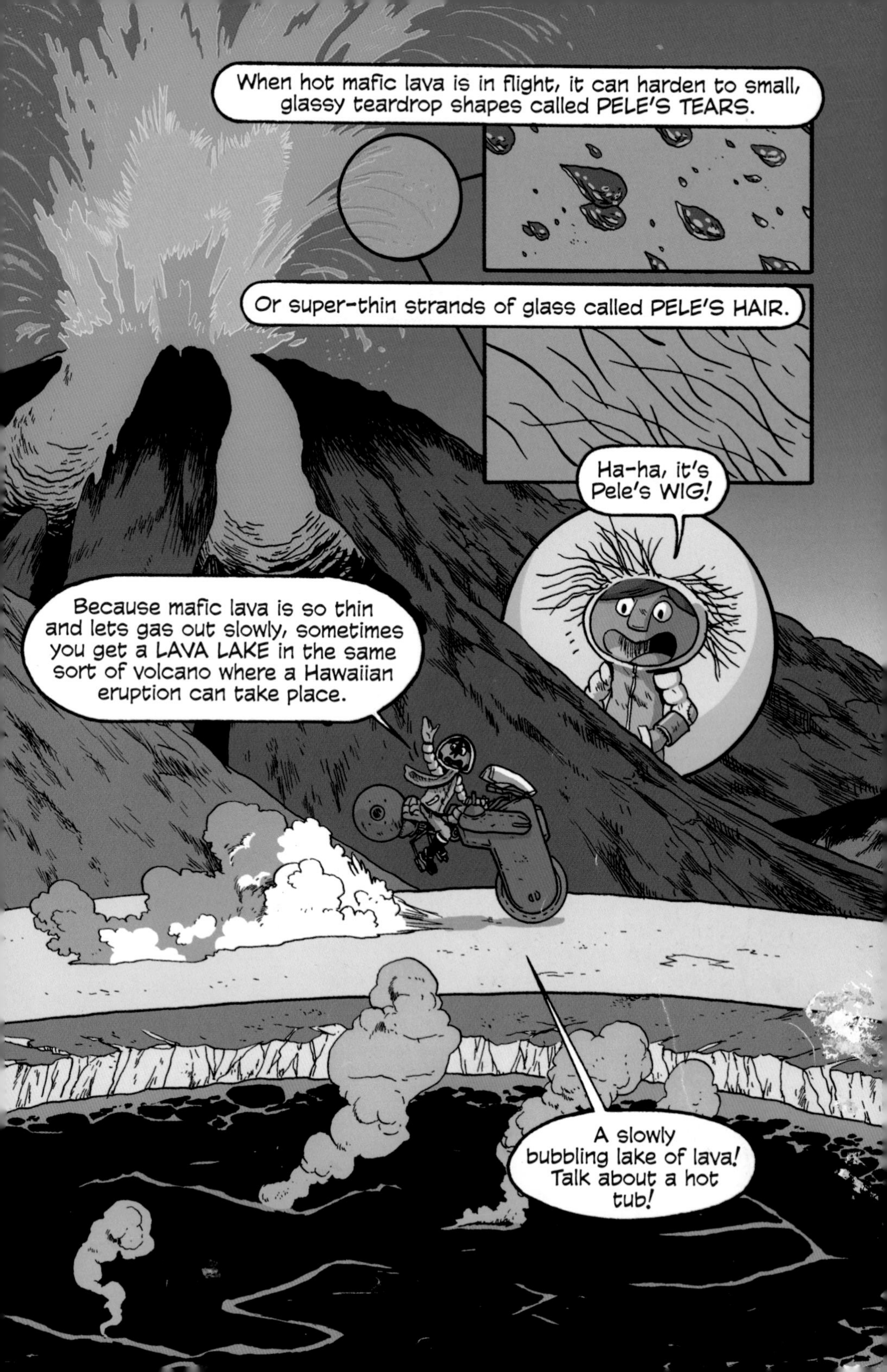
When hot mafic lava is in flight, it can harden to small, glassy teardrop shapes called PELE'S TEARS.
Or super-thin strands of glass called PELE'S HAIR.
Ha-ha, it's Pele's WIG!
Because mafic lava is so thin and lets gas out slowly, sometimes you get a LAVA LAKE in the same sort of volcano where a Hawaiian eruption can take place.
A slowly bubbling lake of lava! Talk about a hot tub!

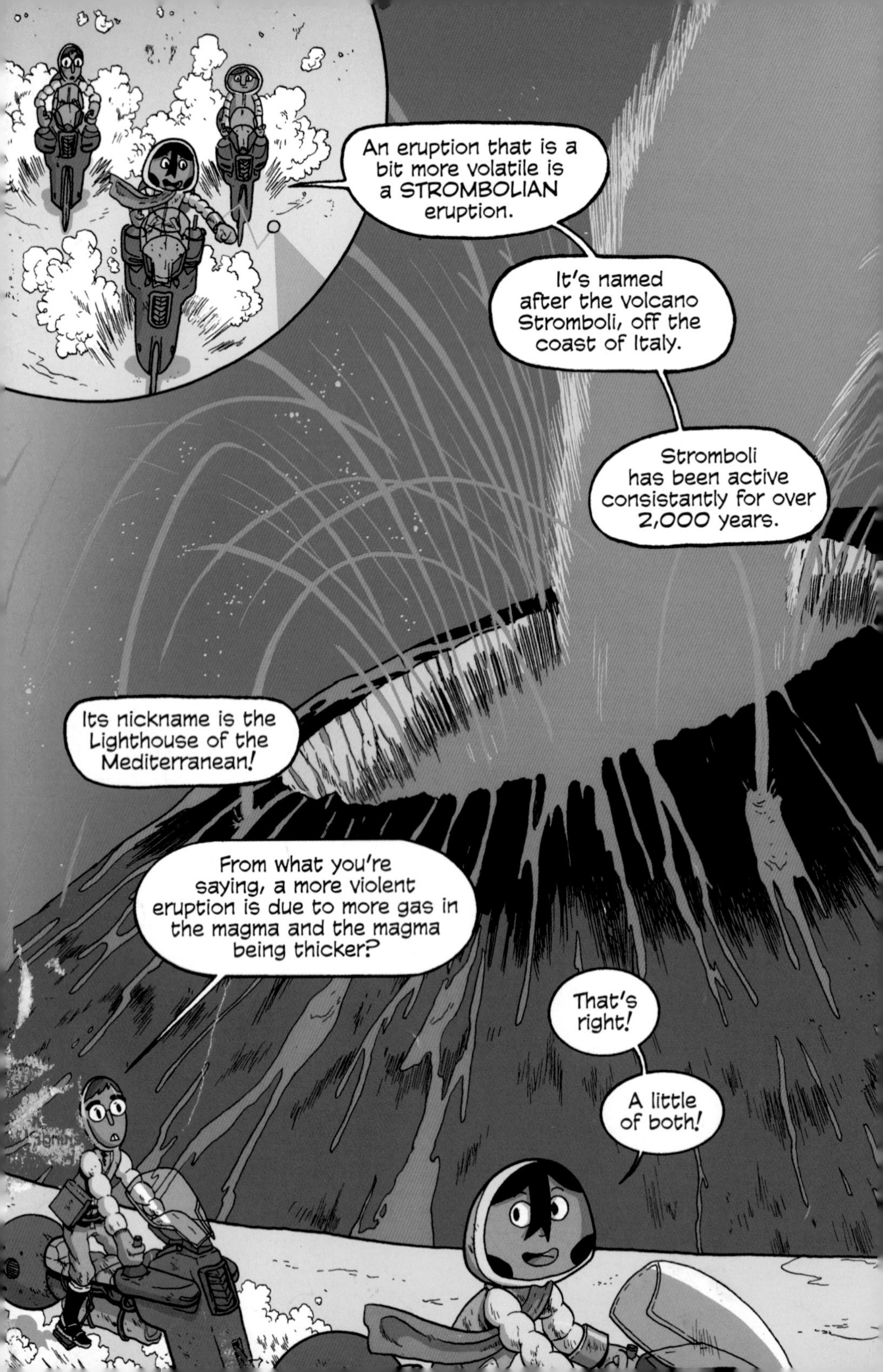
An eruption that is a bit more volatile is a STROMBOLIAN eruption.
It's named after the volcano Stromboli, off the coast of Italy.
Stromboli has been active consistantly for over 2,000 years.
Its nickname is the Lighthouse of the Mediterranean!
From what you're saying, a more violent eruption is due to more gas in the magma and the magma being thicker?
That's right!
A little of both!

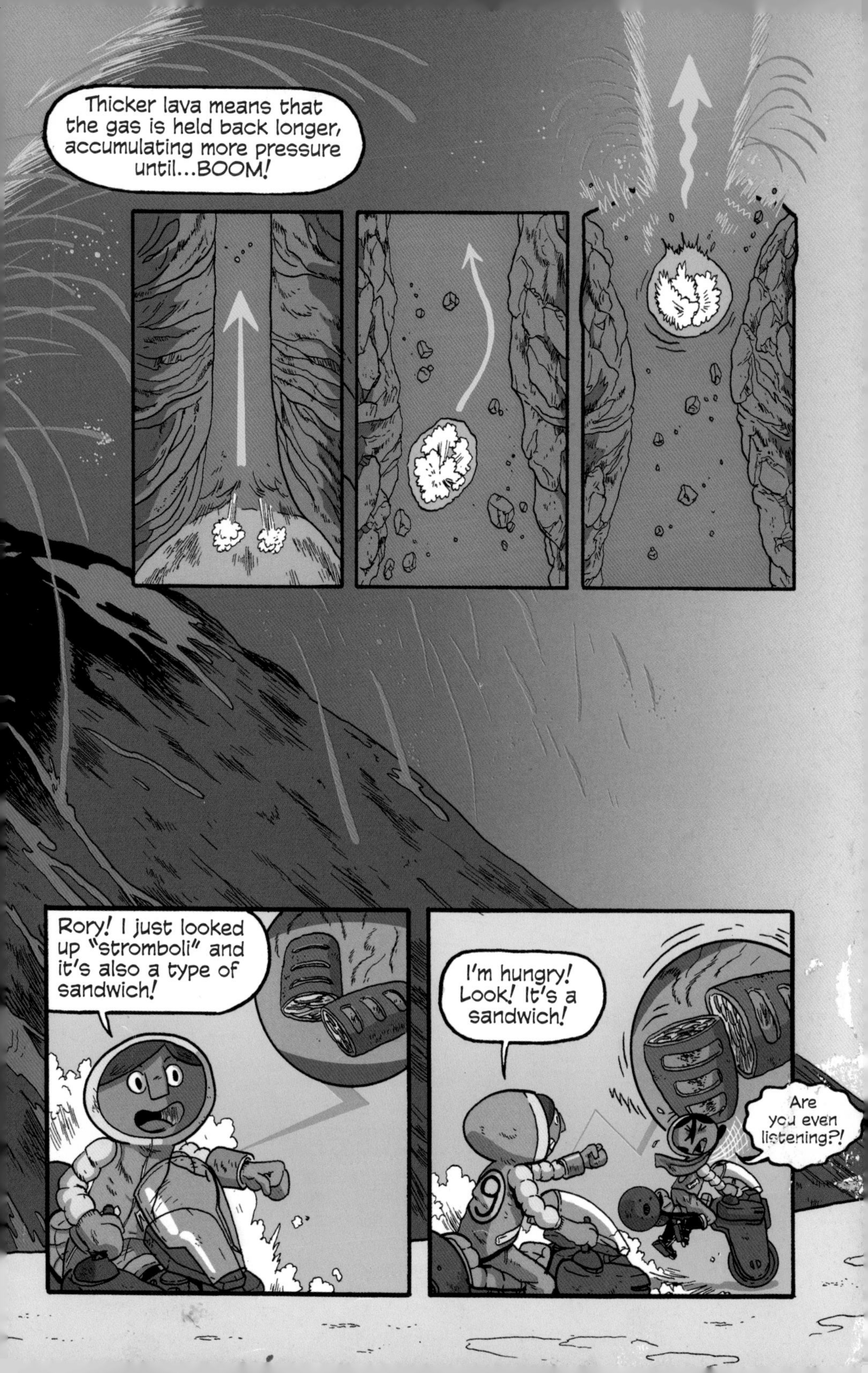
Thicker lava means that the gas is held back longer, accumulating more pressure until...BOOM!
Rory! I just looked up "stromboli" and it's also a type of sandwich!
I'm hungry! Look! It's a sandwich!
Are you even listening?!

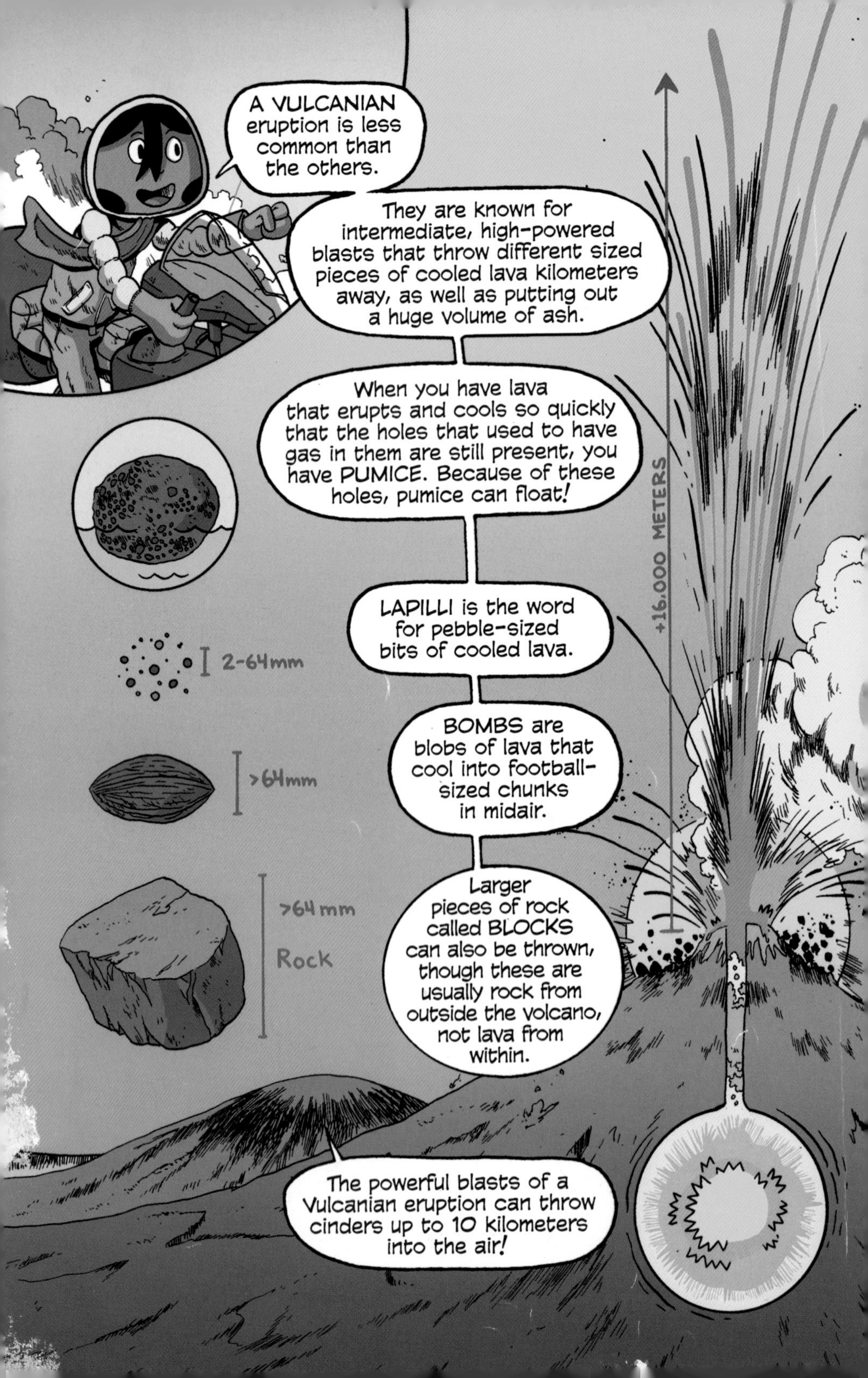
A VULCANIAN eruption is less common than the others.
They are known for intermediate, high-powered blasts that throw different sized pieces of cooled lava kilometers away, as well as putting out a huge volume of ash.
When you have lava that erupts and cools so quickly that the holes that used to have gas in them are still present, you have PUMICE. Because of these holes, pumice can float!
LAPILLI is the word for pebble-sized bits of cooled lava.
2-64mm
BOMBS are blobs of lava that cool into football-sized chunks in midair.
>64mm
Larger pieces of rock called BLOCKS can also be thrown, though these are usually rock from outside the volcano, not lava from within.
>64 mm
Rock
+16,000 METERS
The powerful blasts of a Vulcanian eruption can throw cinders up to 10 kilometers into the air!

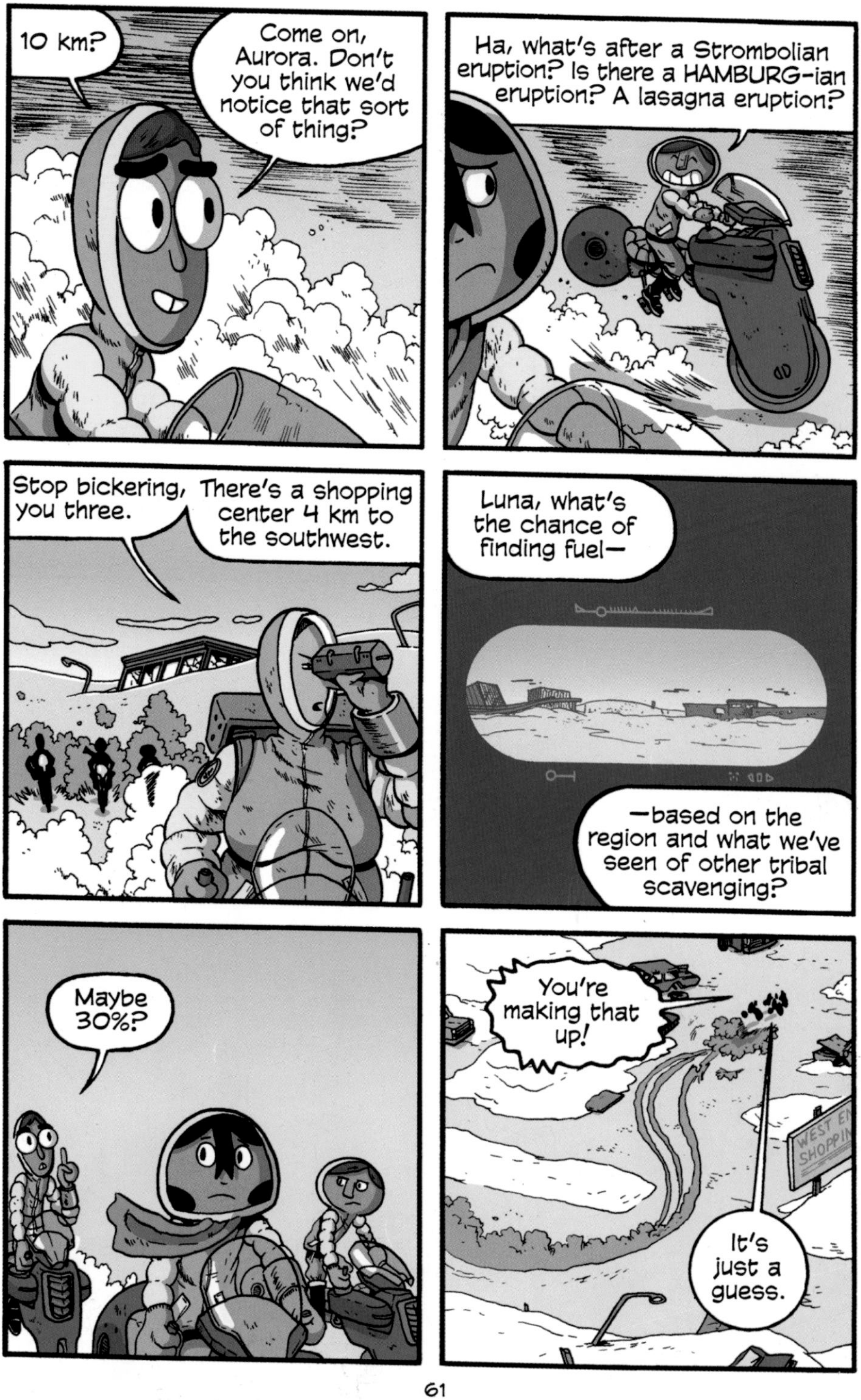
10 km?
Come on, Aurora. Don't you think we'd notice that sort of thing?
Ha, what's after a Strombolian eruption? Is there a HAMBURG-ian eruption? A lasagna eruption?
Stop bickering, you three.
There's a shopping center 4 km to the southwest.
Luna, what's the chance of finding fuel—
—based on the region and what we've seen of other tribal scavenging?
Maybe 30%?
You're making that up!
It's just a guess.

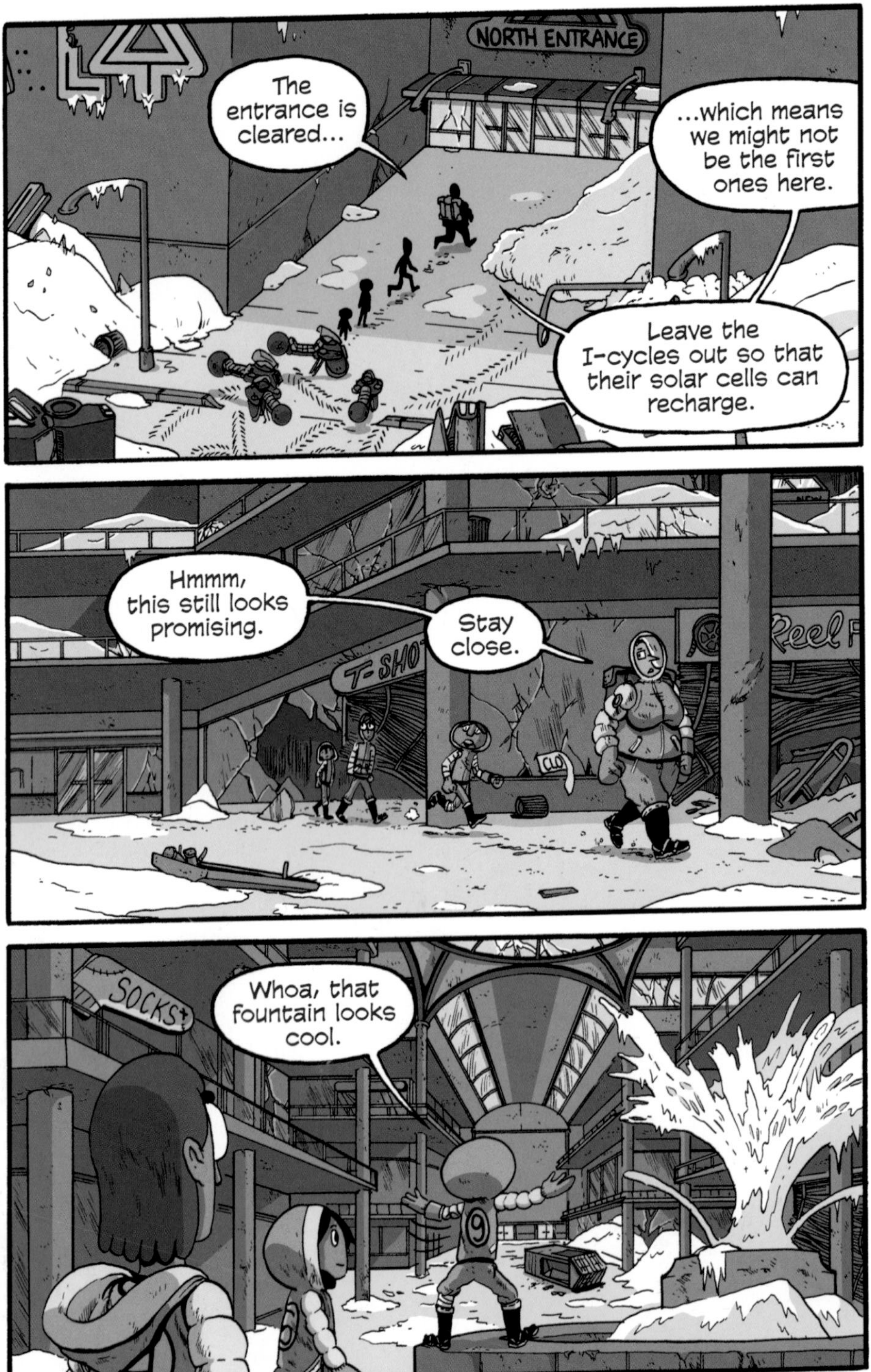
NORTH ENTRANCE
The entrance is cleared...
...which means we might not be the first ones here.
Leave the I-cycles out so that their solar cells can recharge.
Hmmm, this still looks promising.
Stay close.
Whoa, that fountain looks cool.
SOCKS

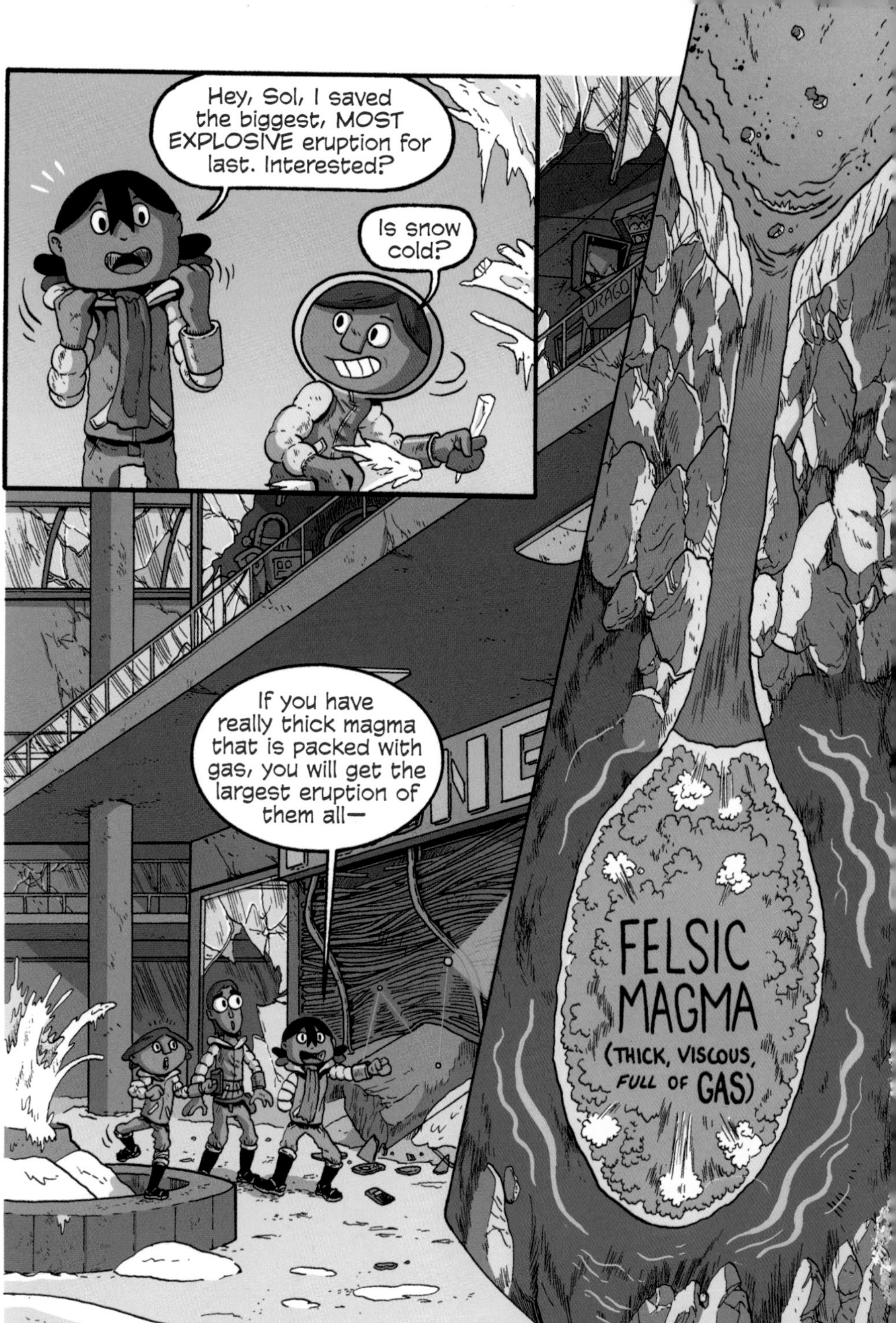
Hey, Sol, I saved the biggest, MOST EXPLOSIVE eruption for last. Interested?
Is snow cold?
If you have really thick magma that is packed with gas, you will get the largest eruption of them all—
FELSIC MAGMA
(THICK, VISCOUS, FULL OF GAS)

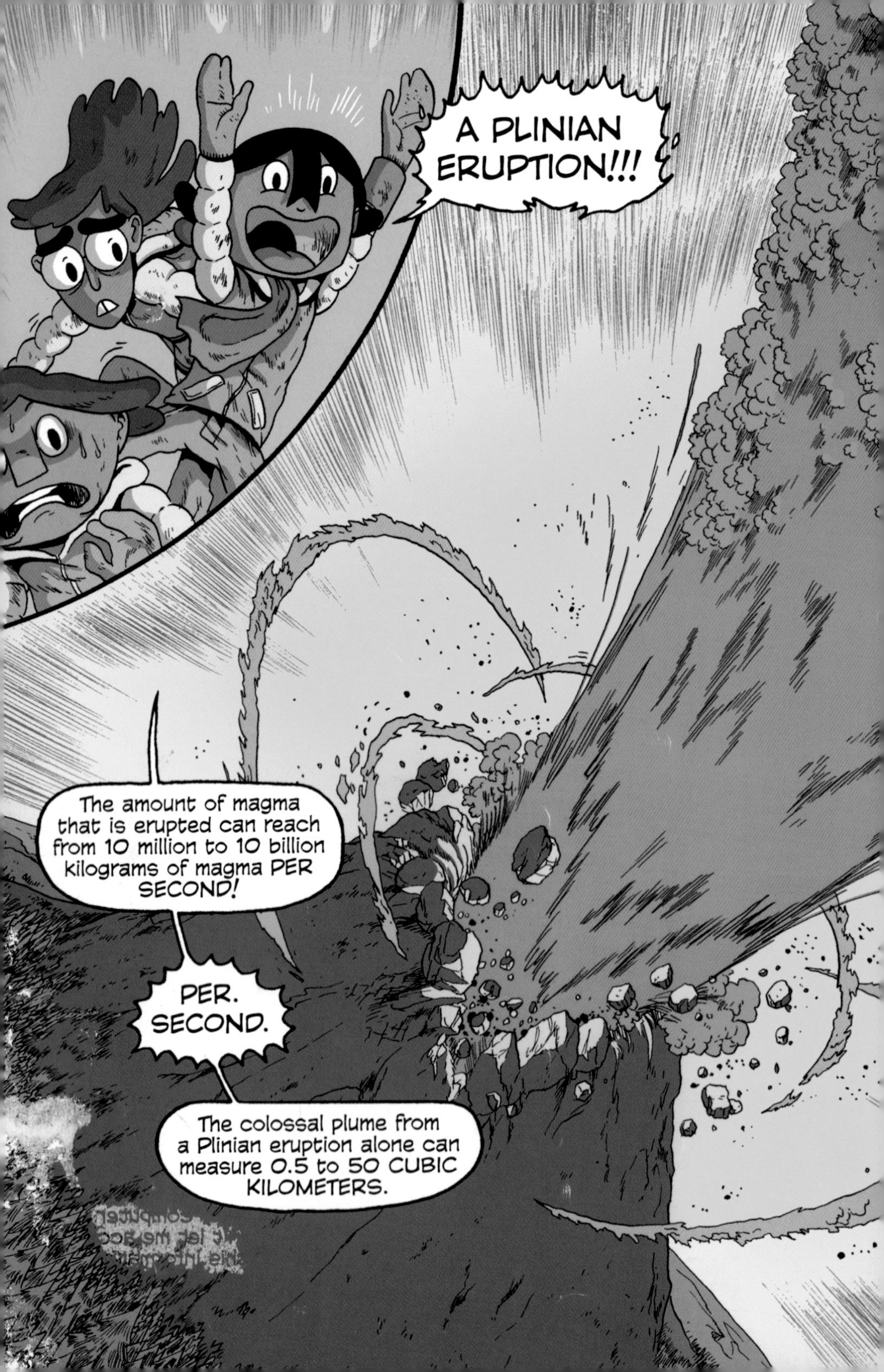
A PLINIAN ERUPTION!!!
The amount of magma that is erupted can reach from 10 million to 10 billion kilograms of magma PER SECOND!
PER. SECOND.
The colossal plume from a Plinian eruption alone can measure 0.5 to 50 CUBIC KILOMETERS.

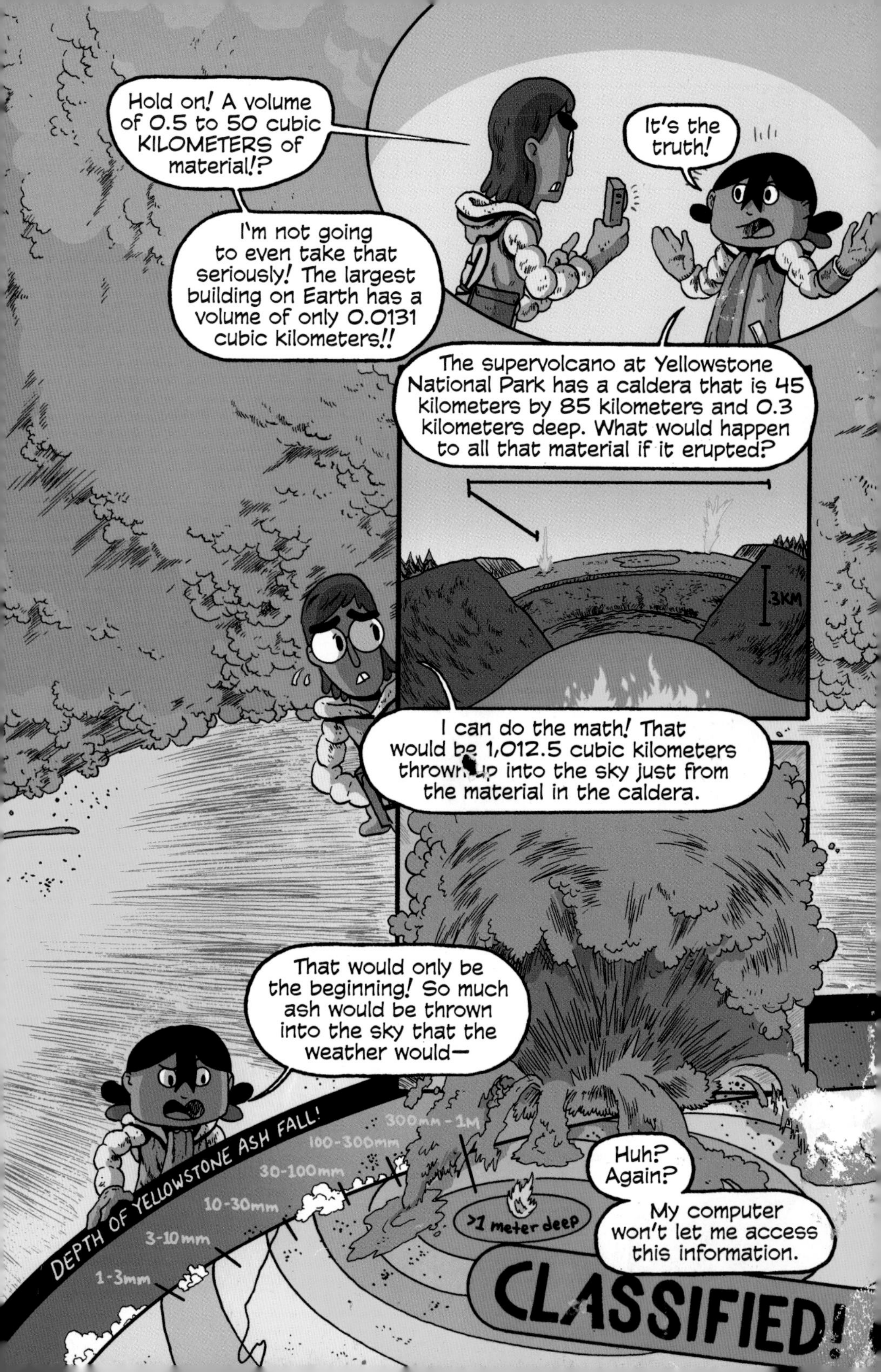
Hold on! A volume of 0.5 to 50 cubic KILOMETERS of material!?
I'm not going to even take that seriously! The largest building on Earth has a volume of only 0.0131 cubic kilometers!!
It's the truth!
The supervolcano at Yellowstone National Park has a caldera that is 45 kilometers by 85 kilometers and 0.3 kilometers deep. What would happen to all that material if it erupted?
.3KM
I can do the math! That would be 1,012.5 cubic kilometers thrown up into the sky just from the material in the caldera.
That would only be the beginning! So much ash would be thrown into the sky that the weather would—
DEPTH OF YELLOWSTONE ASH FALL!
300mm-1M
100-300mm
30-100mm
10-30mm
3-10mm
1-3mm
>1 meter deep
Huh? Again?
My computer won't let me access this information.
CLASSIFIED!

The Plinian column, or plume, is initially propelled into the sky through the sheer, pressure-packed power of the eruption.

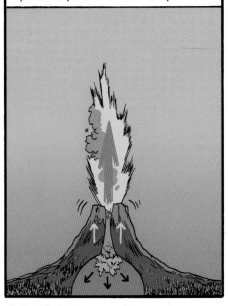

The plume is further raised by upward currents of air called CONVECTION CURRENTS.

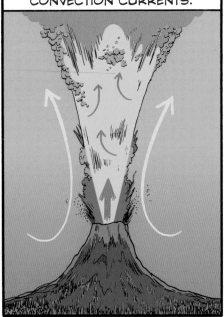

As the pressure and density of the plume balance out with that of the surrounding air, the plume levels off in what is called the "umbrella region."

When there is not enough pressure to maintain the plume, all or part of it collapses and falls toward the ground.

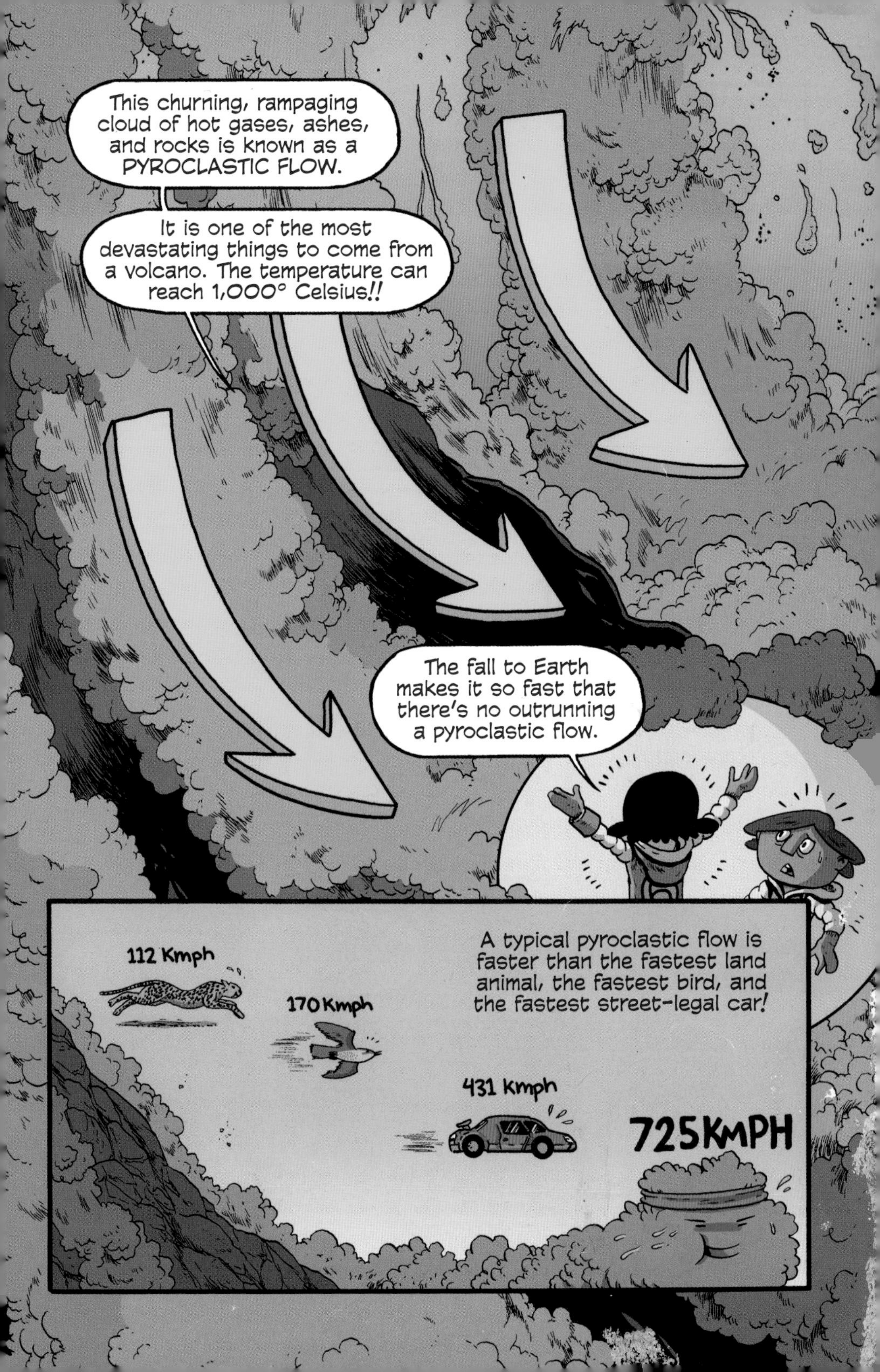
This churning, rampaging cloud of hot gases, ashes, and rocks is known as a PYROCLASTIC FLOW.
It is one of the most devastating things to come from a volcano. The temperature can reach 1,000° Celsius!!
The fall to Earth makes it so fast that there's no outrunning a pyroclastic flow.
A typical pyroclastic flow is faster than the fastest land animal, the fastest bird, and the fastest street-legal car!
112 Kmph
170 Kmph
431 Kmph
725 KMPH

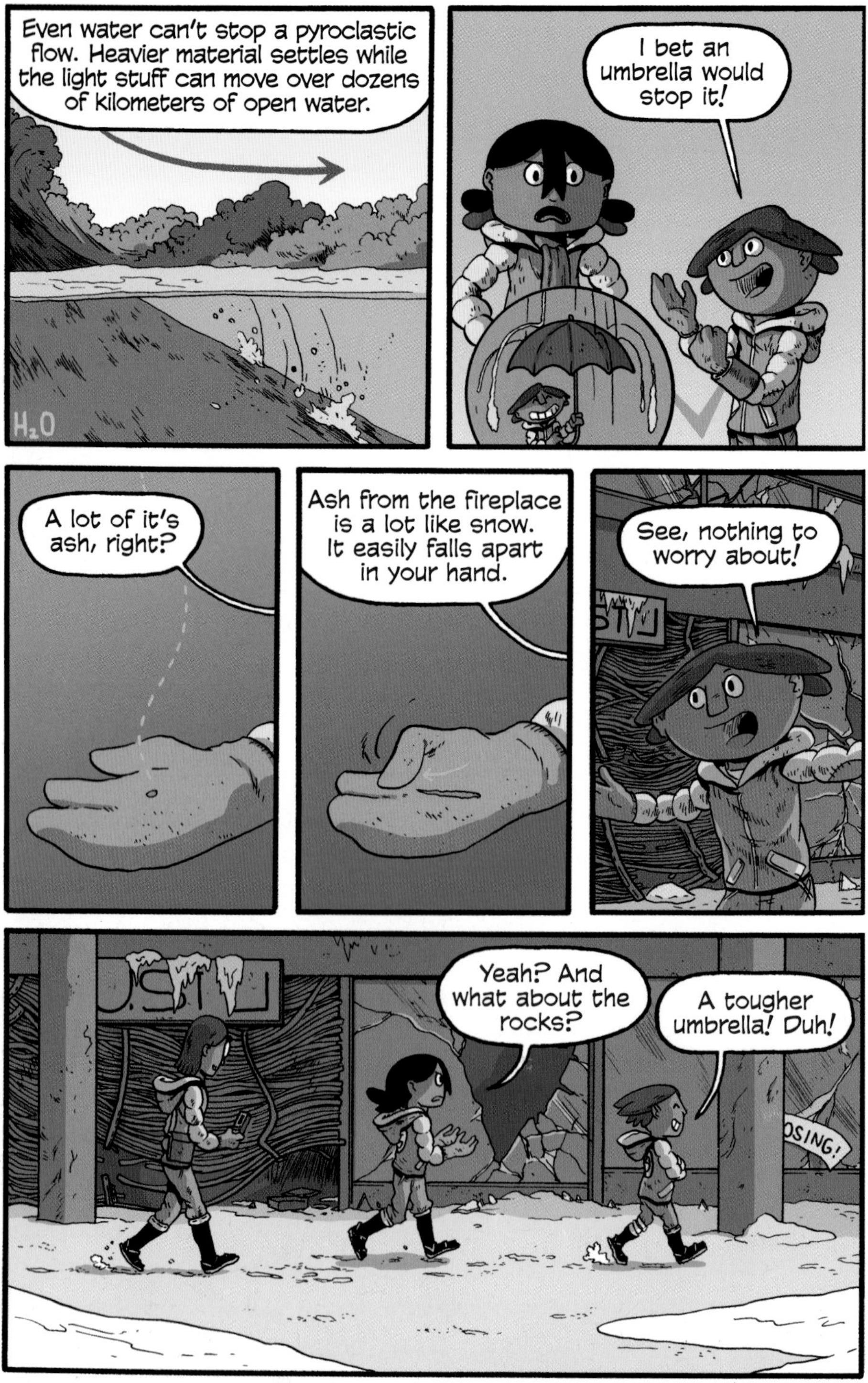
Even water can't stop a pyroclastic flow. Heavier material settles while the light stuff can move over dozens of kilometers of open water.
H2O
I bet an umbrella would stop it!
A lot of it's ash, right?
Ash from the fireplace is a lot like snow. It easily falls apart in your hand.
See, nothing to worry about!
Yeah? And what about the rocks?
A tougher umbrella! Duh!
OSING!

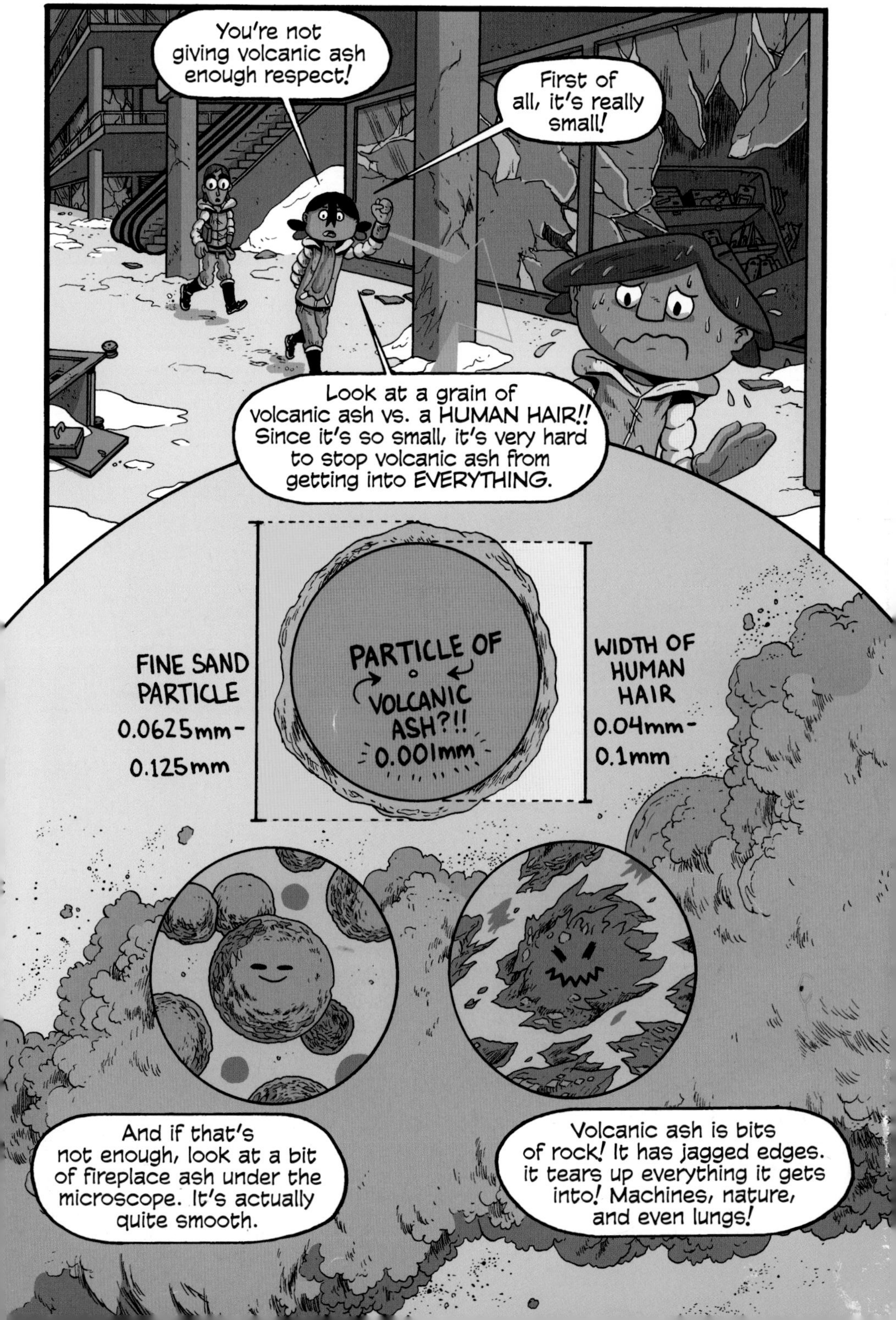
You're not giving volcanic ash enough respect!
First of all, it's really small!
Look at a grain of volcanic ash vs. a HUMAN HAIR!! Since it's so small, it's very hard to stop volcanic ash from getting into EVERYTHING.
FINE SAND PARTICLE 0.0625mm - 0.125mm
PARTICLE OF VOLCANIC ASH?!! 0.001mm
WIDTH OF HUMAN HAIR 0.04mm - 0.1mm
And if that's not enough, look at a bit of fireplace ash under the microscope. It's actually quite smooth.
Volcanic ash is bits of rock! It has jagged edges. it tears up everything it gets into! Machines, nature, and even lungs!

Because the particles are so light, they can travel a great distance on the wind. Mt. St. Helens' eruption sent ash as far as 3,200 km away!

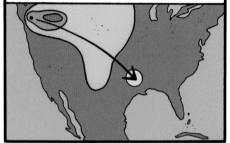

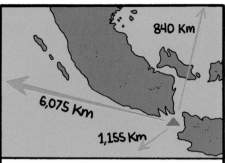

840 Km

6,075 Km

1,155 Km

Krakatau's eruption sent ash over 6,000 km away! And that year the weather was CRAZY!

It—

CLASSIFIED

Huh? Classified again?

Why does it keep doing that?!

A layer of ash 1 mm thick will ground airplanes.

1 cm will make grazing impossible for livestock.

10 cm can collapse houses.

100 cm will destroy a young forest.

500 cm will destroy ANY forest.

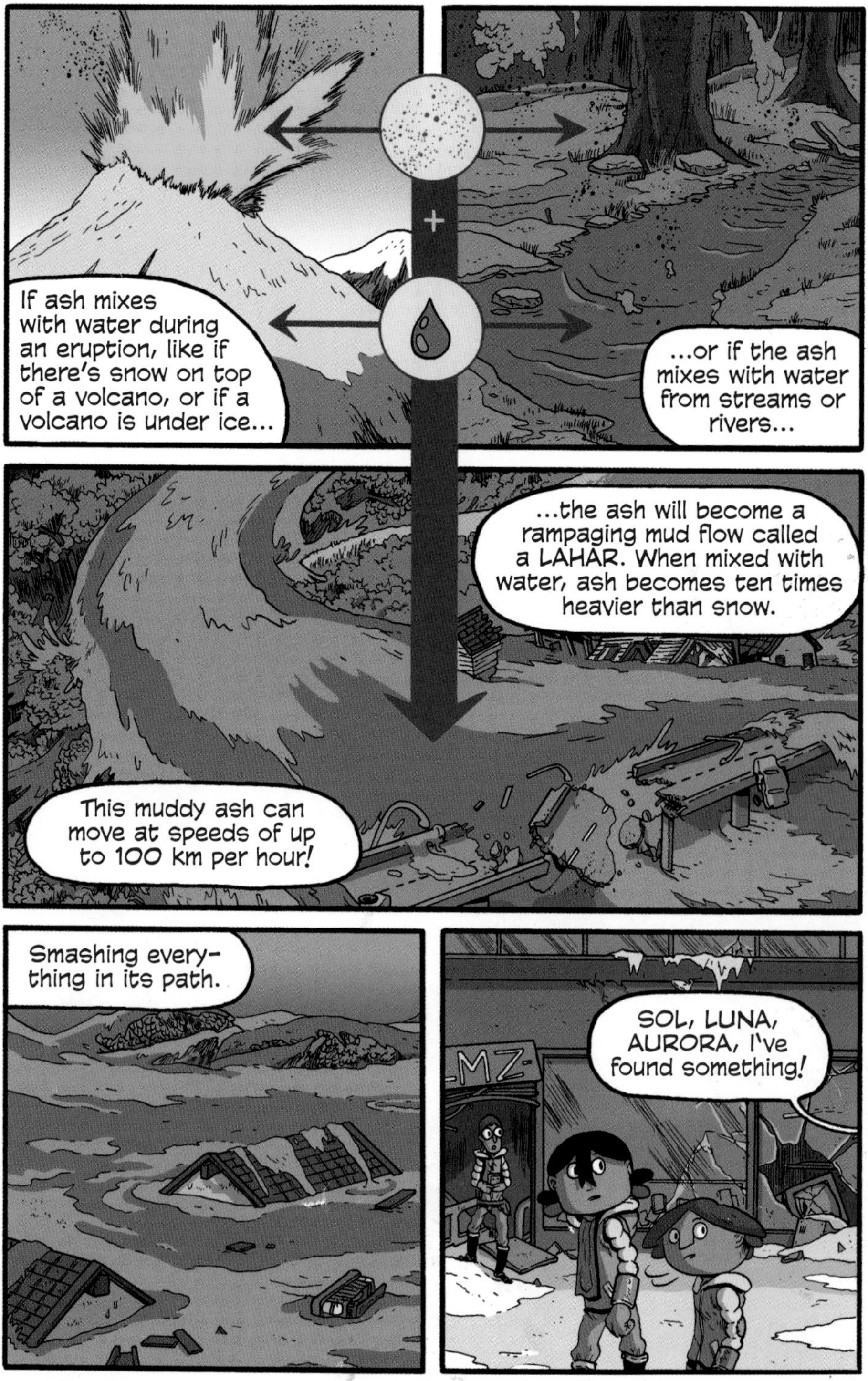
If ash mixes with water during an eruption, like if there's snow on top of a volcano, or if a volcano is under ice...
+
...or if the ash mixes with water from streams or rivers...
...the ash will become a rampaging mud flow called a LAHAR. When mixed with water, ash becomes ten times heavier than snow.
This muddy ash can move at speeds of up to 100 km per hour!
Smashing everything in its path.
MZ
SOL, LUNA, AURORA, I've found something!

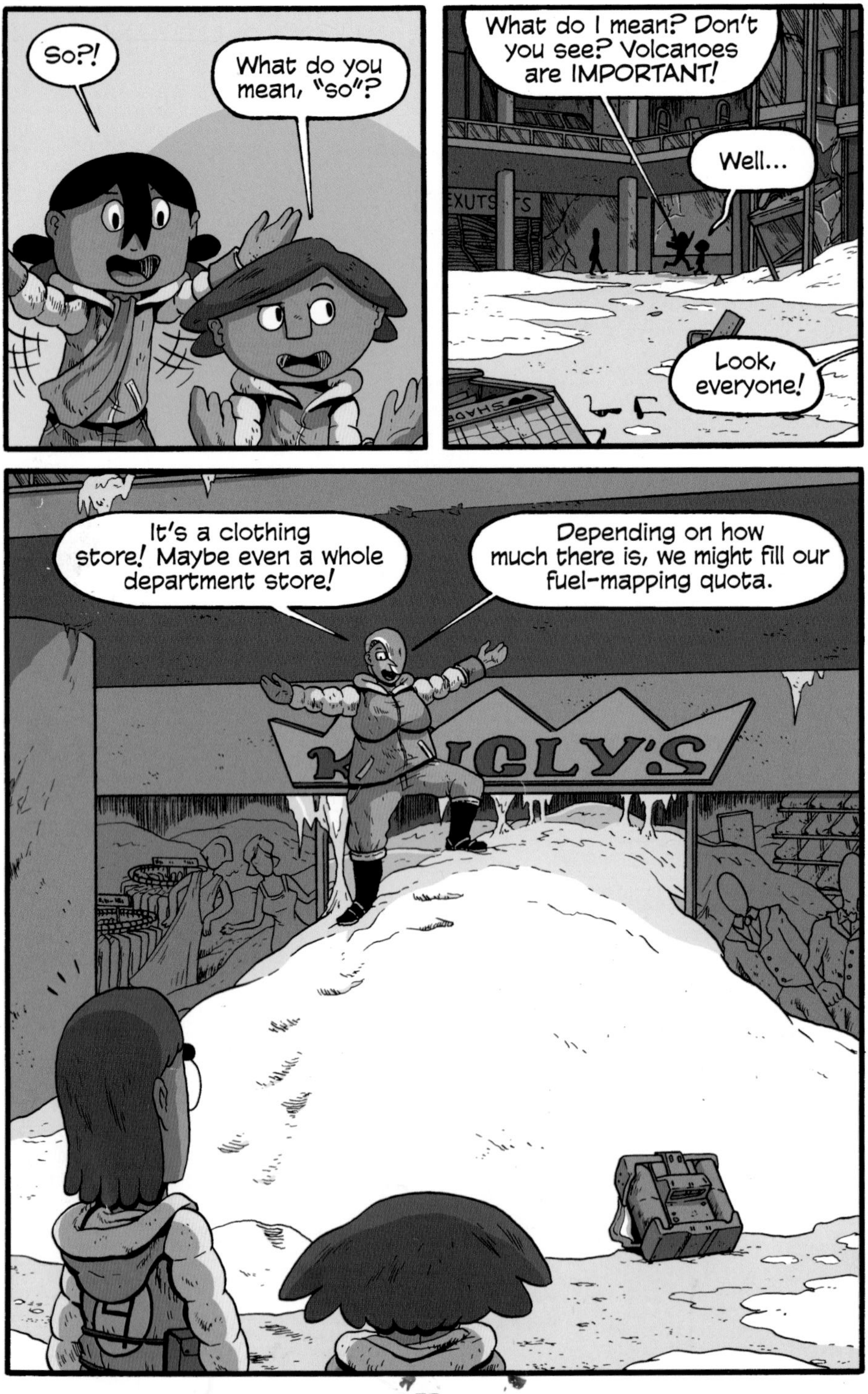
So?!
What do you mean, "so"?
What do I mean? Don't you see? Volcanoes are IMPORTANT!
Well...
Look, everyone!
It's a clothing store! Maybe even a whole department store!
Depending on how much there is, we might fill our fuel-mapping quota.

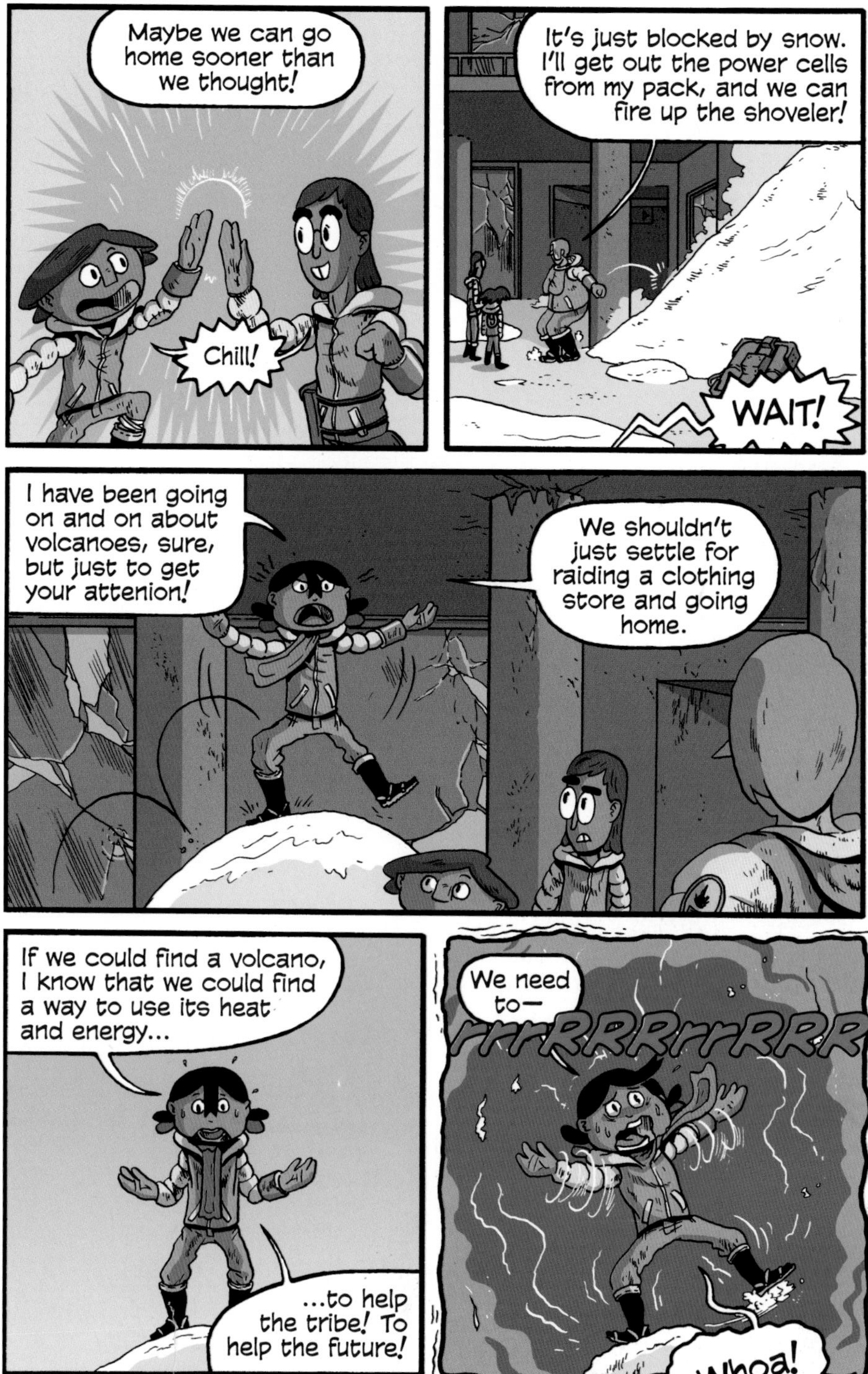
Maybe we can go home sooner than we thought!
Chill!
It's just blocked by snow. I'll get out the power cells from my pack, and we can fire up the shoveler!
WAIT!
I have been going on and on about volcanoes, sure, but just to get your attenion!
We shouldn't just settle for raiding a clothing store and going home.
If we could find a volcano, I know that we could find a way to use its heat and energy...
...to help the tribe! To help the future!
We need to—
rrrRRRrrrRRR
Whoa!

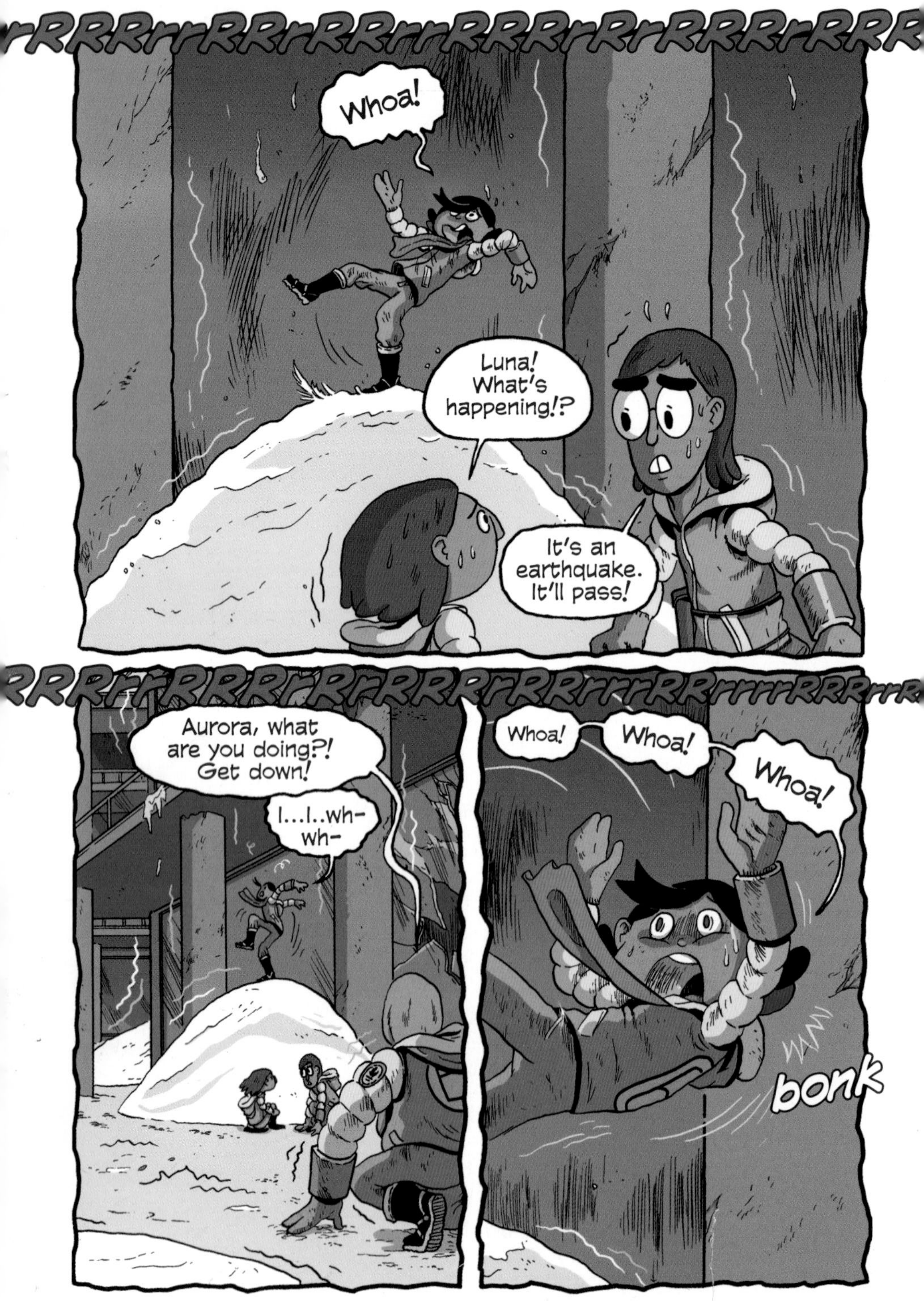
rRRRrrRRrRRrrRRRrRrRRRrRRR
Whoa!
Luna! What's happening!?
It's an earthquake. It'll pass!
RRRrrRRRrRRrRRRrRRRrrrRRrrrrRRRrrR
Aurora, what are you doing?! Get down!
I...I..wh- wh-
Whoa!
Whoa!
Whoa!
bonk

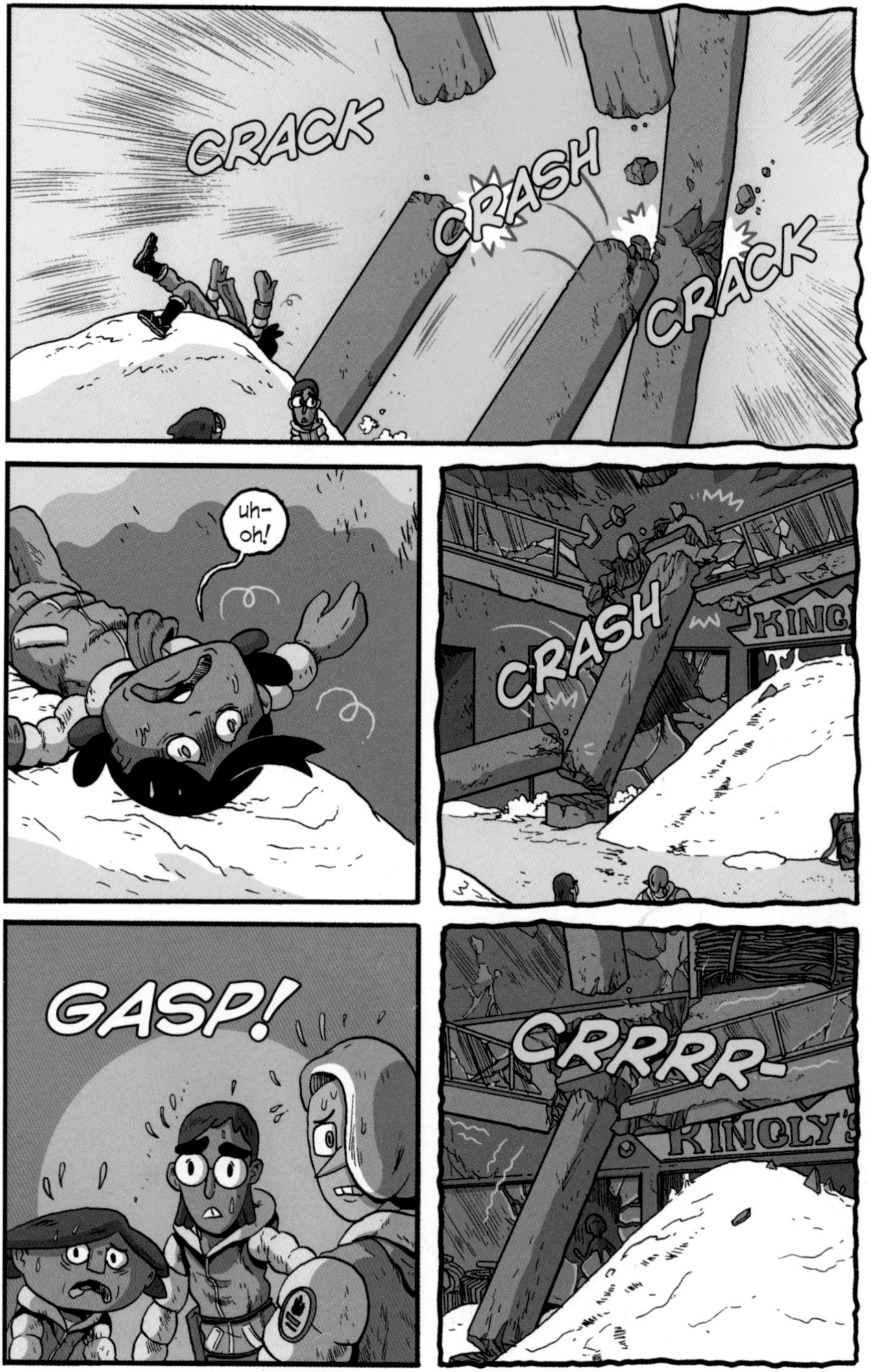
CRACK
CRASH
CRACK
uh-oh!
CRASH
KINGLY'S
GASP!
CRRRR-
KINGLY'S

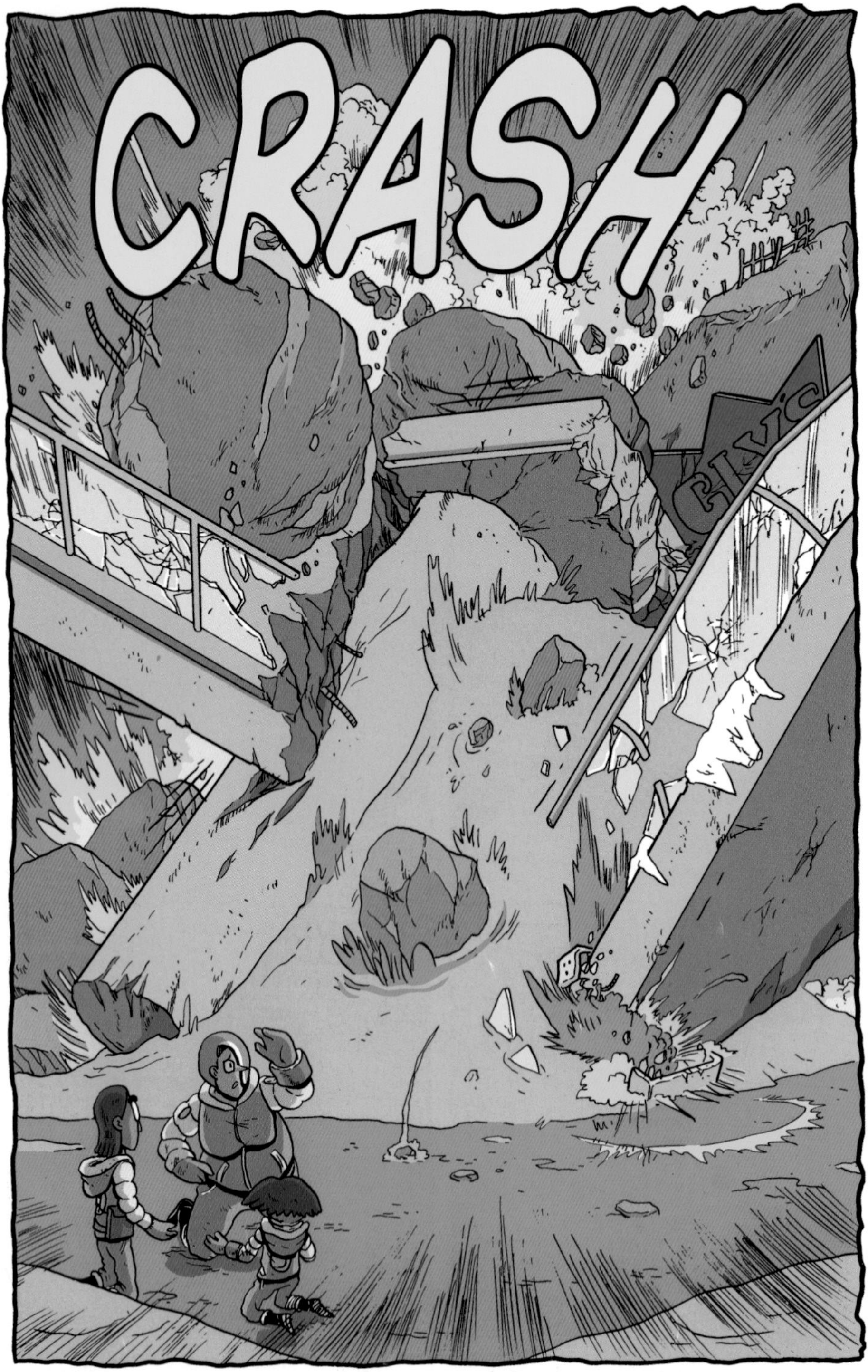
CRASH
CIVIC

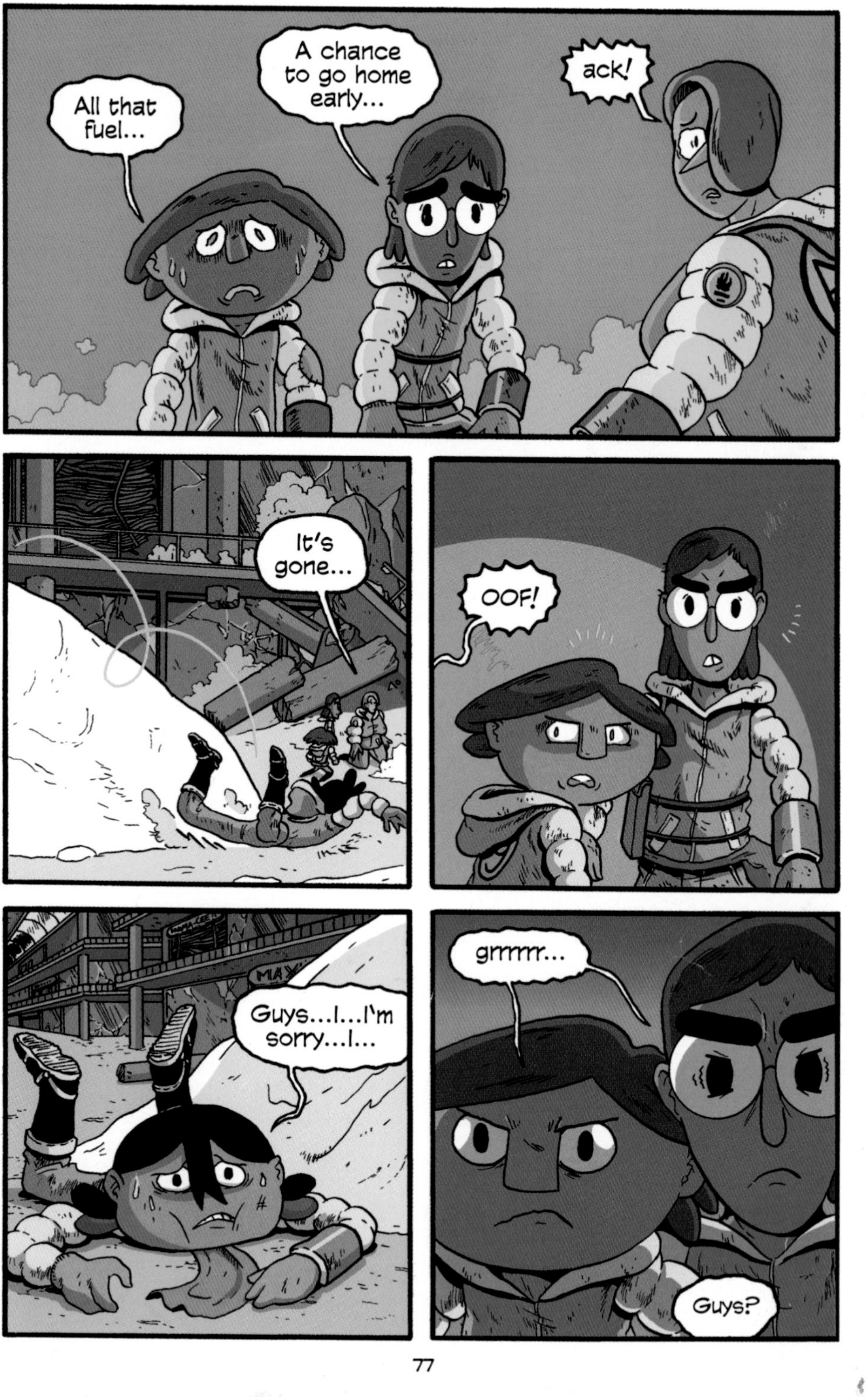
All that fuel...
A chance to go home early...
ack!
It's gone...
OOF!
Guys...I...I'm sorry...I...
grrrrrr...
Guys?

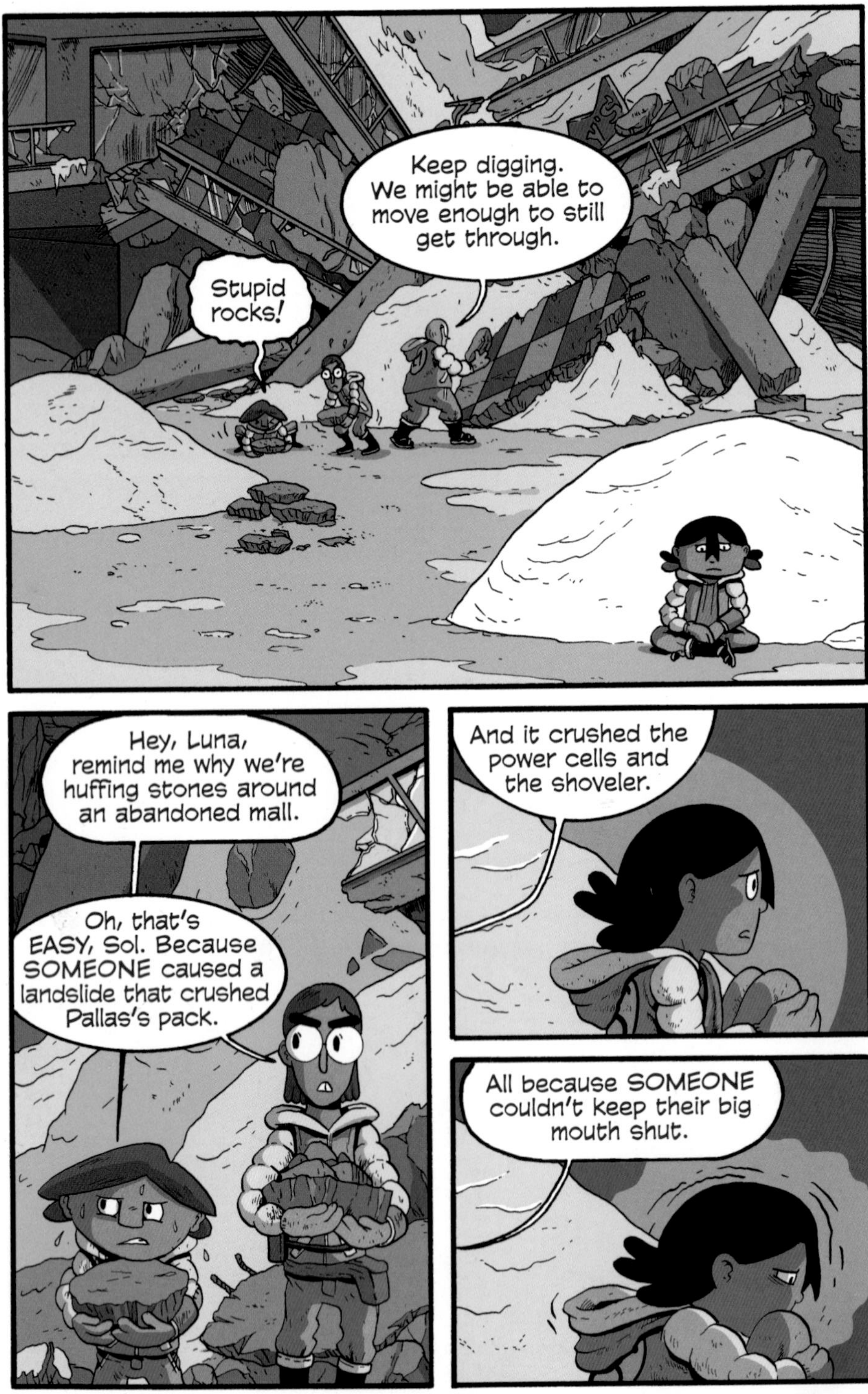

Keep digging. We might be able to move enough to still get through.
Stupid rocks!
Hey, Luna, remind me why we're huffing stones around an abandoned mall.
Oh, that's EASY, Sol. Because SOMEONE caused a landslide that crushed Pallas's pack.
And it crushed the power cells and the shoveler.
All because SOMEONE couldn't keep their big mouth shut.

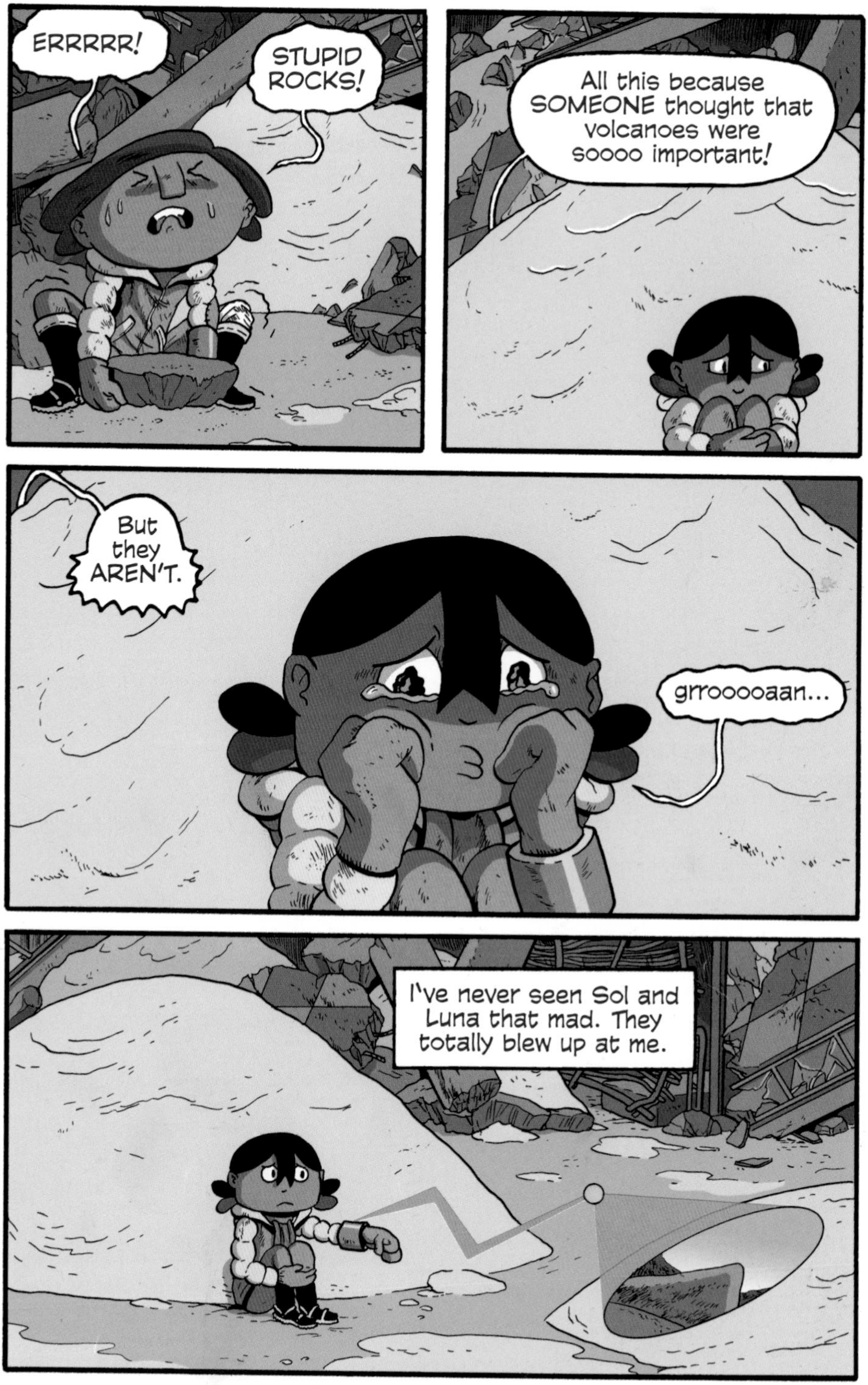
ERRRRR!
STUPID ROCKS!
All this because SOMEONE thought that volcanoes were soooo important!
But they AREN'T.
grrooooaan...
I've never seen Sol and Luna that mad. They totally blew up at me.

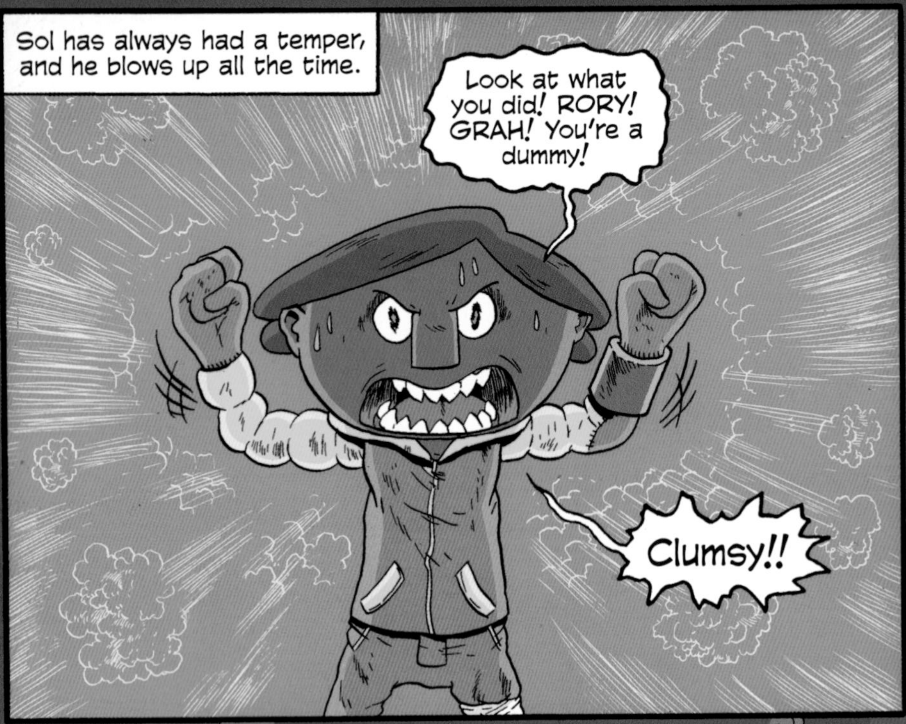
Sol has always had a temper, and he blows up all the time.
Look at what you did! RORY! GRAH! You're a dummy!
Clumsy!!

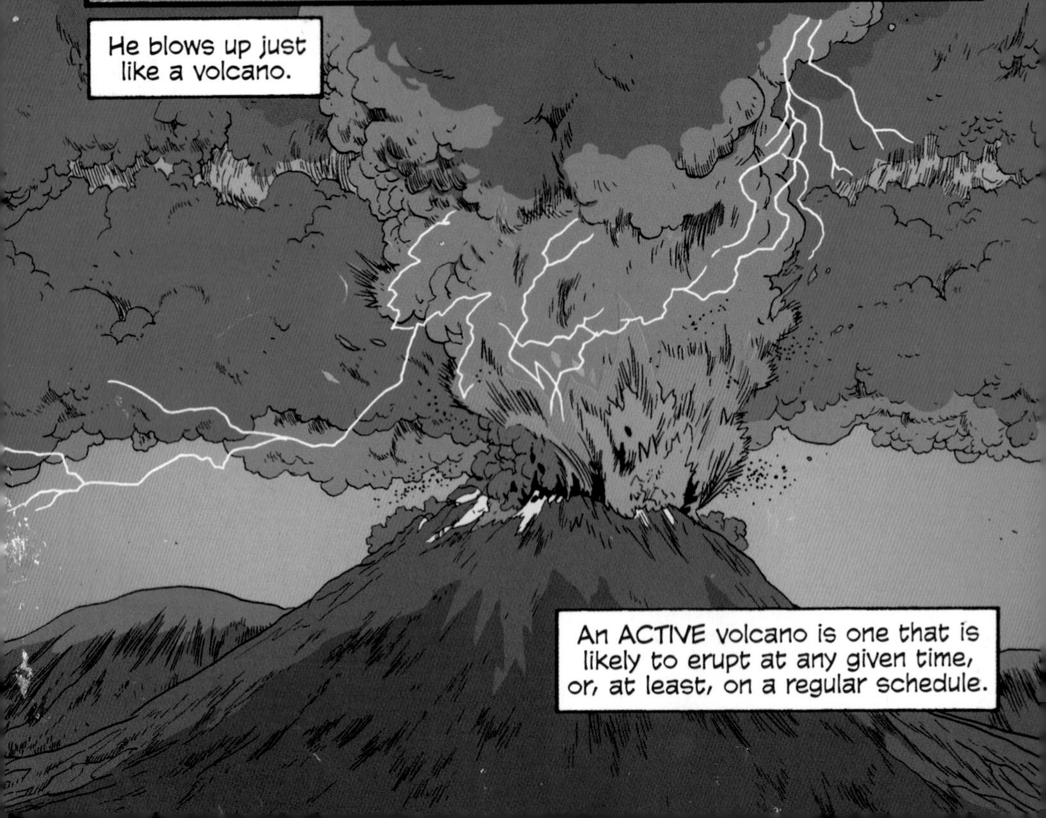
He blows up just like a volcano.
An ACTIVE volcano is one that is likely to erupt at any given time, or, at least, on a regular schedule.

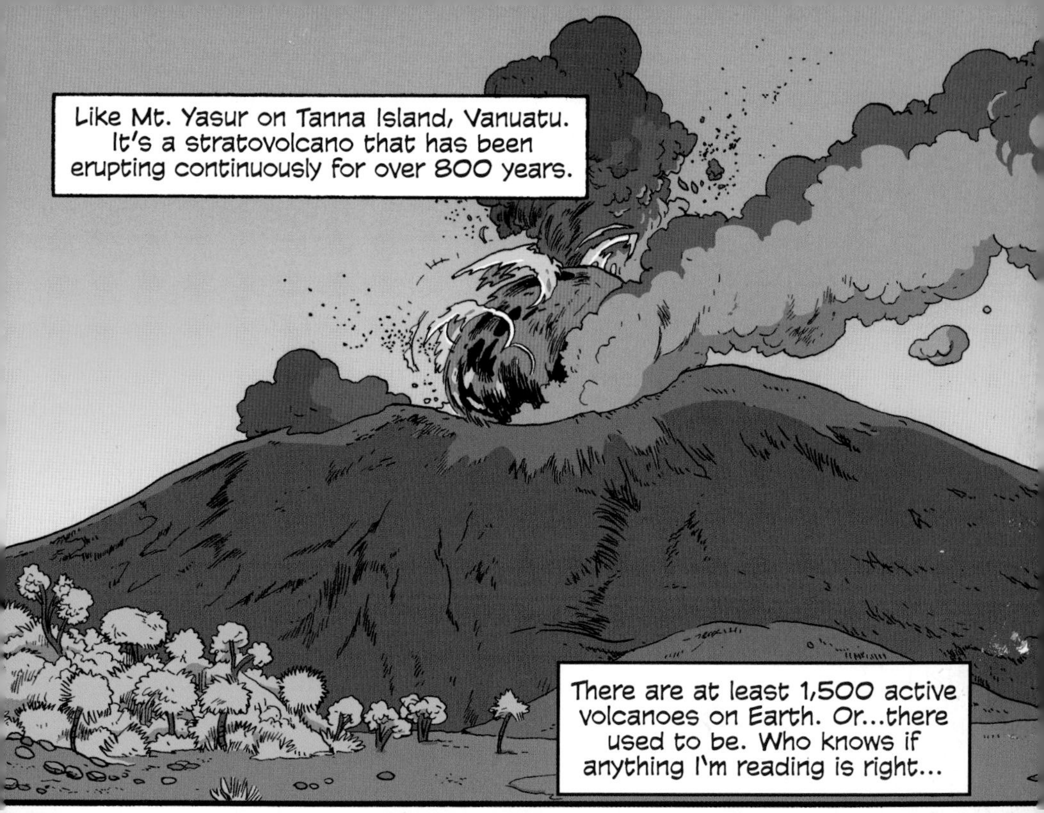
Like Mt. Yasur on Tanna Island, Vanuatu. It's a stratovolcano that has been erupting continuously for over 800 years.
There are at least 1,500 active volcanoes on Earth. Or...there used to be. Who knows if anything I'm reading is right...

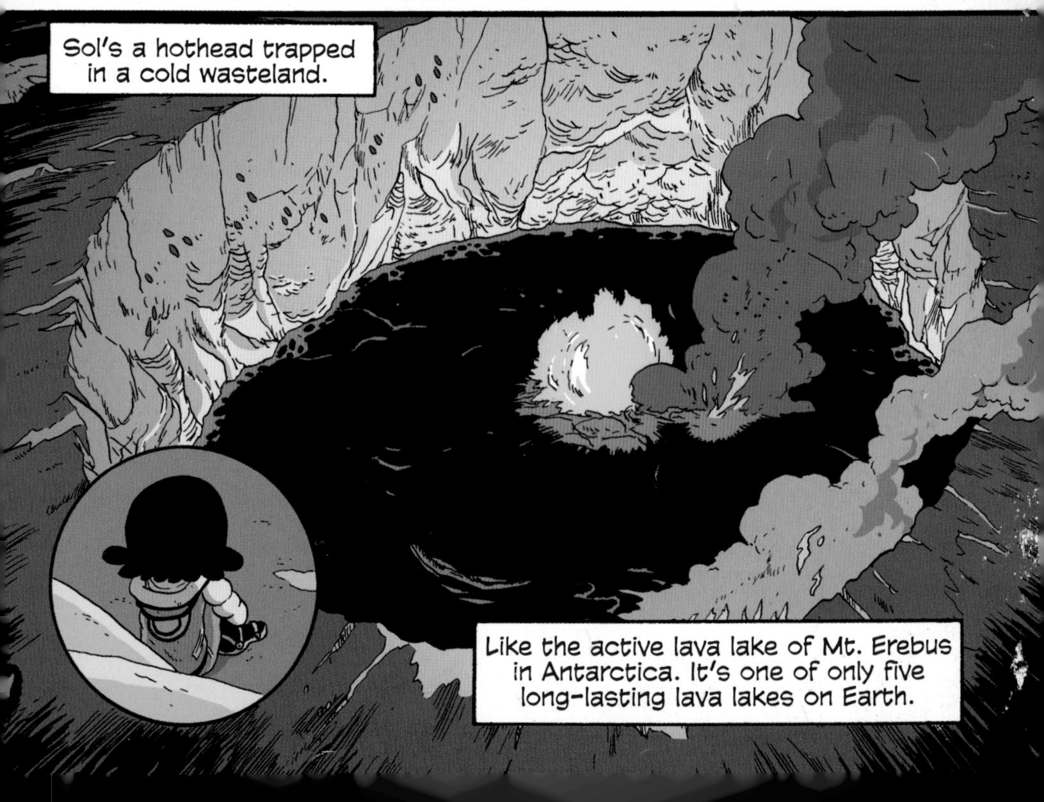
Sol's a hothead trapped in a cold wasteland.
Like the active lava lake of Mt. Erebus in Antarctica. It's one of only five long-lasting lava lakes on Earth.

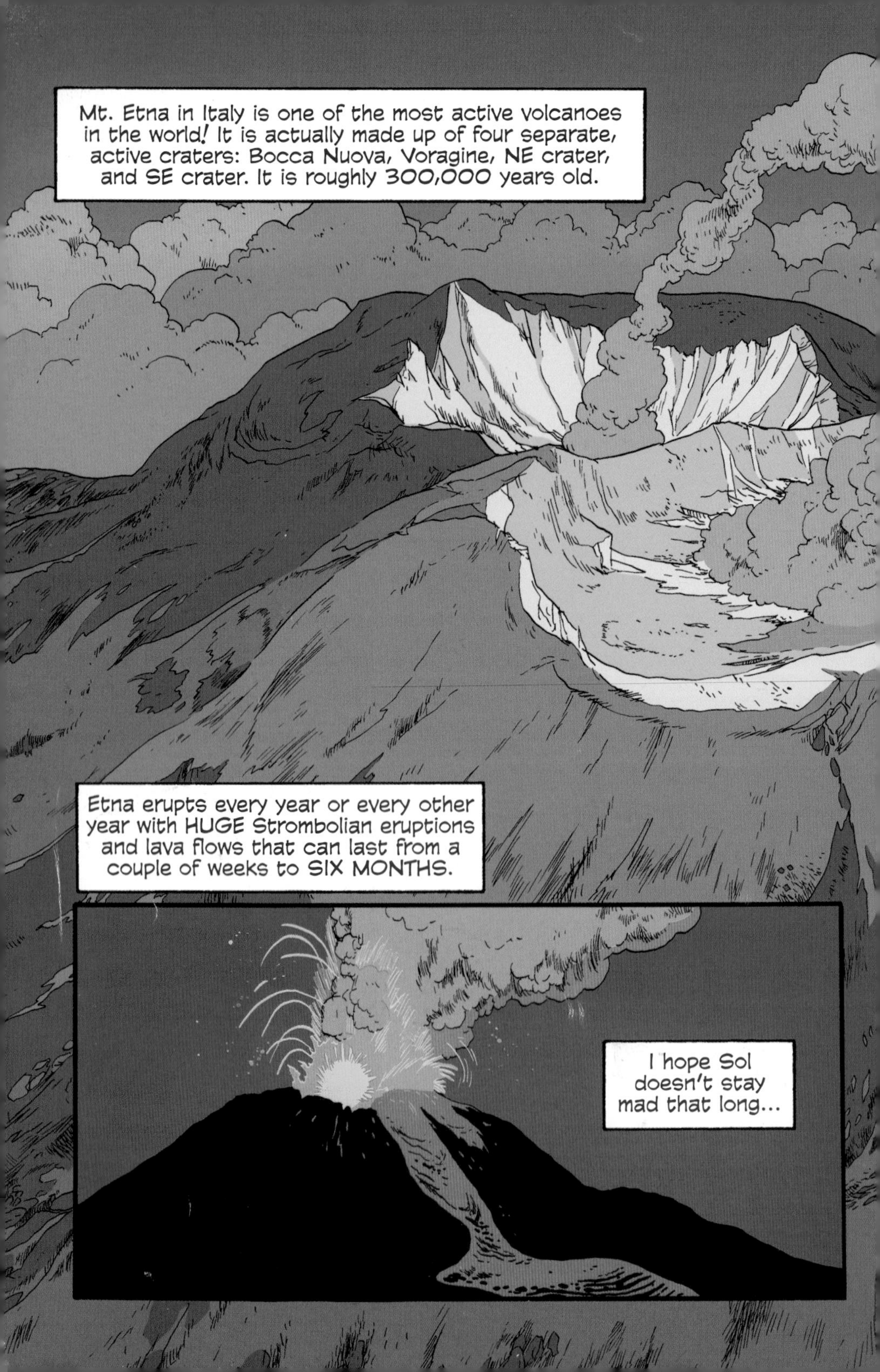
Mt. Etna in Italy is one of the most active volcanoes in the world! It is actually made up of four separate, active craters: Bocca Nuova, Voragine, NE crater, and SE crater. It is roughly 300,000 years old.
Etna erupts every year or every other year with HUGE Strombolian eruptions and lava flows that can last from a couple of weeks to SIX MONTHS.
I hope Sol doesn't stay mad that long...

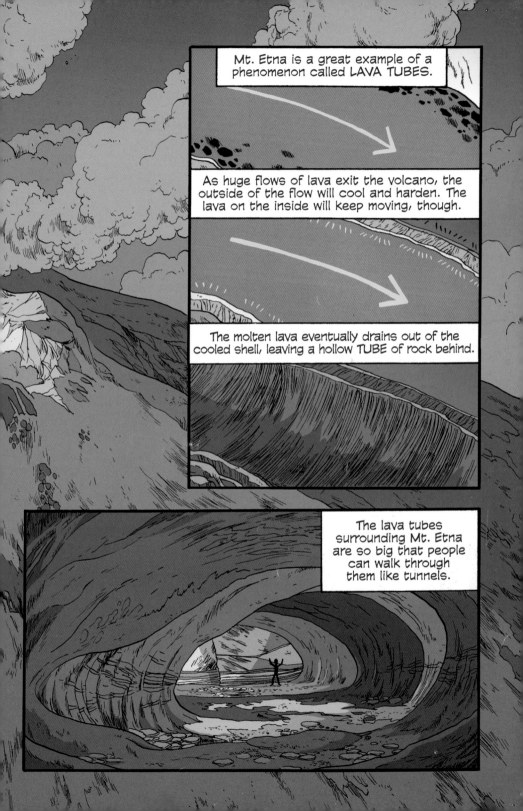

Mt. Etna is a great example of a phenomenon called LAVA TUBES.

As huge flows of lava exit the volcano, the outside of the flow will cool and harden. The lava on the inside will keep moving, though.

The molten lava eventually drains out of the cooled shell, leaving a hollow TUBE of rock behind.

The lava tubes surrounding Mt. Etna are so big that people can walk through them like tunnels.

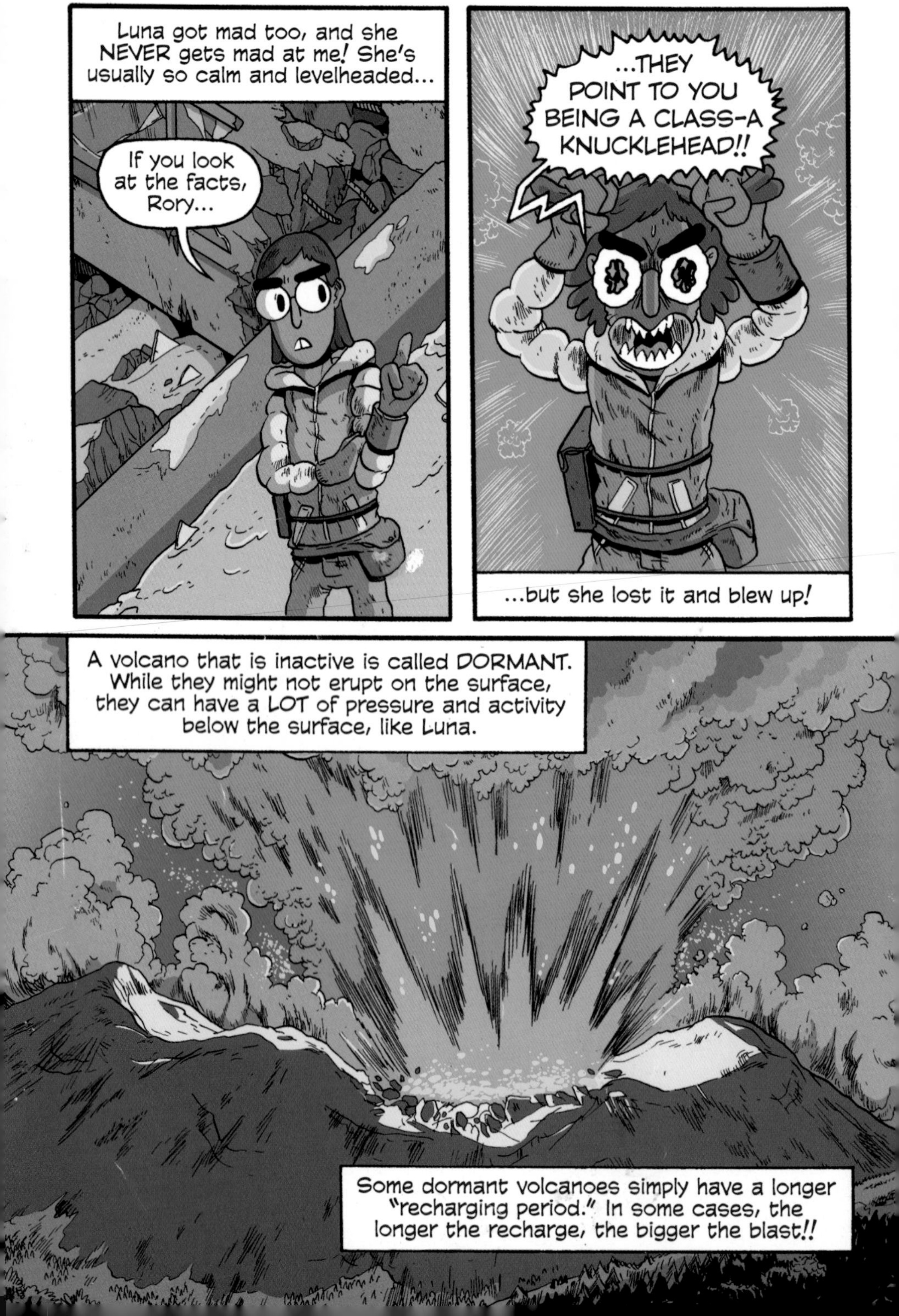
Luna got mad too, and she NEVER gets mad at me! She's usually so calm and levelheaded...
If you look at the facts, Rory...
...THEY POINT TO YOU BEING A CLASS-A KNUCKLEHEAD!!
...but she lost it and blew up!
A volcano that is inactive is called DORMANT. While they might not erupt on the surface, they can have a LOT of pressure and activity below the surface, like Luna.
Some dormant volcanoes simply have a longer "recharging period." In some cases, the longer the recharge, the bigger the blast!!

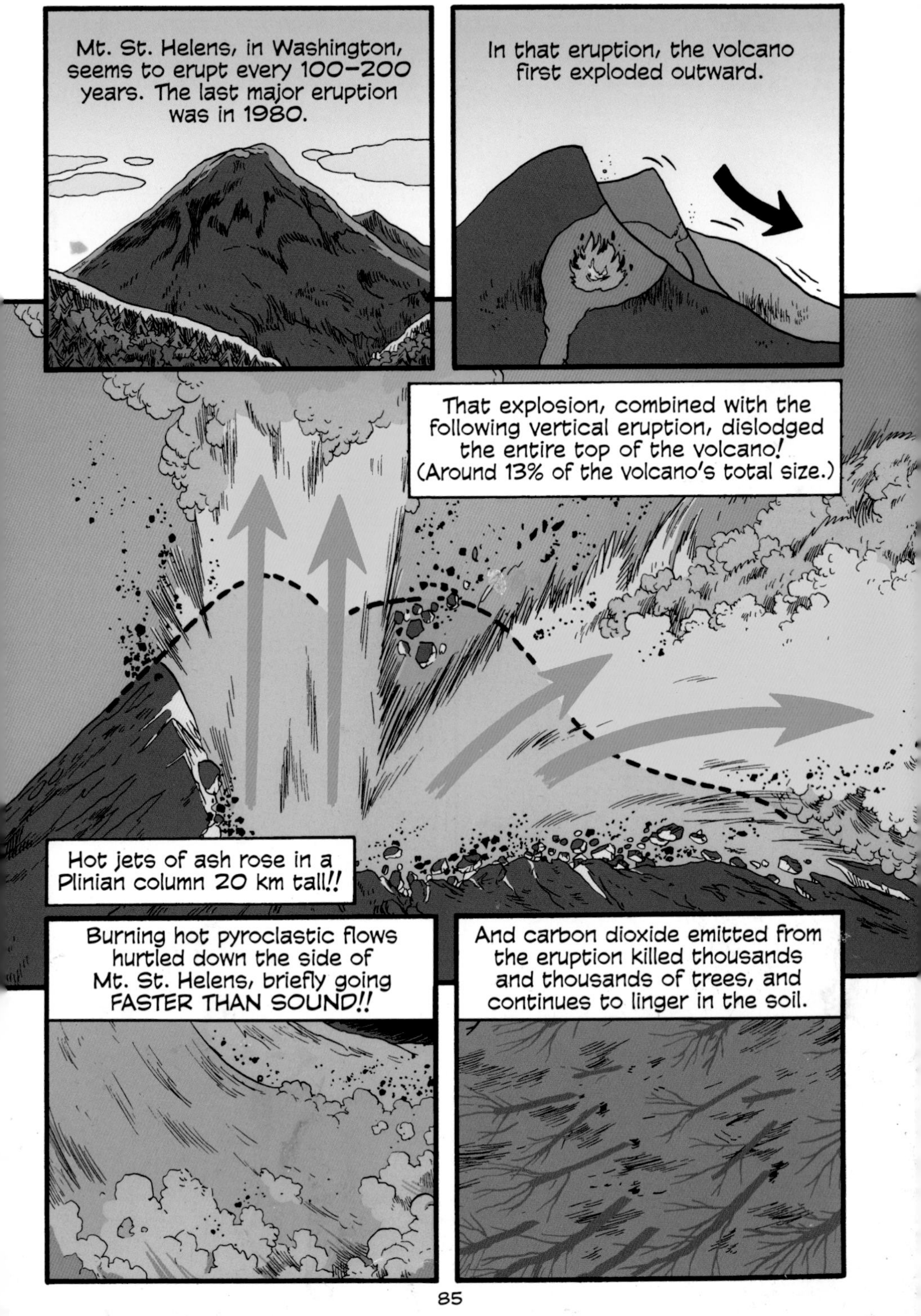
Mt. St. Helens, in Washington, seems to erupt every 100–200 years. The last major eruption was in 1980.
In that eruption, the volcano first exploded outward.
That explosion, combined with the following vertical eruption, dislodged the entire top of the volcano! (Around 13% of the volcano's total size.)
Hot jets of ash rose in a Plinian column 20 km tall!!
Burning hot pyroclastic flows hurtled down the side of Mt. St. Helens, briefly going FASTER THAN SOUND!!
And carbon dioxide emitted from the eruption killed thousands and thousands of trees, and continues to linger in the soil.

One of the most famous eruptions in recorded history was from the dormant volcano, Mt. Vesuvius, in 79 AD.

This eruption permanently changed Vesuvius and destroyed the towns of Pompeii and Herculaneum.

The eruption lasted more than 30 hours, during which 1.5 BILLION kg of material were shot out of the volcano EVERY SECOND.

The initial plume was over 19 km tall!

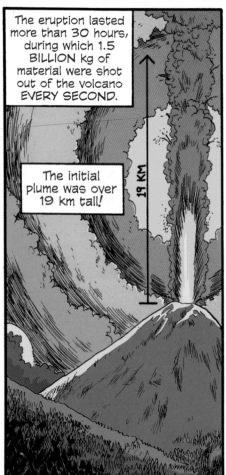

19 KM

Heavier chunks of white pumice were the first to descend on Pompeii and Herculaneum.

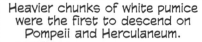

These 140°C rocks were up to 3cm in circumference and caught houses and other structures on fire.

The pyroclastic flows followed...

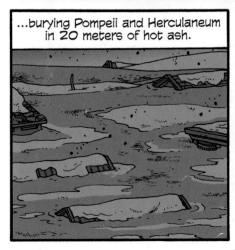

...burying Pompeii and Herculaneum in 20 meters of hot ash.

The ash hardened, preserving the buildings and people trapped inside for future study.

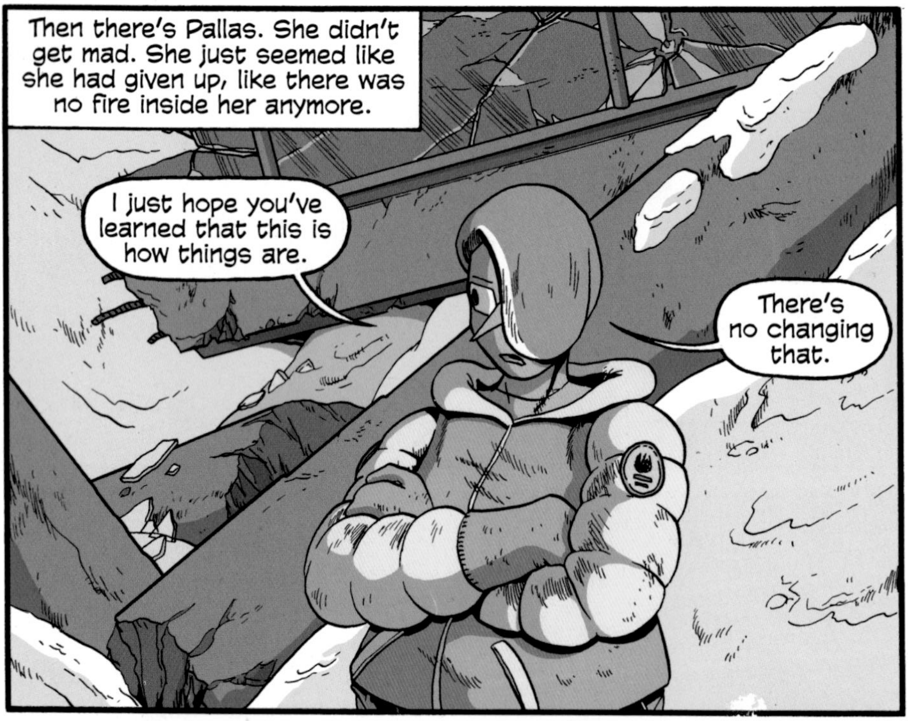
Then there's Pallas. She didn't get mad. She just seemed like she had given up, like there was no fire inside her anymore.
I just hope you've learned that this is how things are.
There's no changing that.

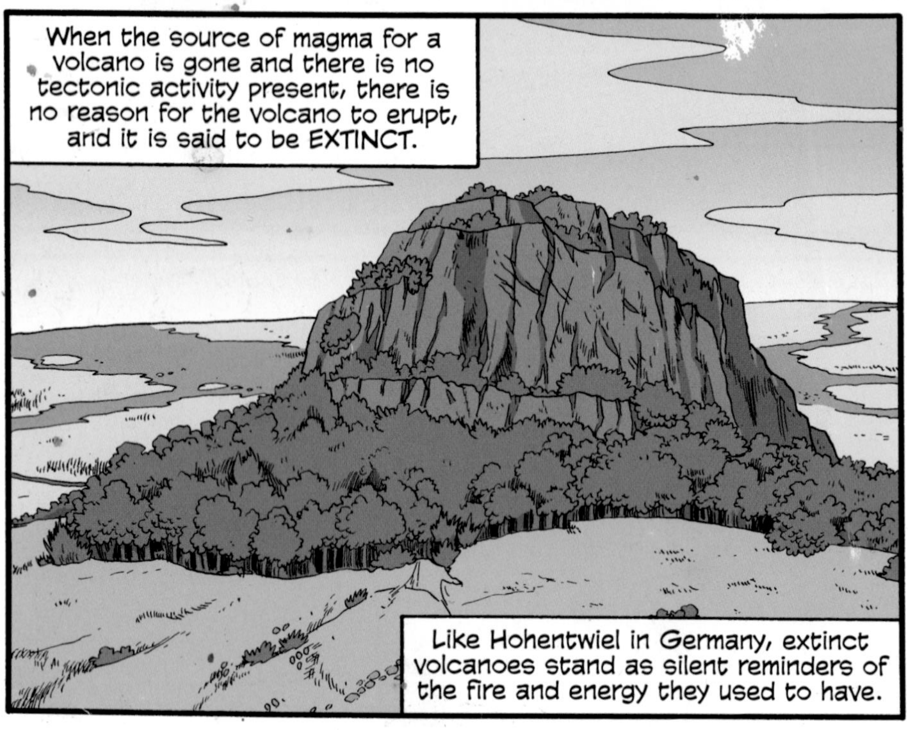
When the source of magma for a volcano is gone and there is no tectonic activity present, there is no reason for the volcano to erupt, and it is said to be EXTINCT.
Like Hohentwiel in Germany, extinct volcanoes stand as silent reminders of the fire and energy they used to have.

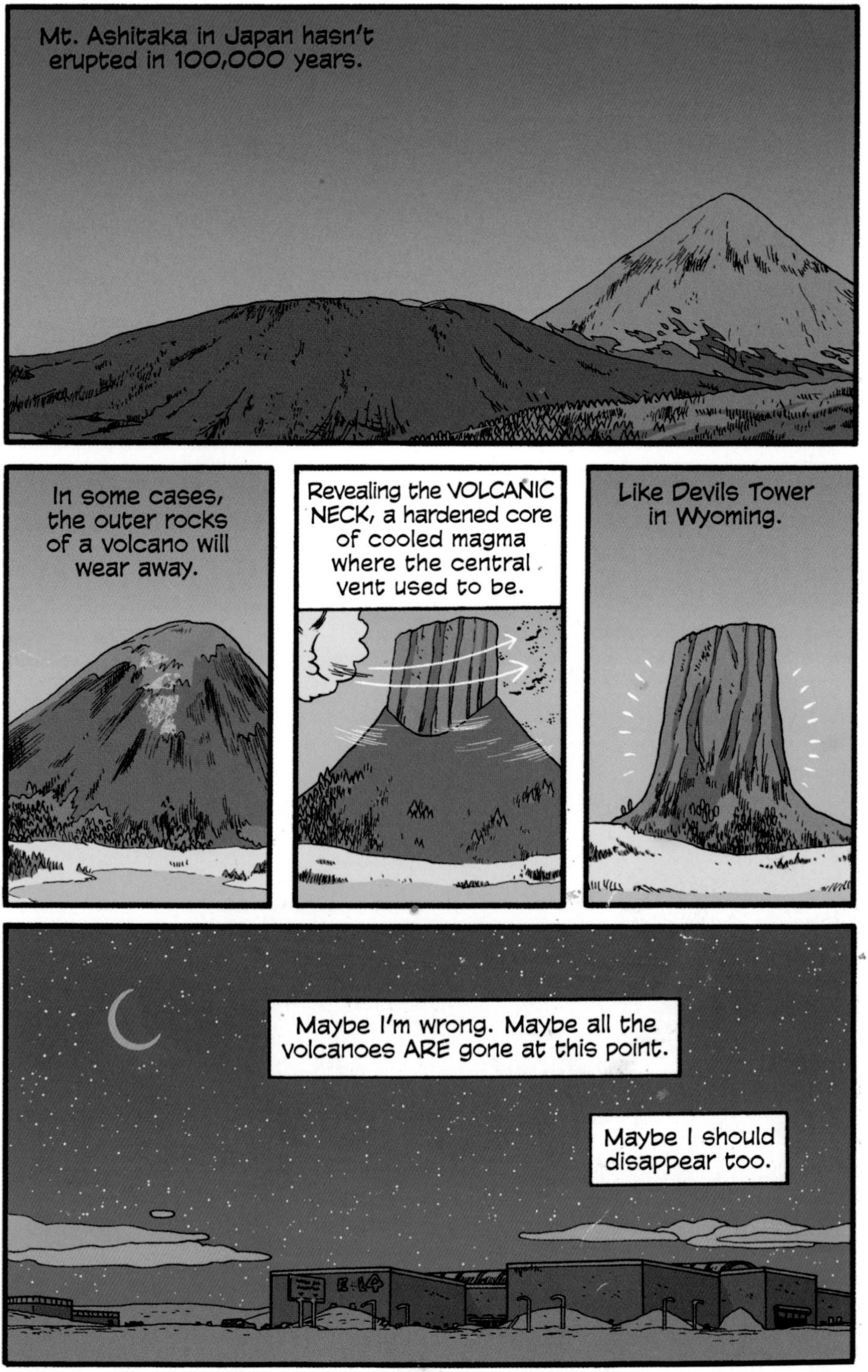
Mt. Ashitaka in Japan hasn't erupted in 100,000 years.
In some cases, the outer rocks of a volcano will wear away.
Revealing the VOLCANIC NECK, a hardened core of cooled magma where the central vent used to be.
Like Devils Tower in Wyoming.
Maybe I'm wrong. Maybe all the volcanoes ARE gone at this point.
Maybe I should disappear too.

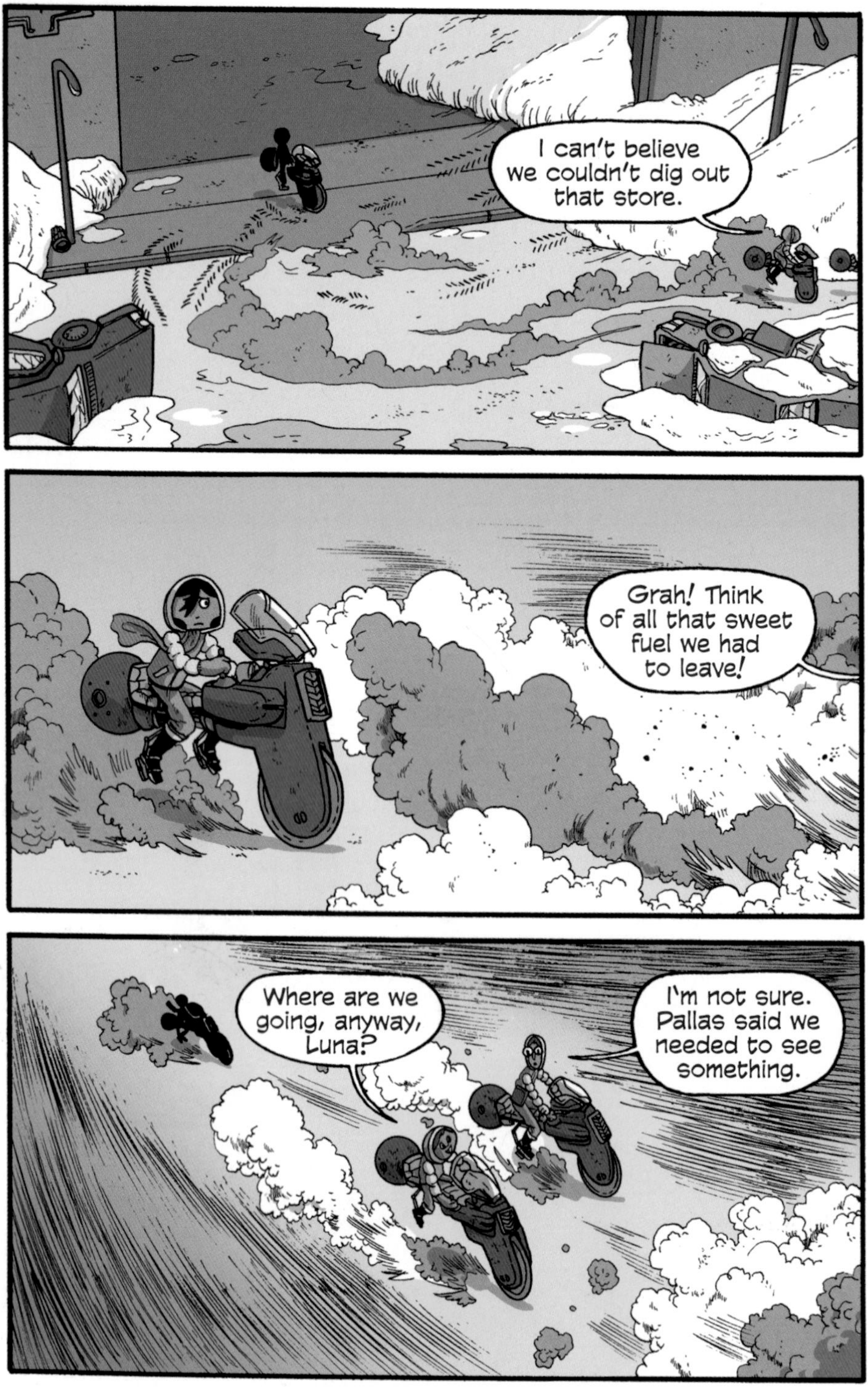
I can't believe we couldn't dig out that store.
Grah! Think of all that sweet fuel we had to leave!
Where are we going, anyway, Luna?
I'm not sure. Pallas said we needed to see something.

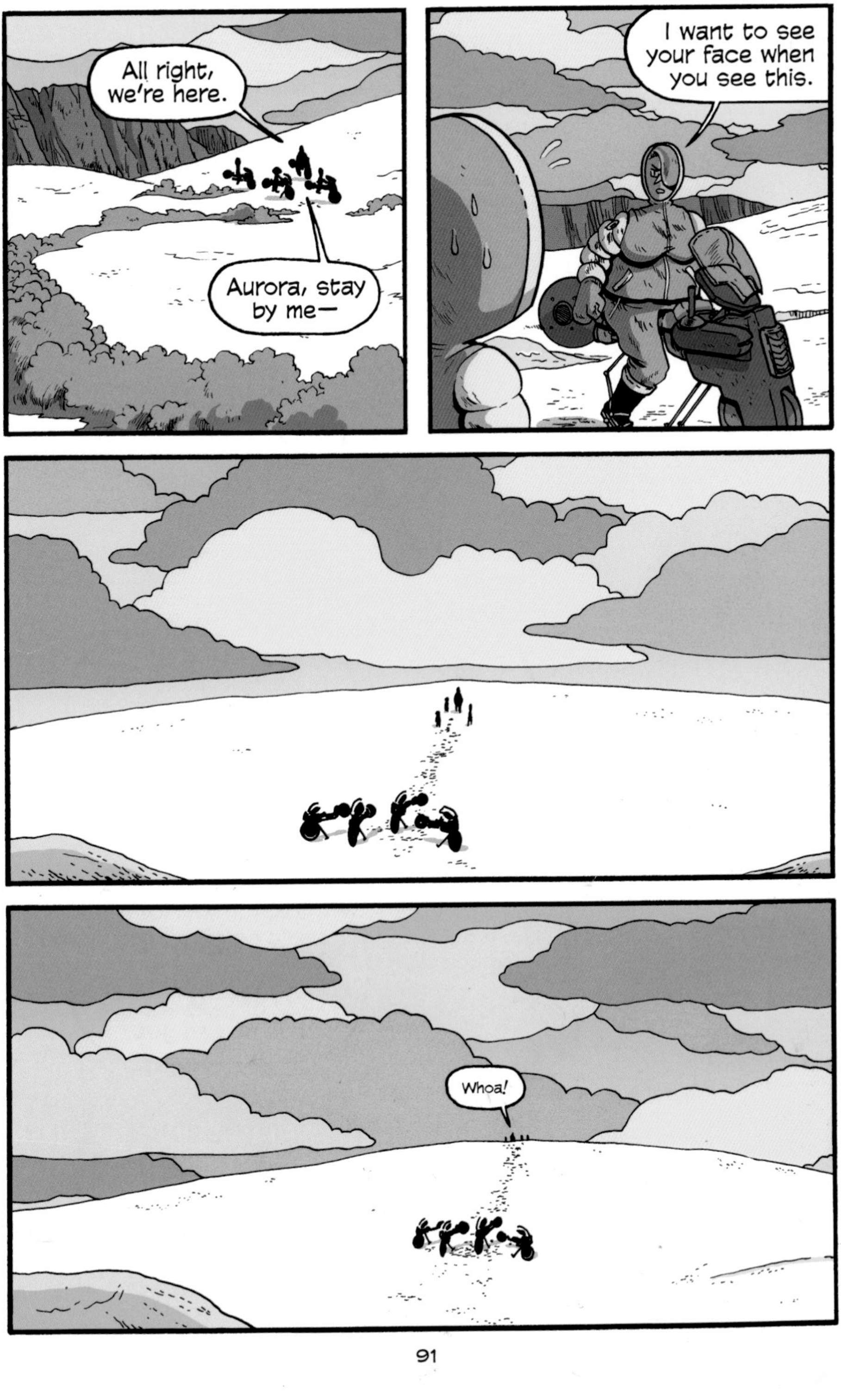
All right, we're here.
Aurora, stay by me—
I want to see your face when you see this.
Whoa!

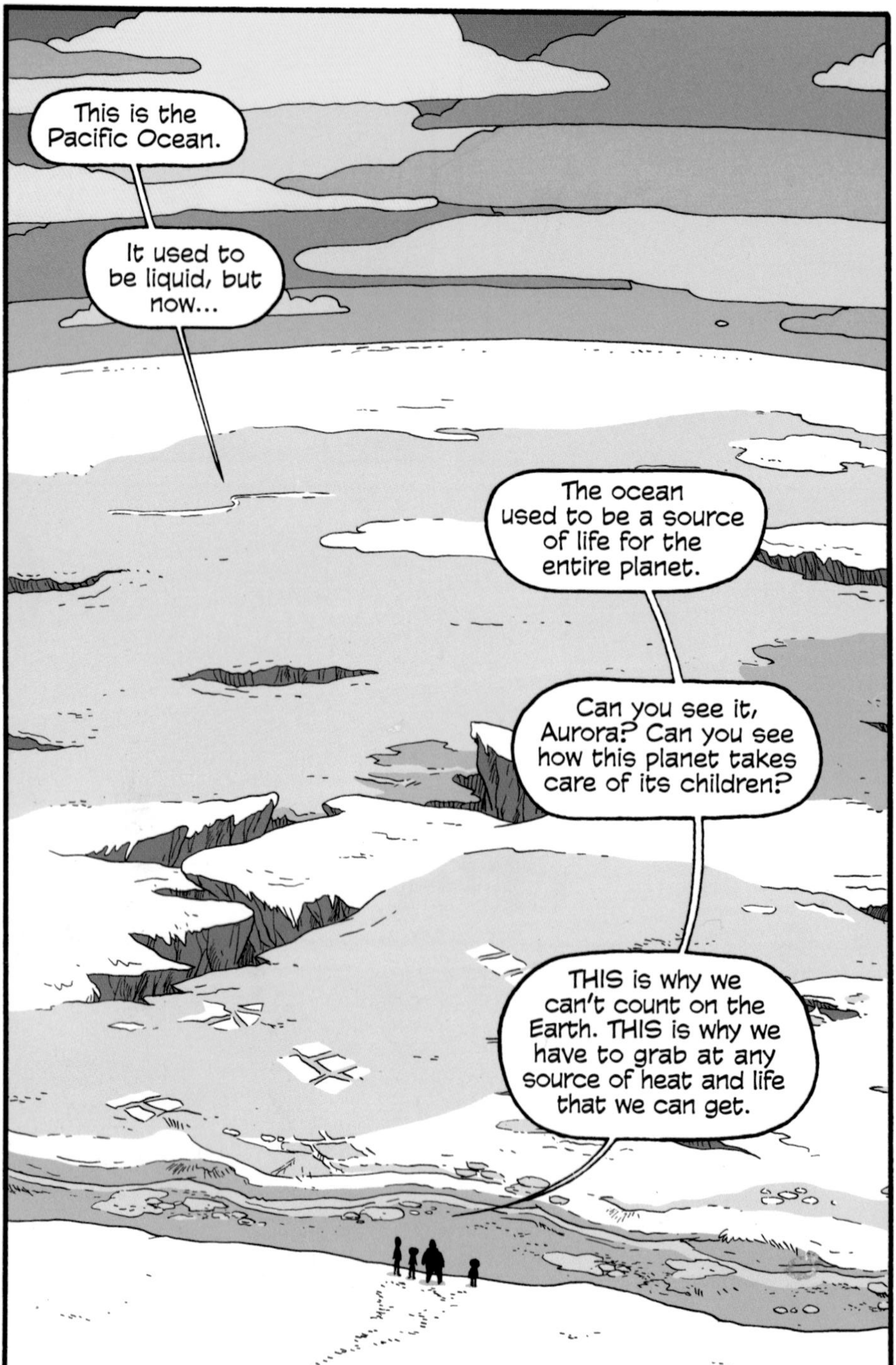
This is the Pacific Ocean.
It used to be liquid, but now...
The ocean used to be a source of life for the entire planet.
Can you see it, Aurora? Can you see how this planet takes care of its children?
THIS is why we can't count on the Earth. THIS is why we have to grab at any source of heat and life that we can get.

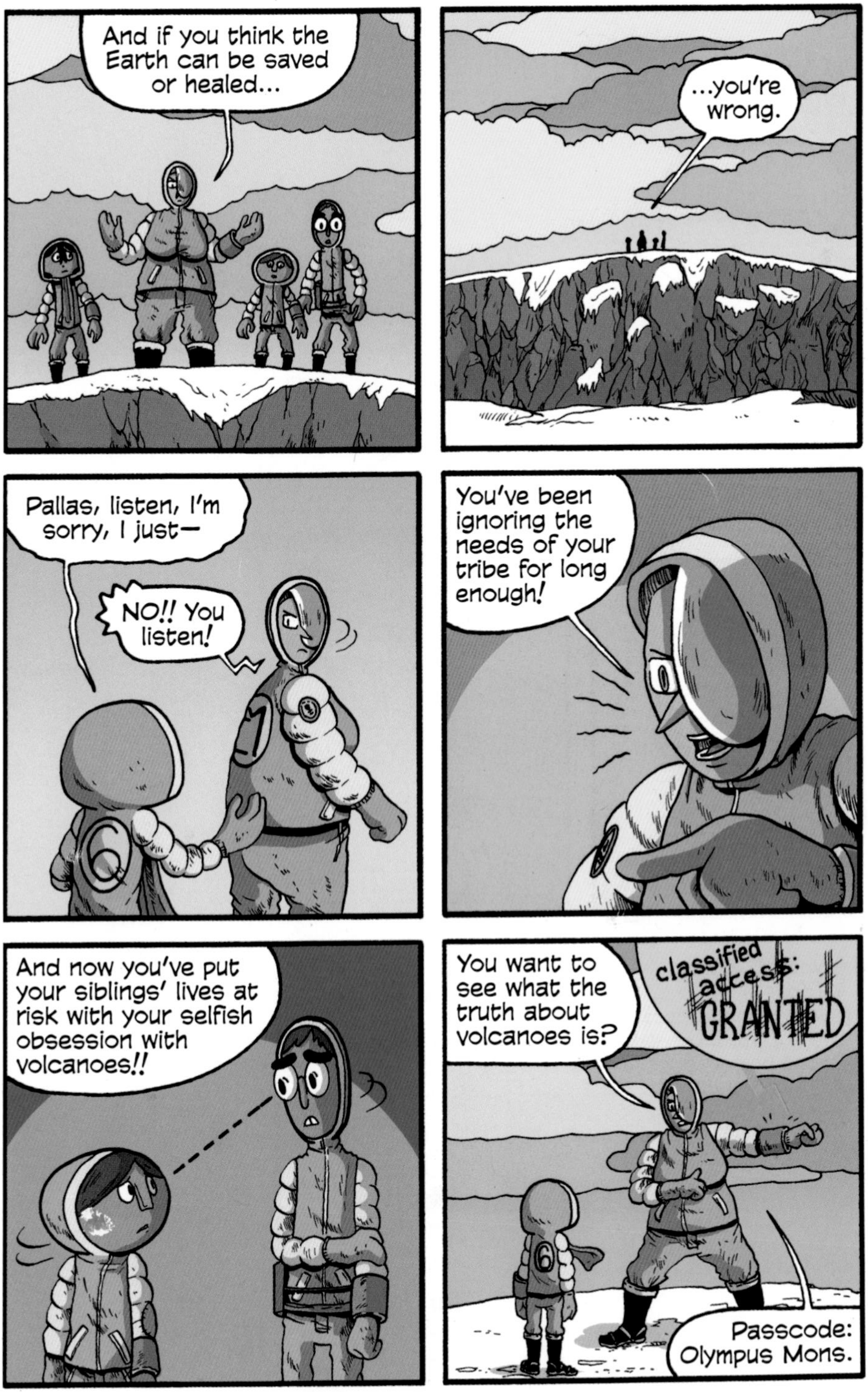
And if you think the Earth can be saved or healed...
...you're wrong.
Pallas, listen, I'm sorry, I just—
NO!! You listen!
You've been ignoring the needs of your tribe for long enough!
And now you've put your siblings' lives at risk with your selfish obsession with volcanoes!!
You want to see what the truth about volcanoes is?
classified access:
GRANTED
Passcode: Olympus Mons.

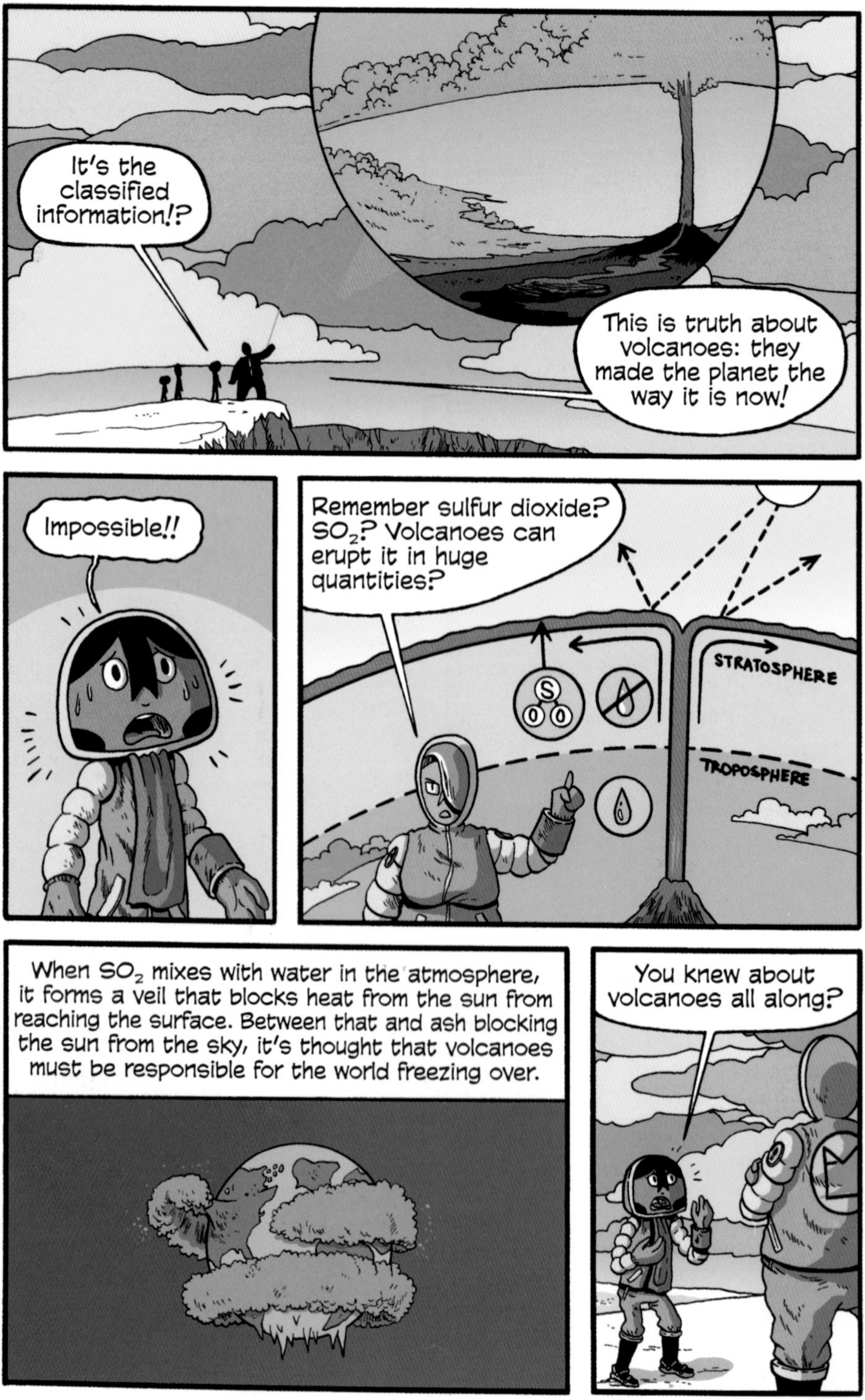
It's the classified information!?
This is truth about volcanoes: they made the planet the way it is now!
Impossible!!
Remember sulfur dioxide? SO2? Volcanoes can erupt it in huge quantities?
STRATOSPHERE
TROPOSPHERE
When SO2 mixes with water in the atmosphere, it forms a veil that blocks heat from the sun from reaching the surface. Between that and ash blocking the sun from the sky, it's thought that volcanoes must be responsible for the world freezing over.
You knew about volcanoes all along?

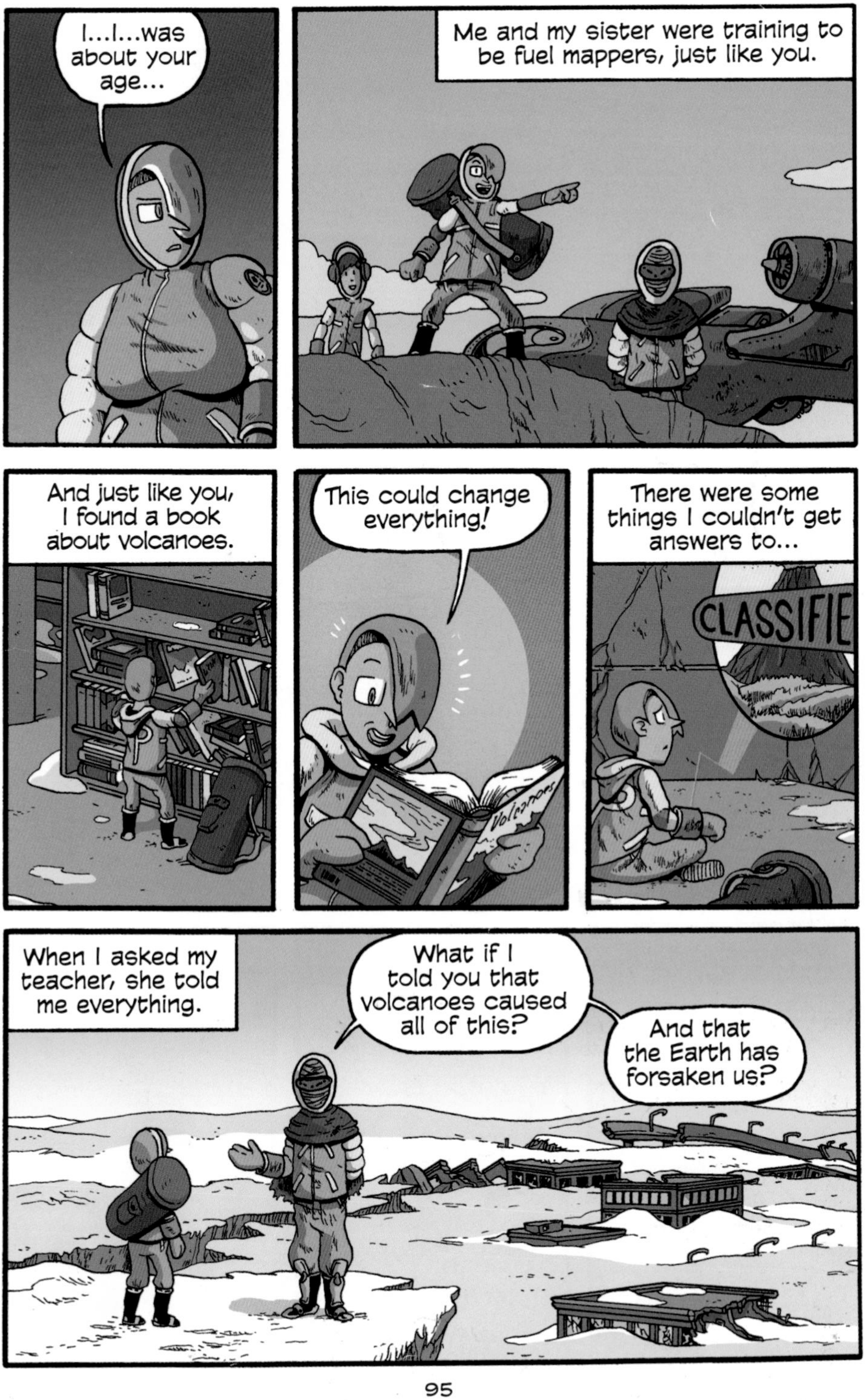

I...I...was about your age...
Me and my sister were training to be fuel mappers, just like you.
And just like you, I found a book about volcanoes.
This could change everything!
Volcanoes
There were some things I couldn't get answers to...
CLASSIFIE
When I asked my teacher, she told me everything.
What if I told you that volcanoes caused all of this?
And that the Earth has forsaken us?

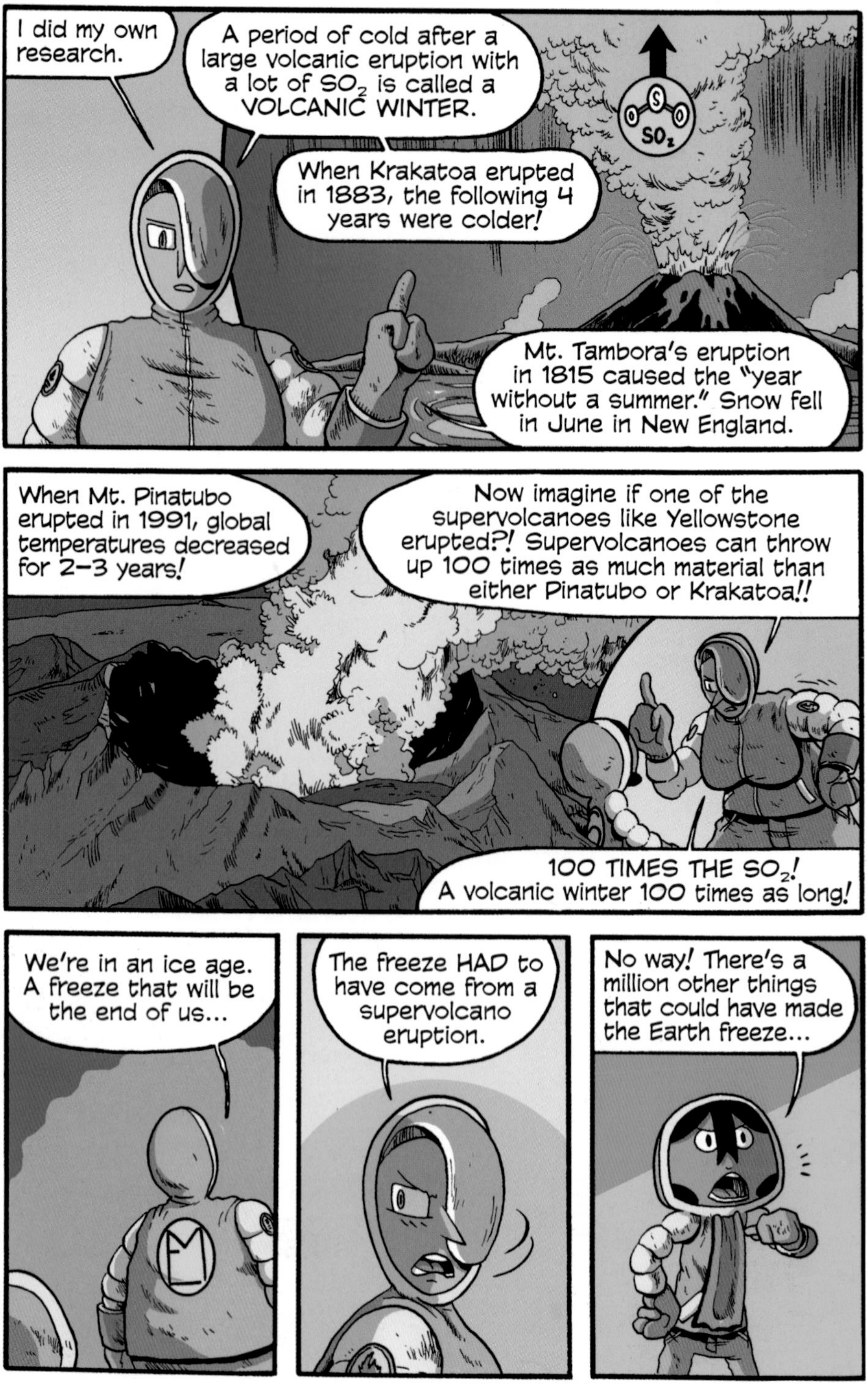
I did my own research.
A period of cold after a large volcanic eruption with a lot of SO_2 is called a VOLCANIC WINTER.
SO_2
When Krakatoa erupted in 1883, the following 4 years were colder!
Mt. Tambora's eruption in 1815 caused the "year without a summer." Snow fell in June in New England.
When Mt. Pinatubo erupted in 1991, global temperatures decreased for 2–3 years!
Now imagine if one of the supervolcanoes like Yellowstone erupted?! Supervolcanoes can throw up 100 times as much material than either Pinatubo or Krakatoa!!
100 TIMES THE SO_2! A volcanic winter 100 times as long!
We're in an ice age. A freeze that will be the end of us...
The freeze HAD to have come from a supervolcano eruption.
No way! There's a million other things that could have made the Earth freeze...

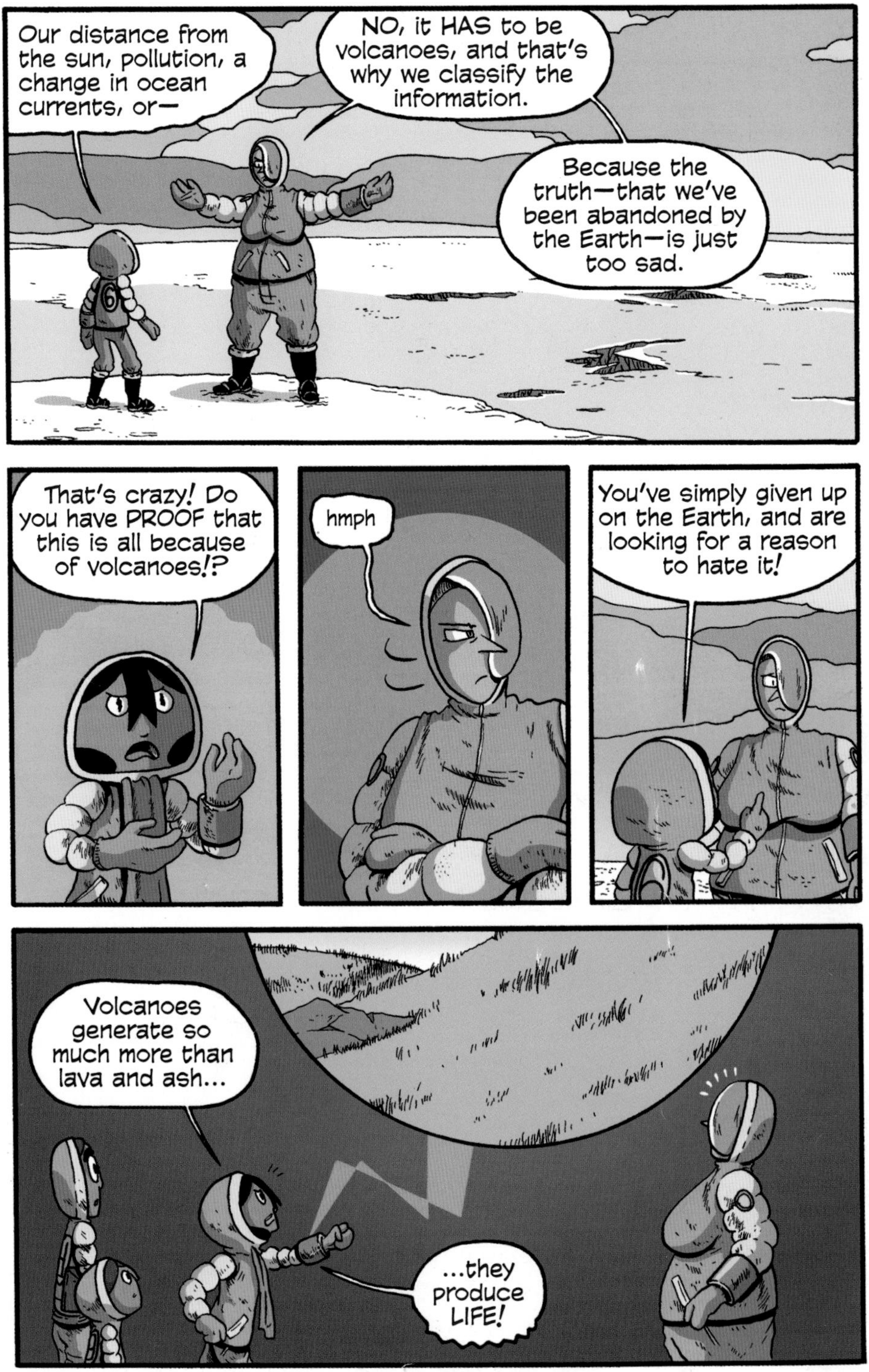

Our distance from the sun, pollution, a change in ocean currents, or—
NO, it HAS to be volcanoes, and that's why we classify the information.
Because the truth—that we've been abandoned by the Earth—is just too sad.
That's crazy! Do you have PROOF that this is all because of volcanoes!?
hmph
You've simply given up on the Earth, and are looking for a reason to hate it!
Volcanoes generate so much more than lava and ash...
...they produce LIFE!

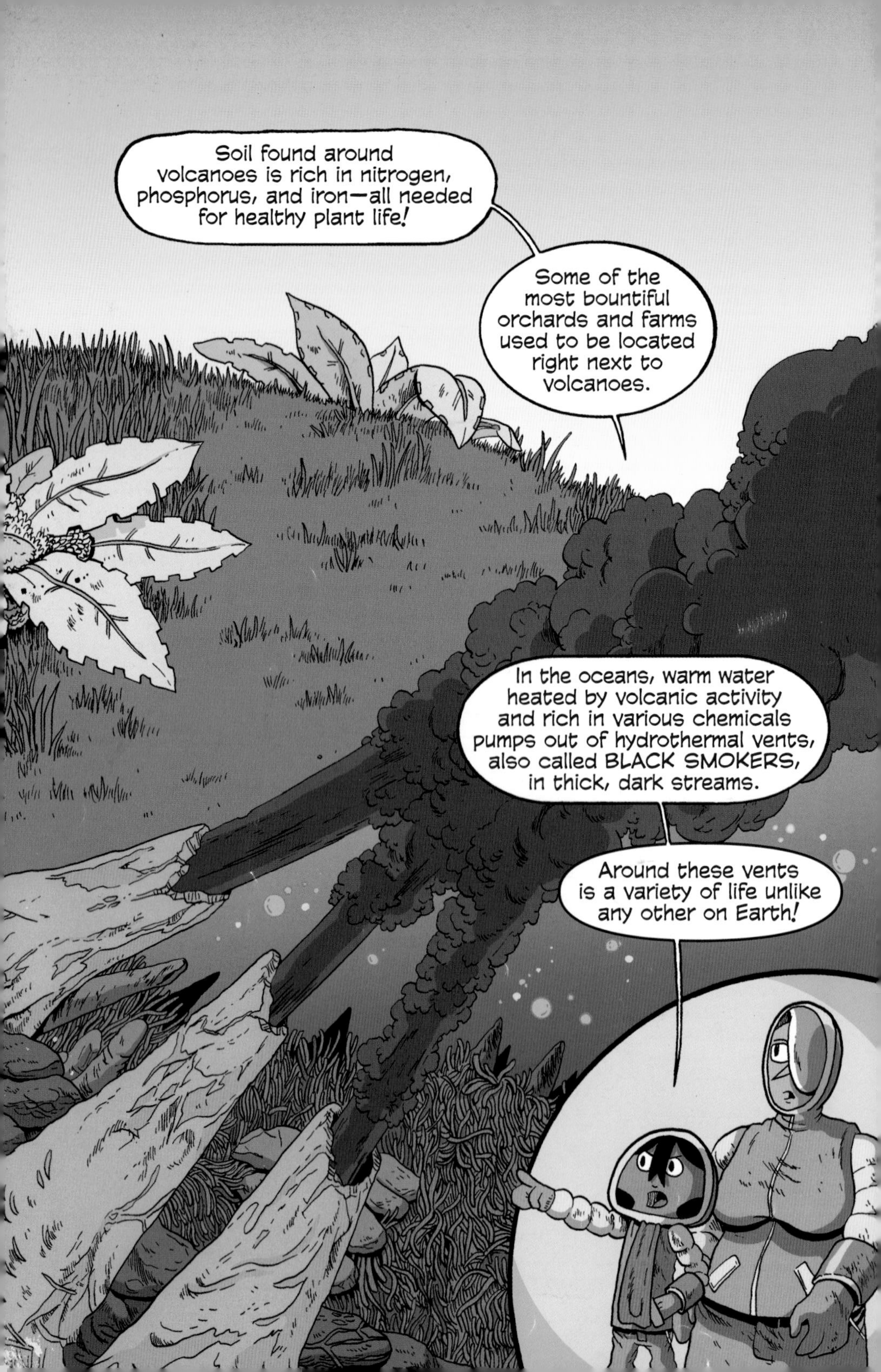
Soil found around volcanoes is rich in nitrogen, phosphorus, and iron—all needed for healthy plant life!
Some of the most bountiful orchards and farms used to be located right next to volcanoes.
In the oceans, warm water heated by volcanic activity and rich in various chemicals pumps out of hydrothermal vents, also called BLACK SMOKERS, in thick, dark streams.
Around these vents is a variety of life unlike any other on Earth!

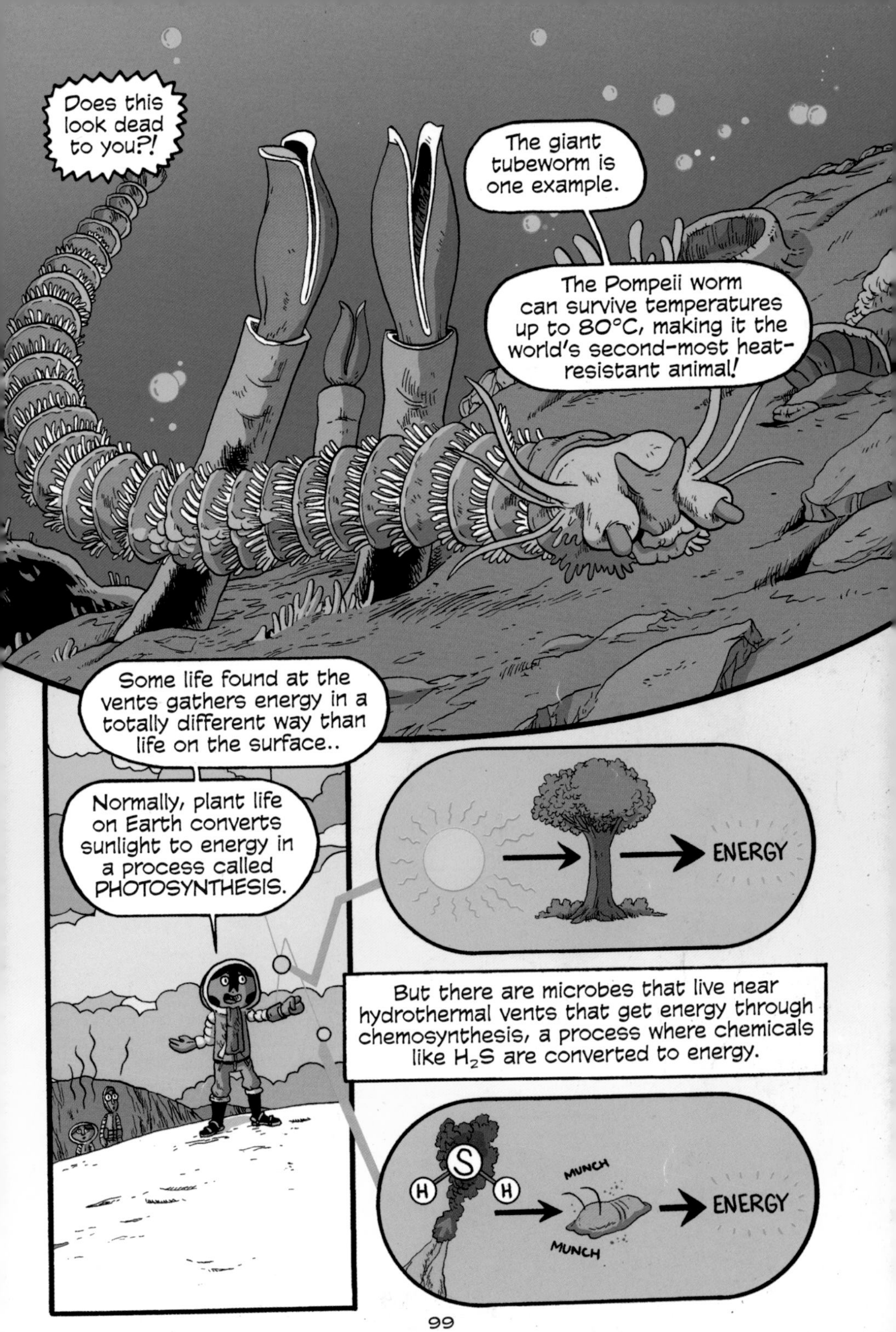
Does this look dead to you?!
The giant tubeworm is one example.
The Pompeii worm can survive temperatures up to 80°C, making it the world's second-most heat-resistant animal!
Some life found at the vents gathers energy in a totally different way than life on the surface..
Normally, plant life on Earth converts sunlight to energy in a process called PHOTOSYNTHESIS.
ENERGY
But there are microbes that live near hydrothermal vents that get energy through chemosynthesis, a process where chemicals like H_2S are converted to energy.
S
H
H
MUNCH
MUNCH
ENERGY

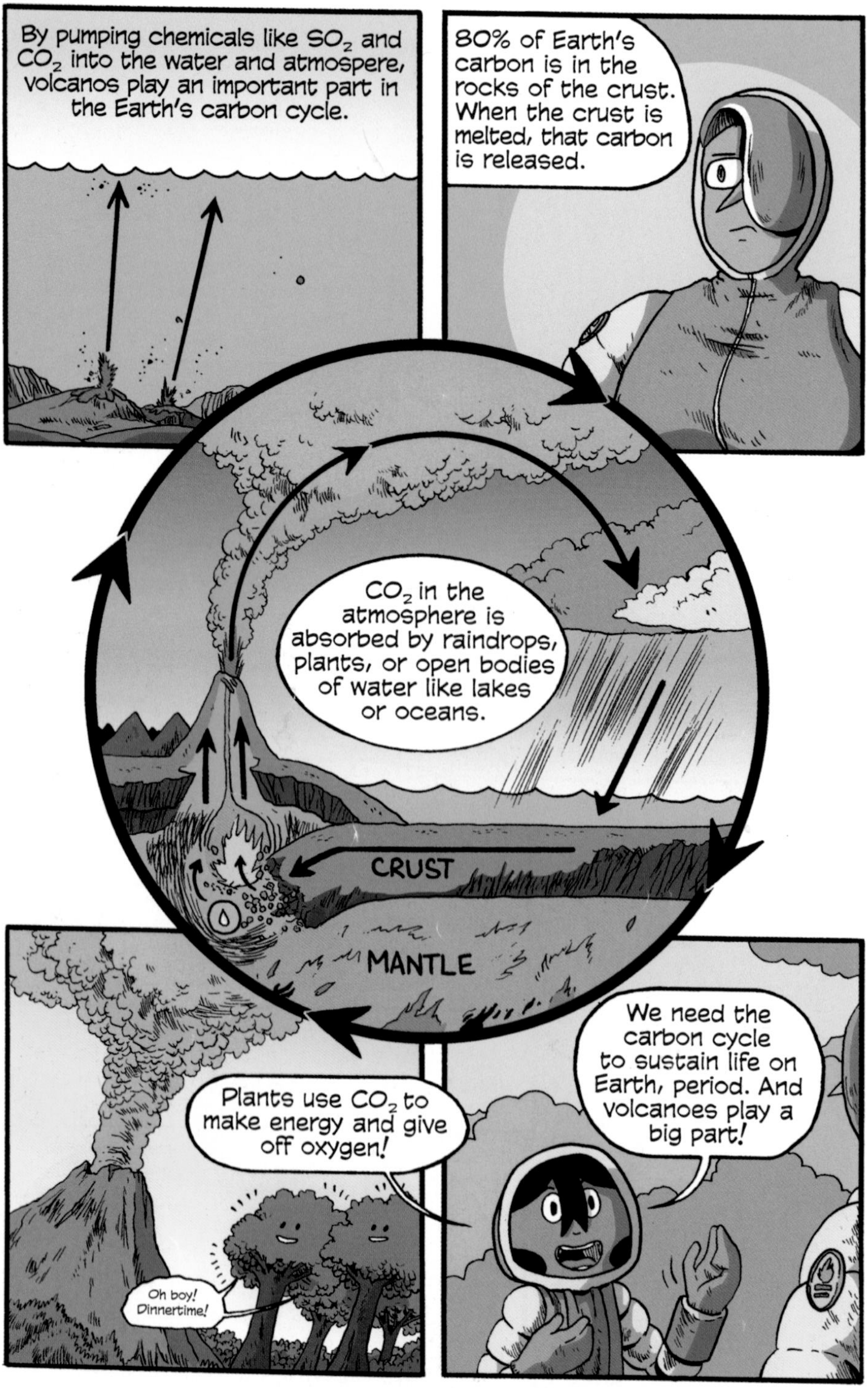
By pumping chemicals like SO_2 and CO_2 into the water and atmospere, volcanos play an important part in the Earth's carbon cycle.
80% of Earth's carbon is in the rocks of the crust. When the crust is melted, that carbon is released.
CO_2 in the atmosphere is absorbed by raindrops, plants, or open bodies of water like lakes or oceans.
CRUST
MANTLE
Plants use CO_2 to make energy and give off oxygen!
Oh boy! Dinnertime!
We need the carbon cycle to sustain life on Earth, period. And volcanoes play a big part!

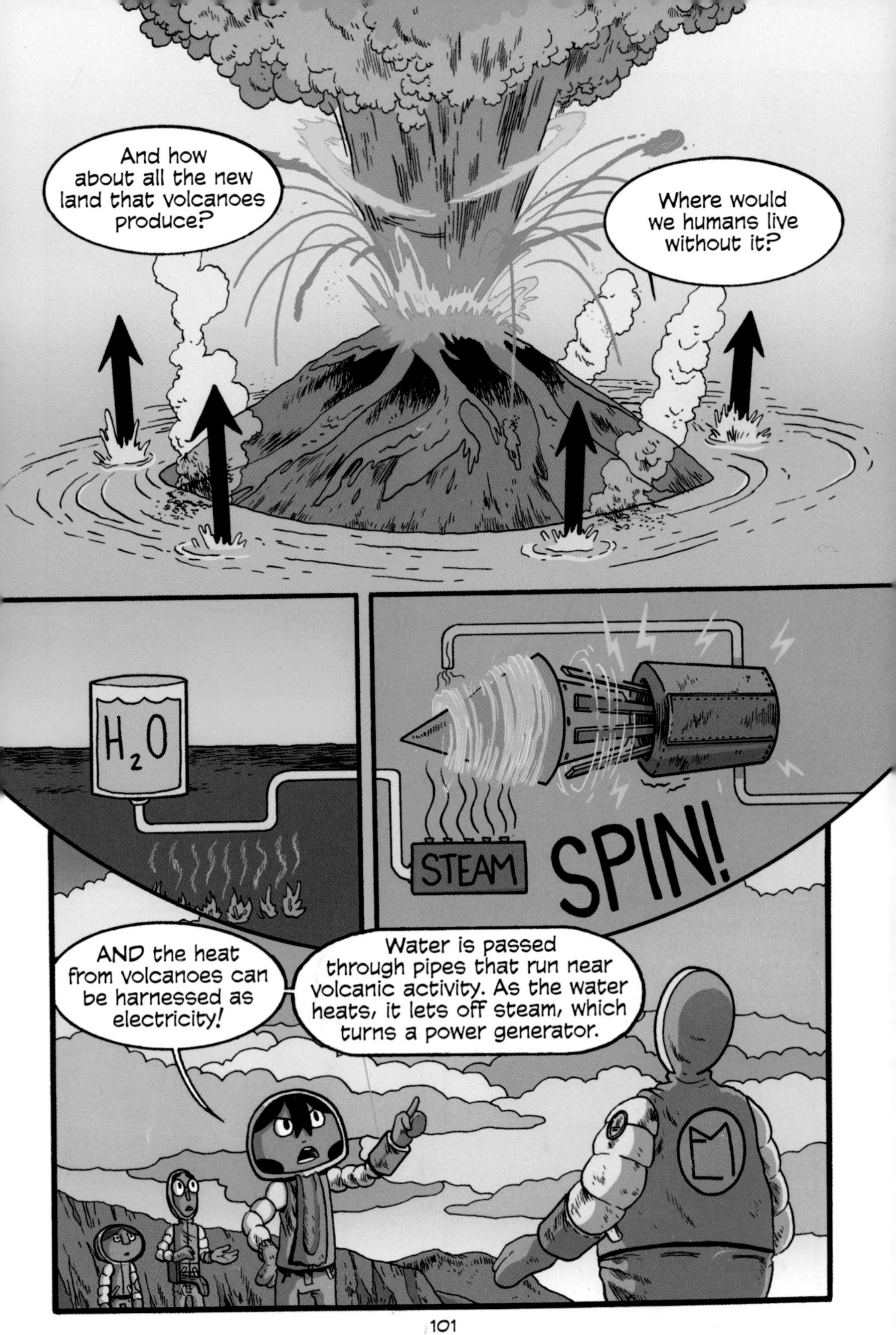
And how about all the new land that volcanoes produce?
Where would we humans live without it?
H2O
STEAM
SPIN!
AND the heat from volcanoes can be harnessed as electricity!
Water is passed through pipes that run near volcanic activity. As the water heats, it lets off steam, which turns a power generator.

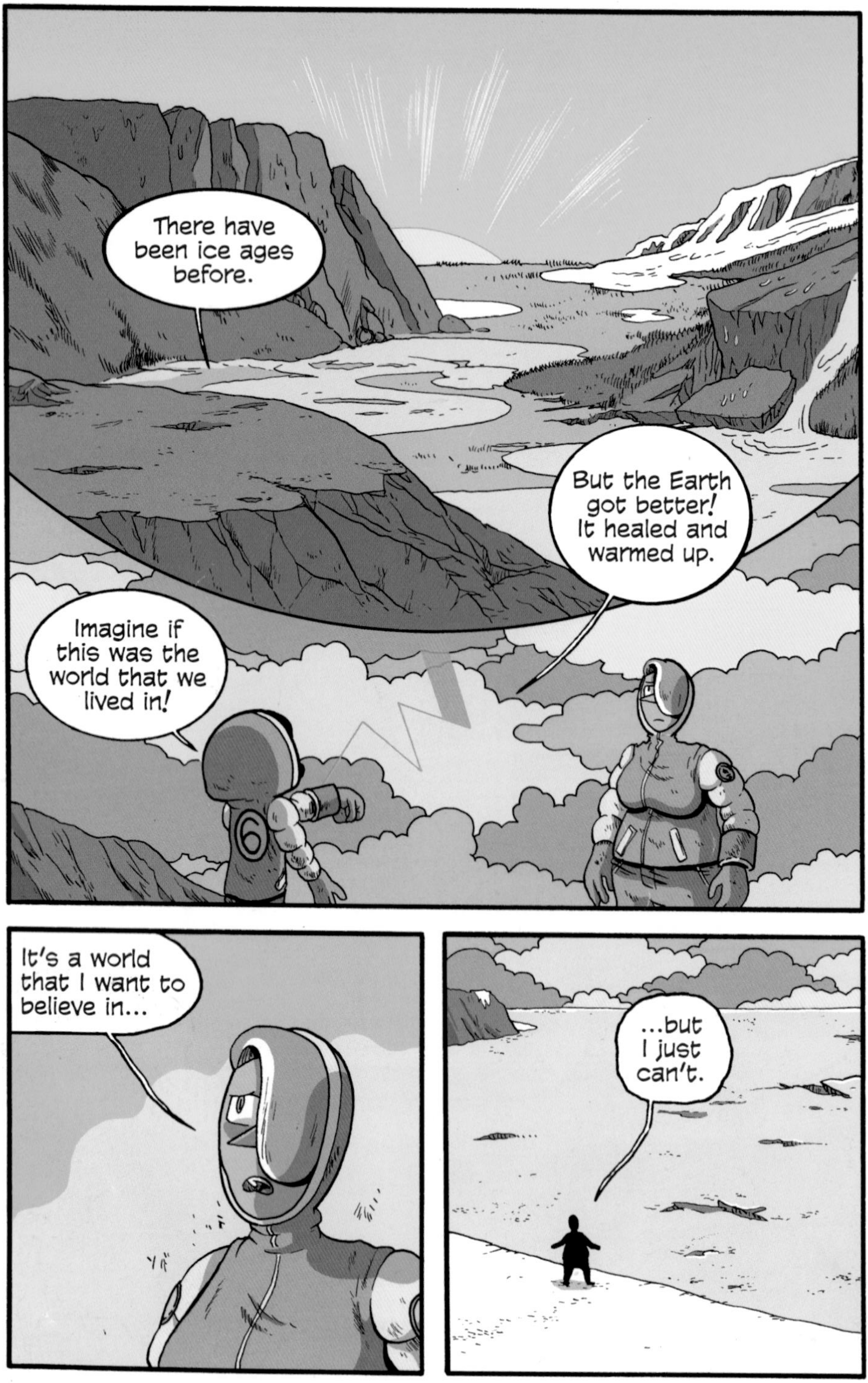
There have been ice ages before.
But the Earth got better! It healed and warmed up.
Imagine if this was the world that we lived in!
It's a world that I want to believe in...
...but I just can't.

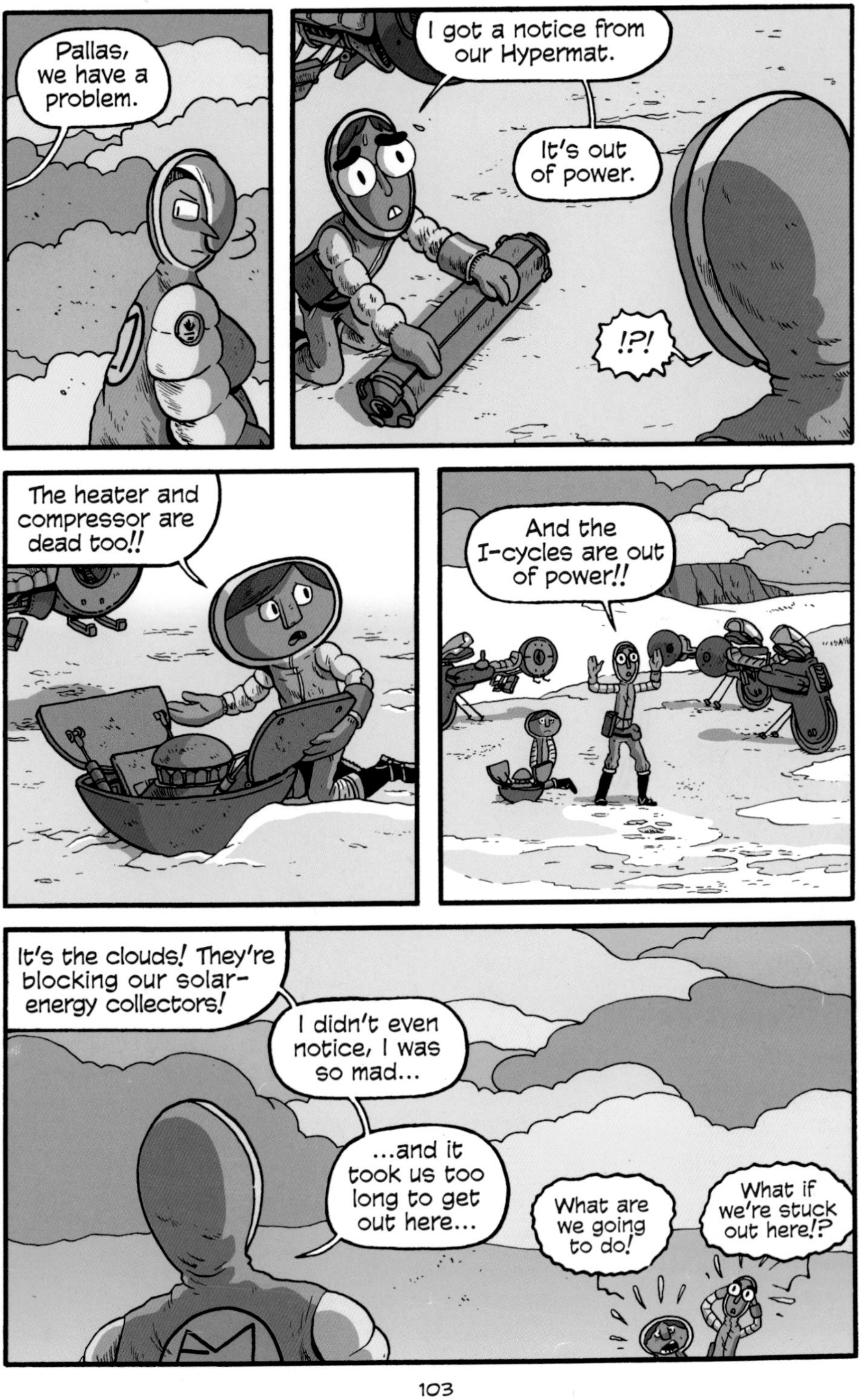
Pallas, we have a problem.
I got a notice from our Hypermat.
It's out of power.
!?!
The heater and compressor are dead too!!
And the I-cycles are out of power!!
It's the clouds! They're blocking our solar-energy collectors!
I didn't even notice, I was so mad...
...and it took us too long to get out here...
What are we going to do!
What if we're stuck out here!?

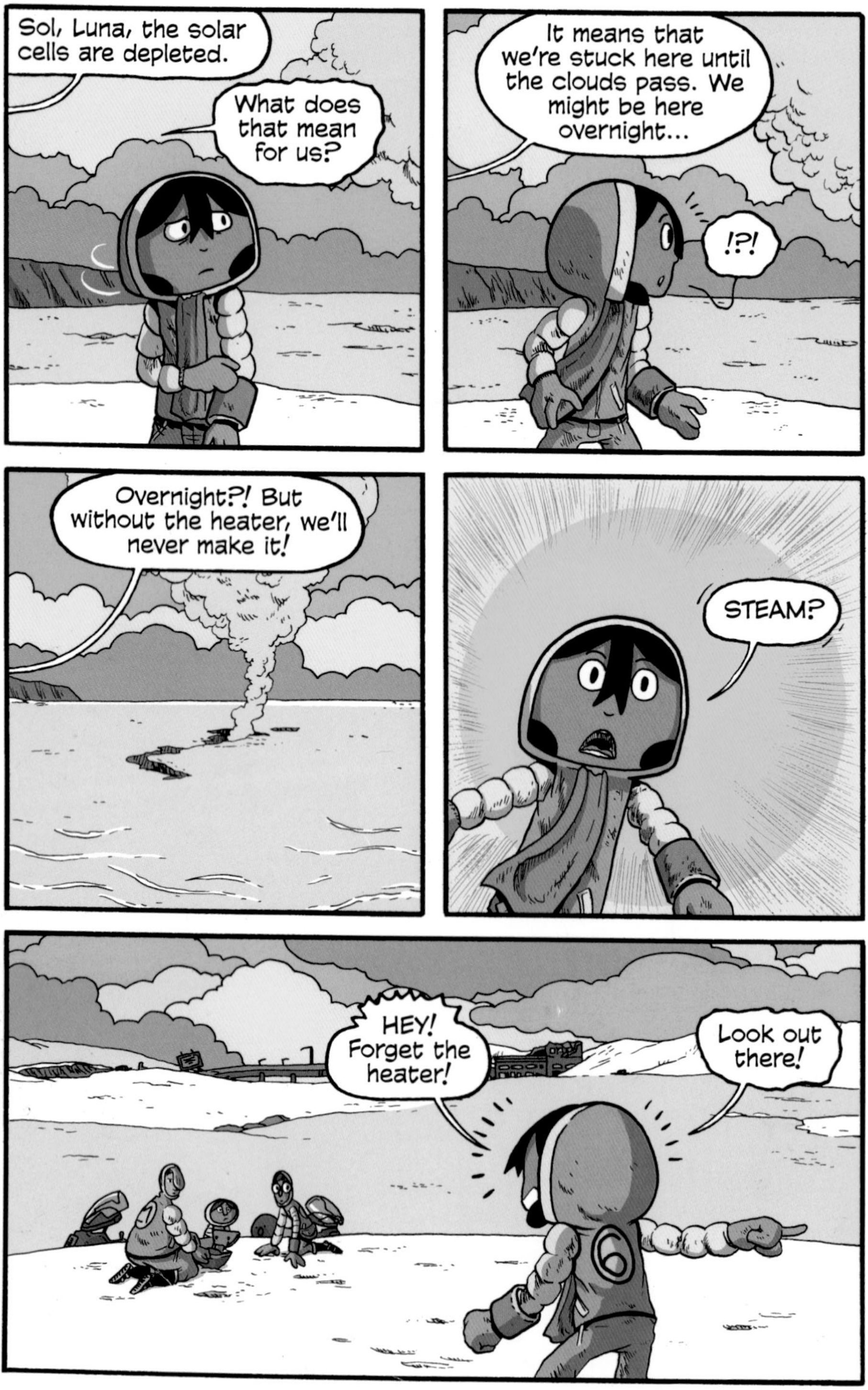
Sol, Luna, the solar cells are depleted.
What does that mean for us?
It means that we're stuck here until the clouds pass. We might be here overnight...
!?!
Overnight?! But without the heater, we'll never make it!
STEAM?
HEY! Forget the heater!
Look out there!

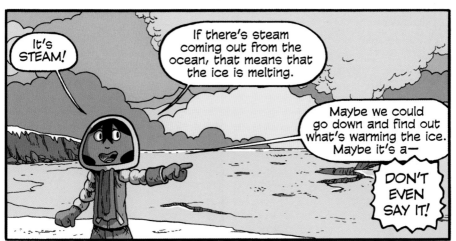

It's STEAM!

If there's steam coming out from the ocean, that means that the ice is melting.

Maybe we could go down and find out what's warming the ice. Maybe it's a—

DON'T EVEN SAY IT!

If you hadn't caused a landslide and smashed my pack and the backup power cells, we wouldn't be in this mess!!

Ooooh, I'm so mad I could—

PALLAS!

WHAT?!

That's our SISTER! We're the only ones who get to yell at her.

She's obsessed, but she's the only one with a good idea of how to get out of this mess!

We say that we try to find what's warming the ice!

Guys! You...

105

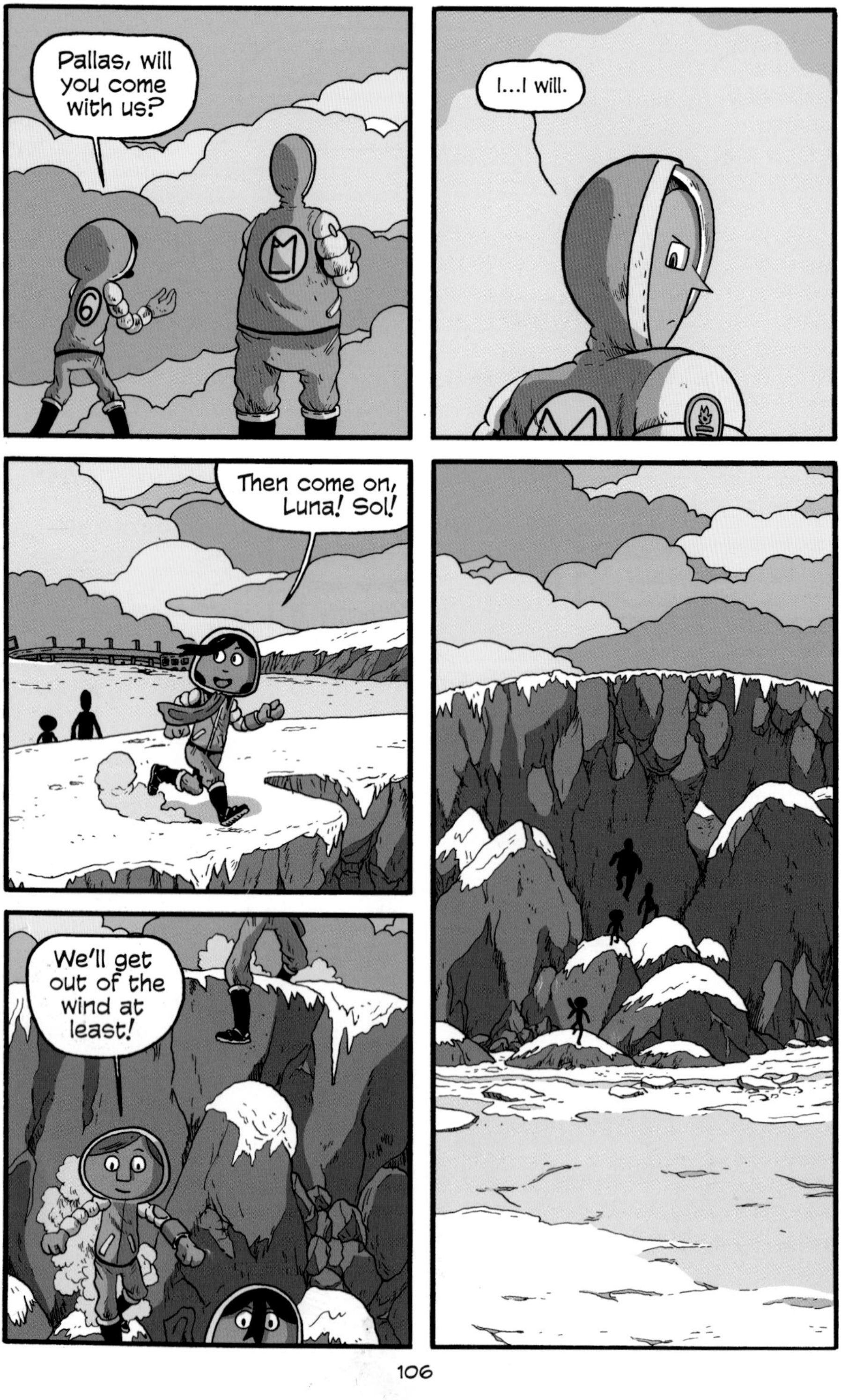
Pallas, will you come with us?
I...I will.
Then come on, Luna! Sol!
We'll get out of the wind at least!

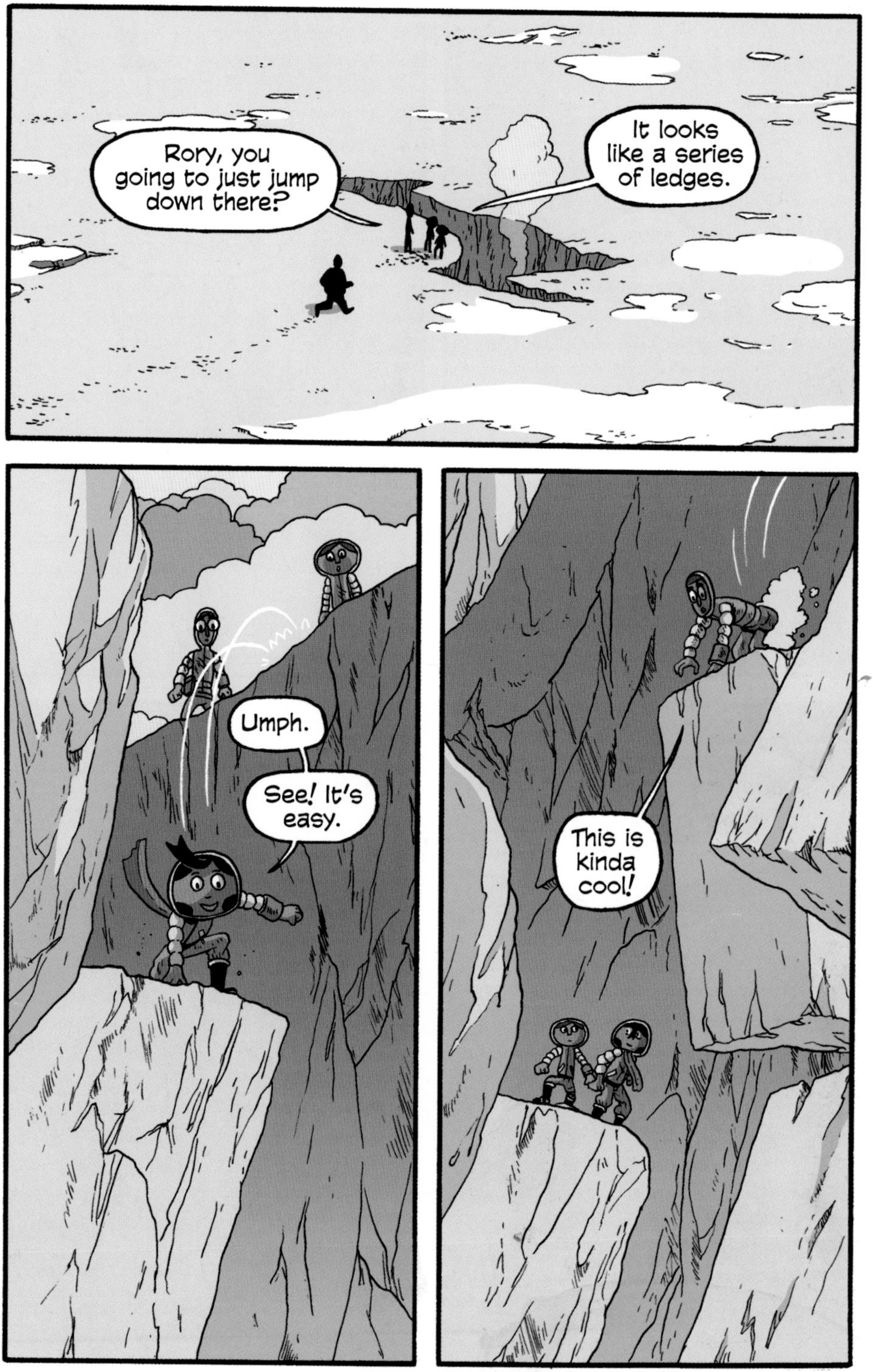
Rory, you going to just jump down there?
It looks like a series of ledges.
Umph.
See! It's easy.
This is kinda cool!

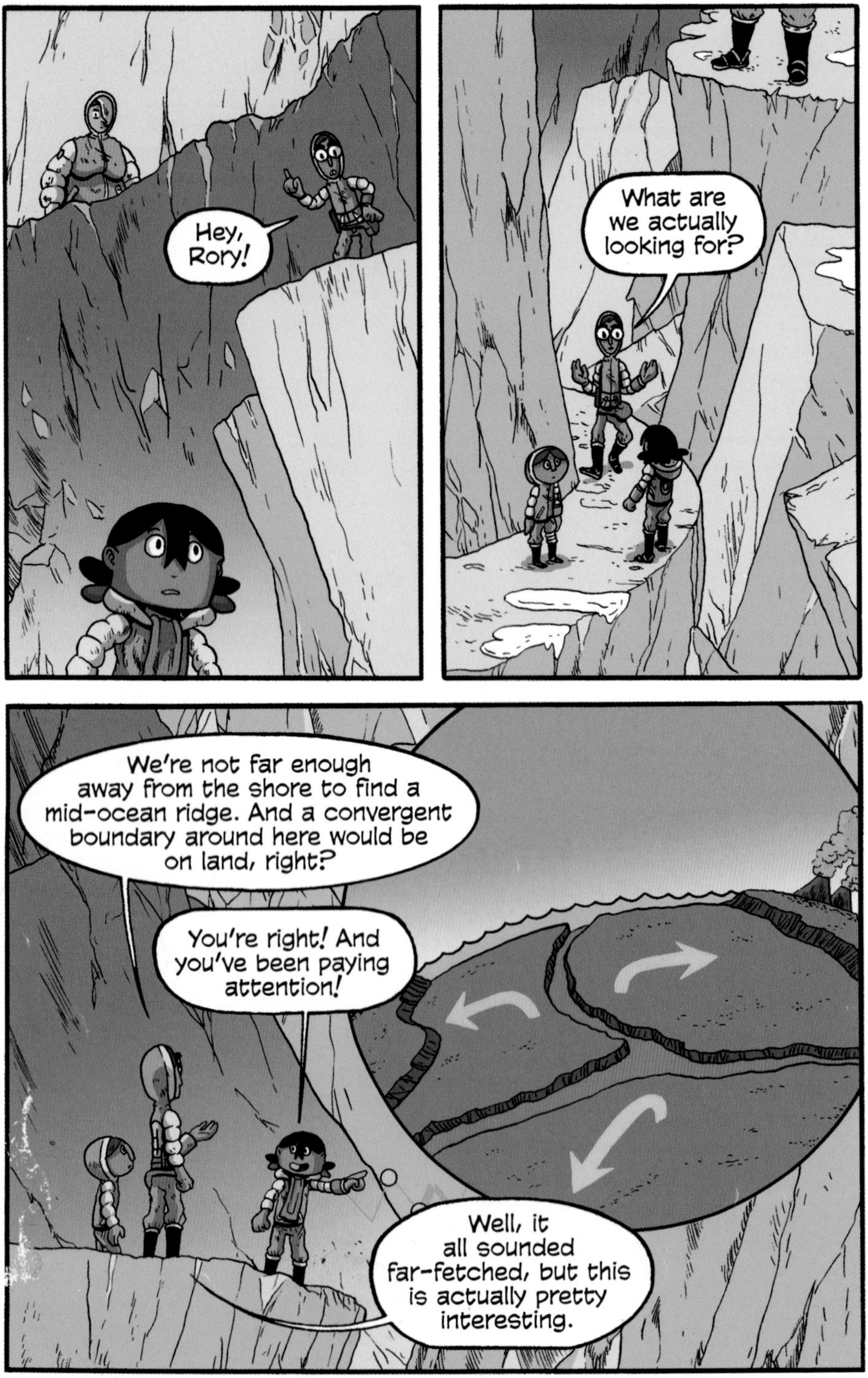
Hey, Rory!
What are we actually looking for?
We're not far enough away from the shore to find a mid-ocean ridge. And a convergent boundary around here would be on land, right?
You're right! And you've been paying attention!
Well, it all sounded far-fetched, but this is actually pretty interesting.

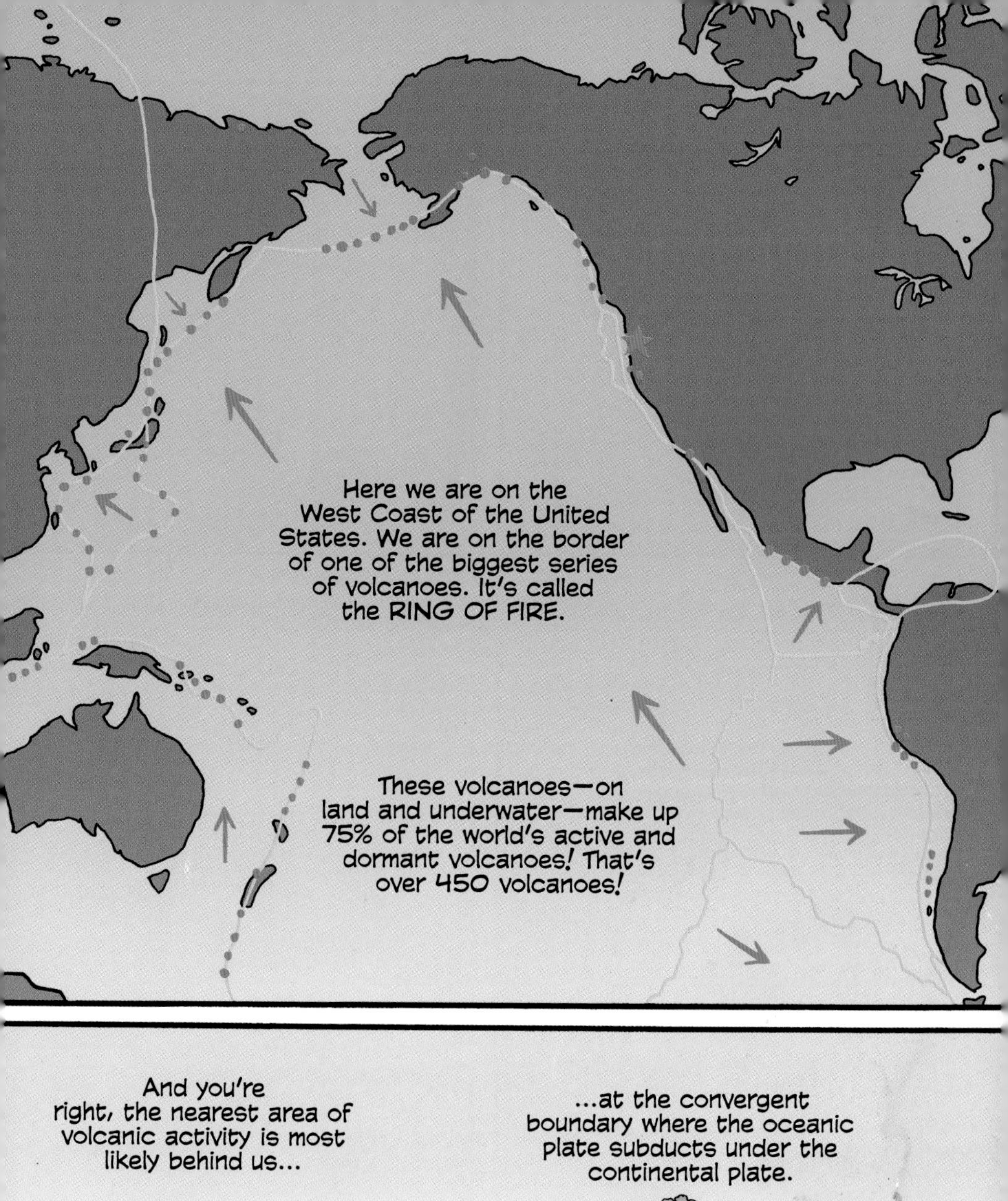
Here we are on the West Coast of the United States. We are on the border of one of the biggest series of volcanoes. It's called the RING OF FIRE.
These volcanoes—on land and underwater—make up 75% of the world's active and dormant volcanoes! That's over 450 volcanoes!

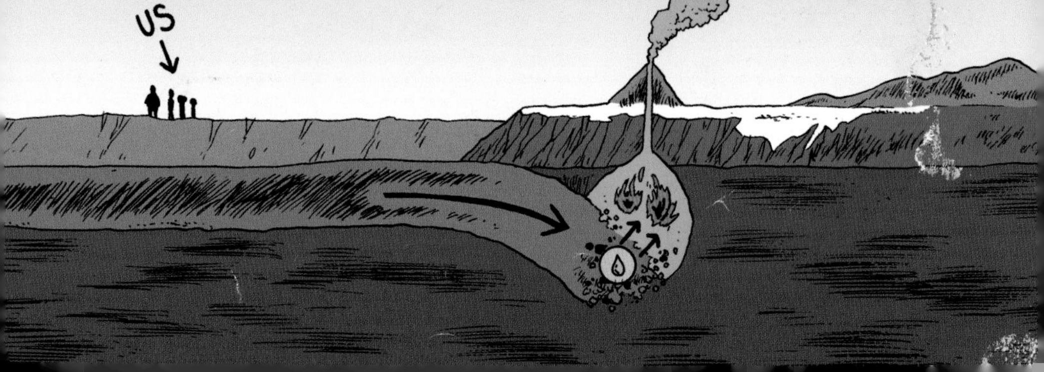
And you're right, the nearest area of volcanic activity is most likely behind us...
...at the convergent boundary where the oceanic plate subducts under the continental plate.
US

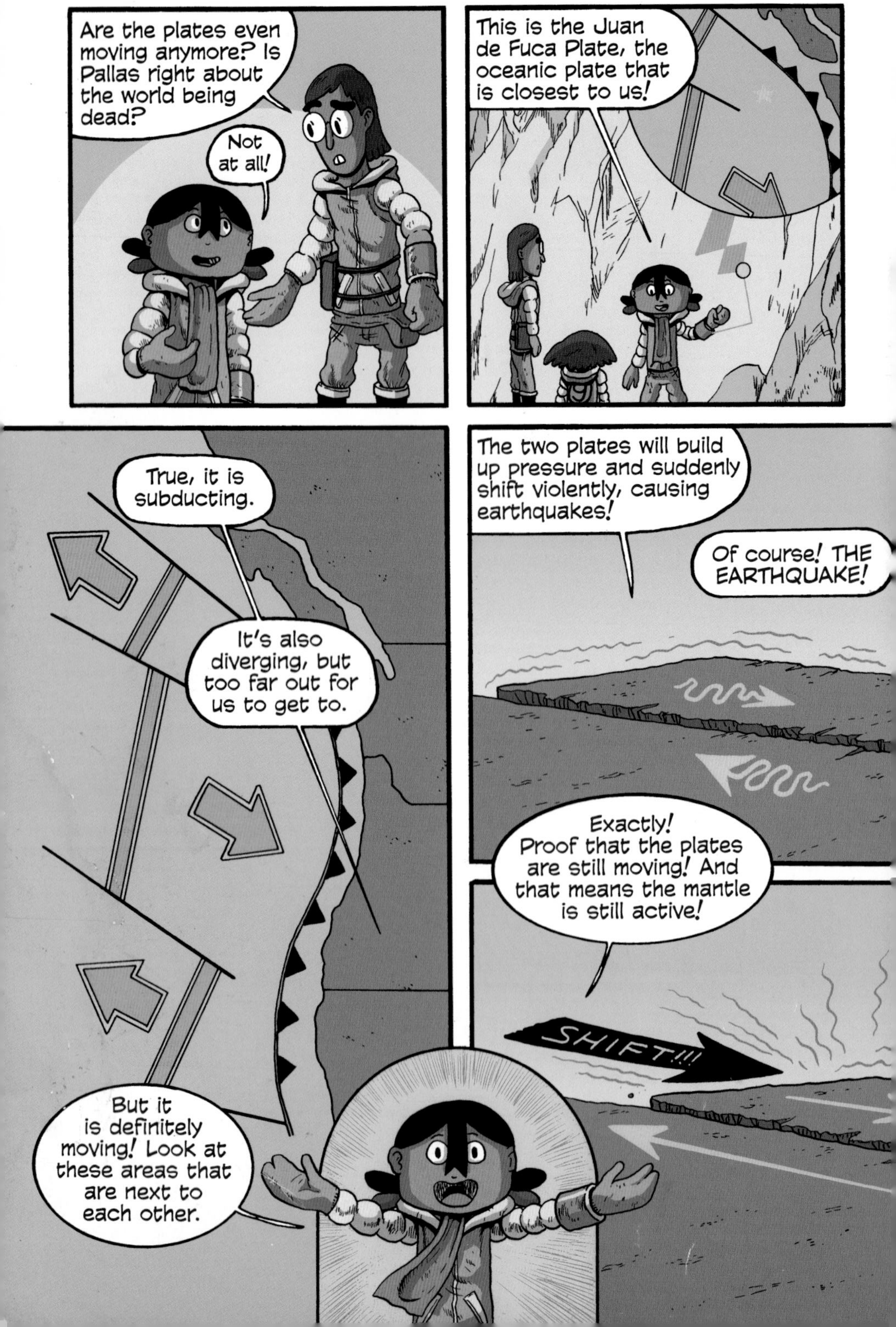
Are the plates even moving anymore? Is Pallas right about the world being dead?
Not at all!
This is the Juan de Fuca Plate, the oceanic plate that is closest to us!
True, it is subducting.
It's also diverging, but too far out for us to get to.
But it is definitely moving! Look at these areas that are next to each other.
The two plates will build up pressure and suddenly shift violently, causing earthquakes!
Of course! THE EARTHQUAKE!
Exactly! Proof that the plates are still moving! And that means the mantle is still active!
SHIFT!!!

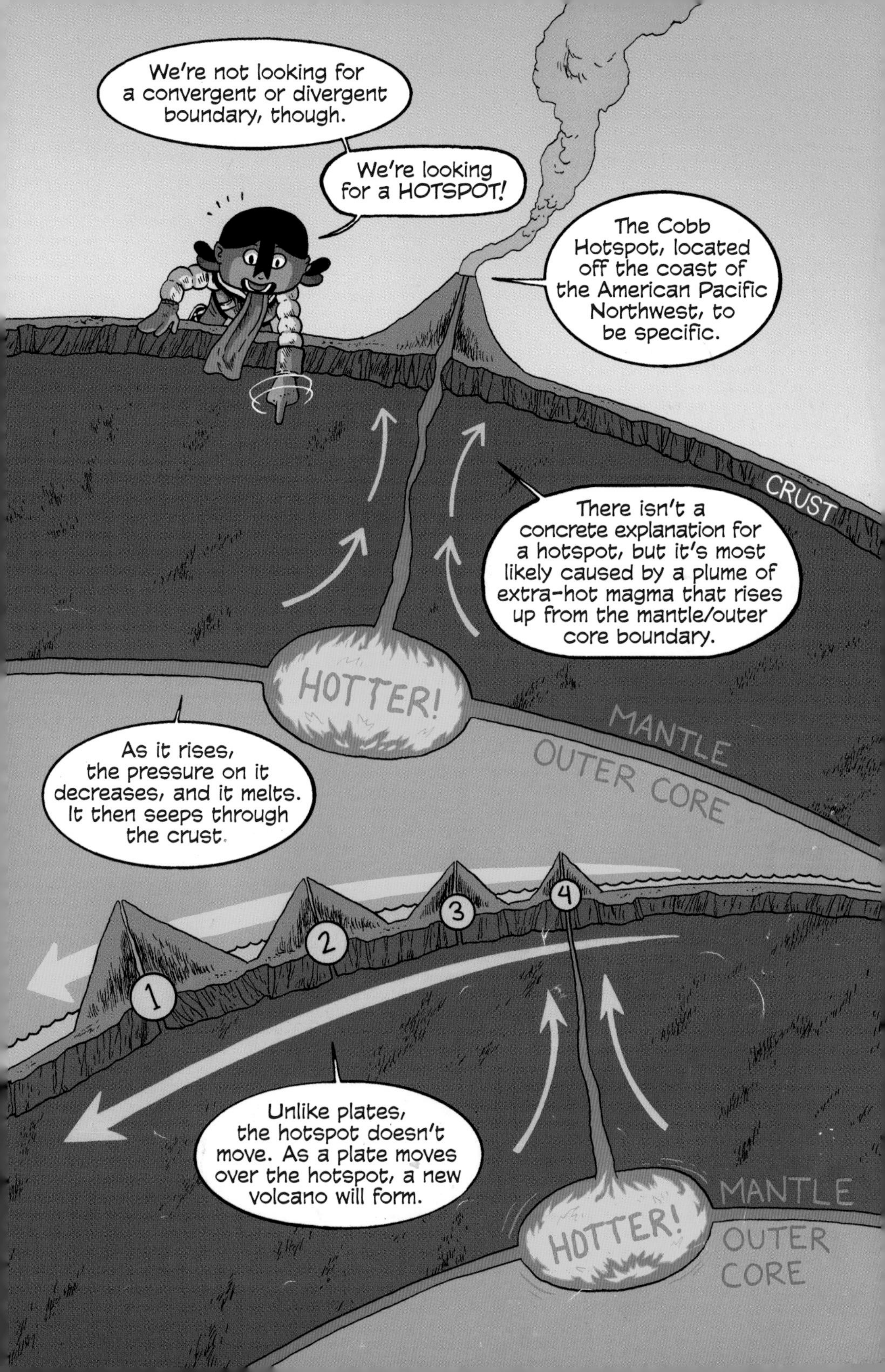
We're not looking for a convergent or divergent boundary, though.
We're looking for a HOTSPOT!
The Cobb Hotspot, located off the coast of the American Pacific Northwest, to be specific.
CRUST
There isn't a concrete explanation for a hotspot, but it's most likely caused by a plume of extra-hot magma that rises up from the mantle/outer core boundary.
HOTTER!
MANTLE
OUTER CORE
As it rises, the pressure on it decreases, and it melts. It then seeps through the crust.
1
2
3
4
Unlike plates, the hotspot doesn't move. As a plate moves over the hotspot, a new volcano will form.
HOTTER!
MANTLE
OUTER CORE

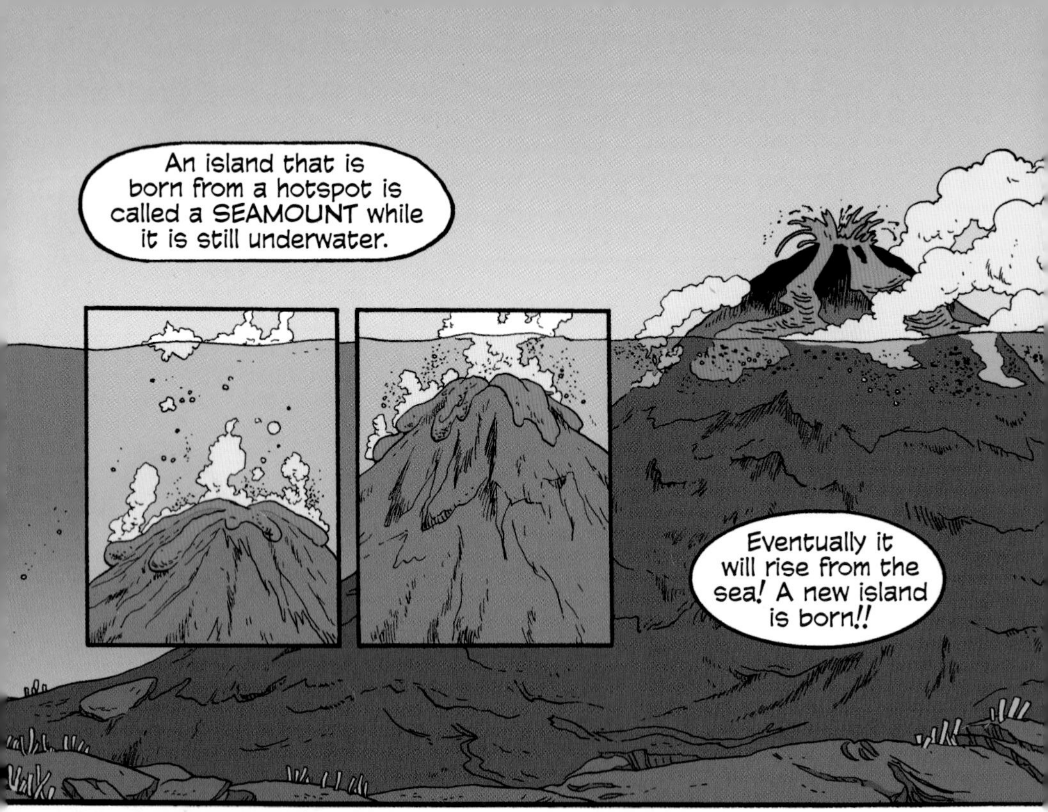
An island that is born from a hotspot is called a SEAMOUNT while it is still underwater.
Eventually it will rise from the sea! A new island is born!!

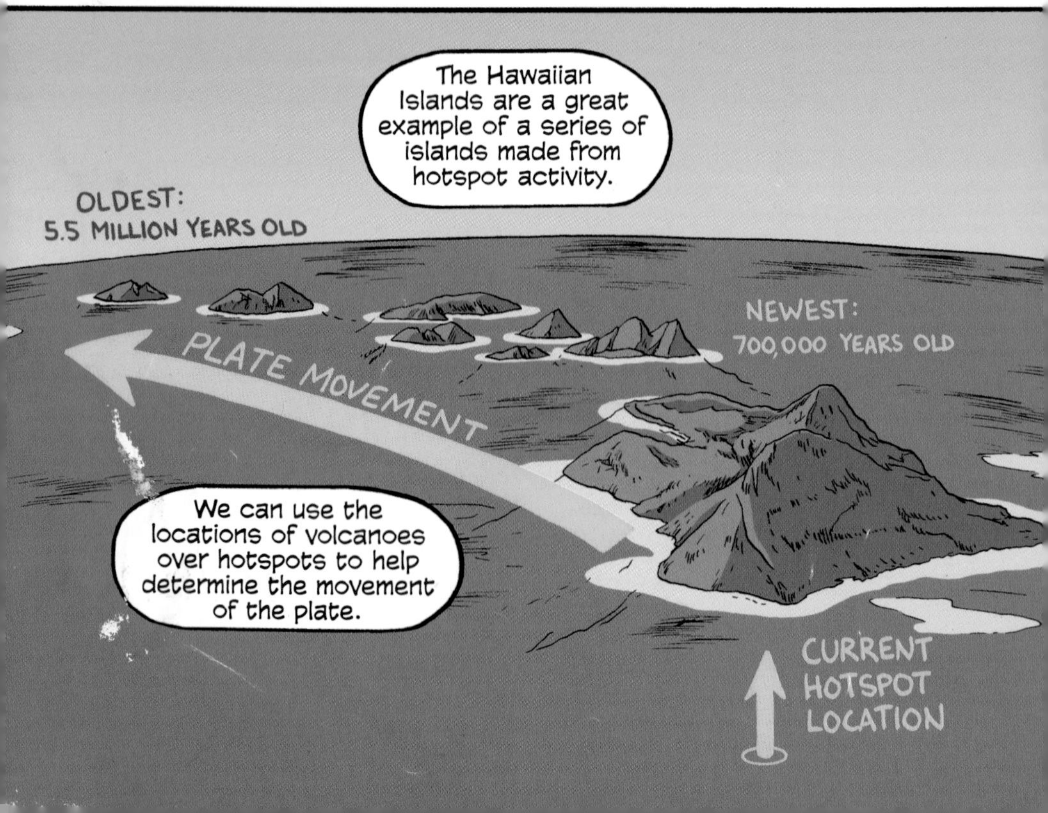
The Hawaiian Islands are a great example of a series of islands made from hotspot activity.
OLDEST: 5.5 MILLION YEARS OLD
NEWEST: 700,000 YEARS OLD
PLATE MOVEMENT
We can use the locations of volcanoes over hotspots to help determine the movement of the plate.
CURRENT HOTSPOT LOCATION

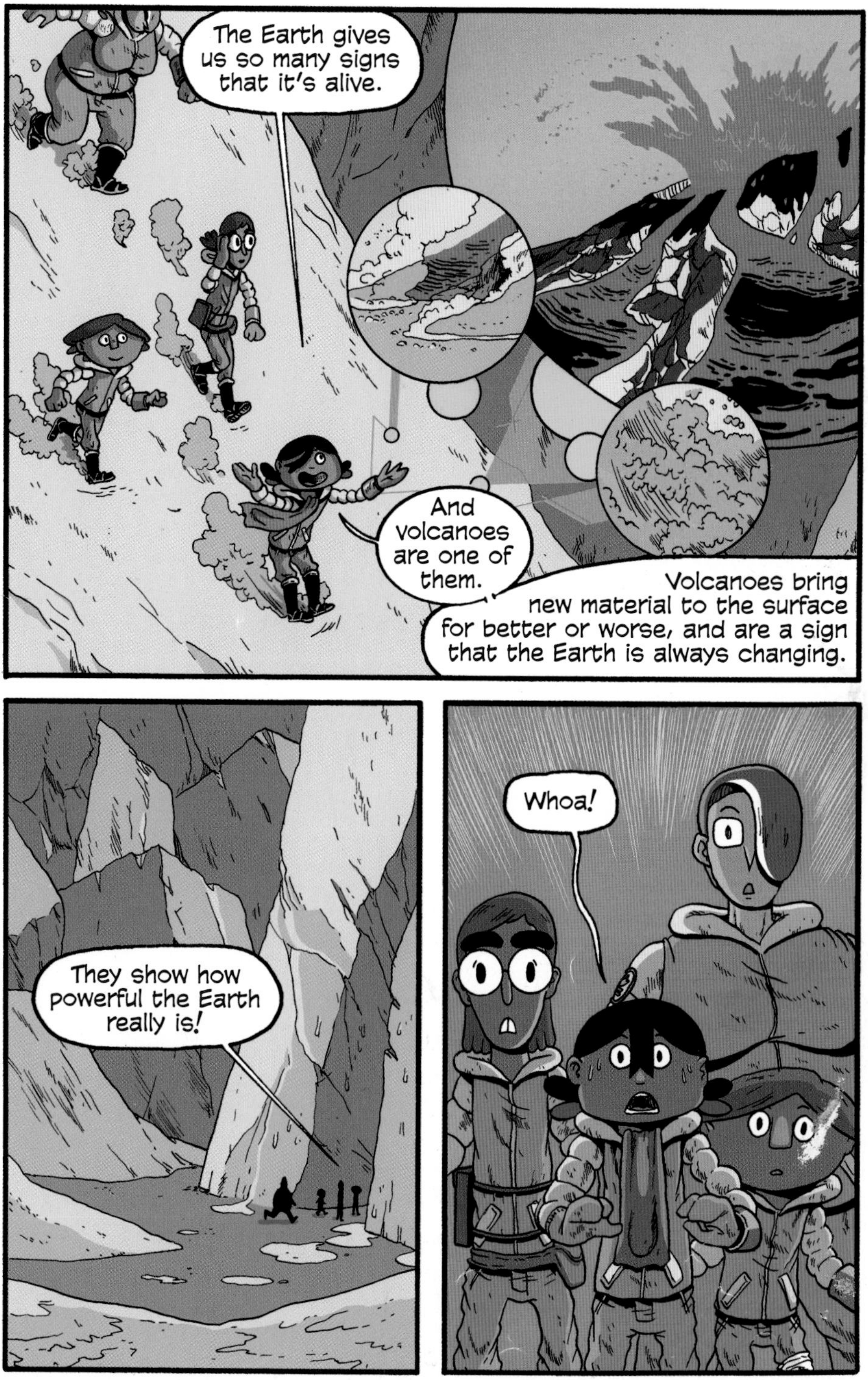
The Earth gives us so many signs that it's alive.
And volcanoes are one of them.
Volcanoes bring new material to the surface for better or worse, and are a sign that the Earth is always changing.
They show how powerful the Earth really is!
Whoa!

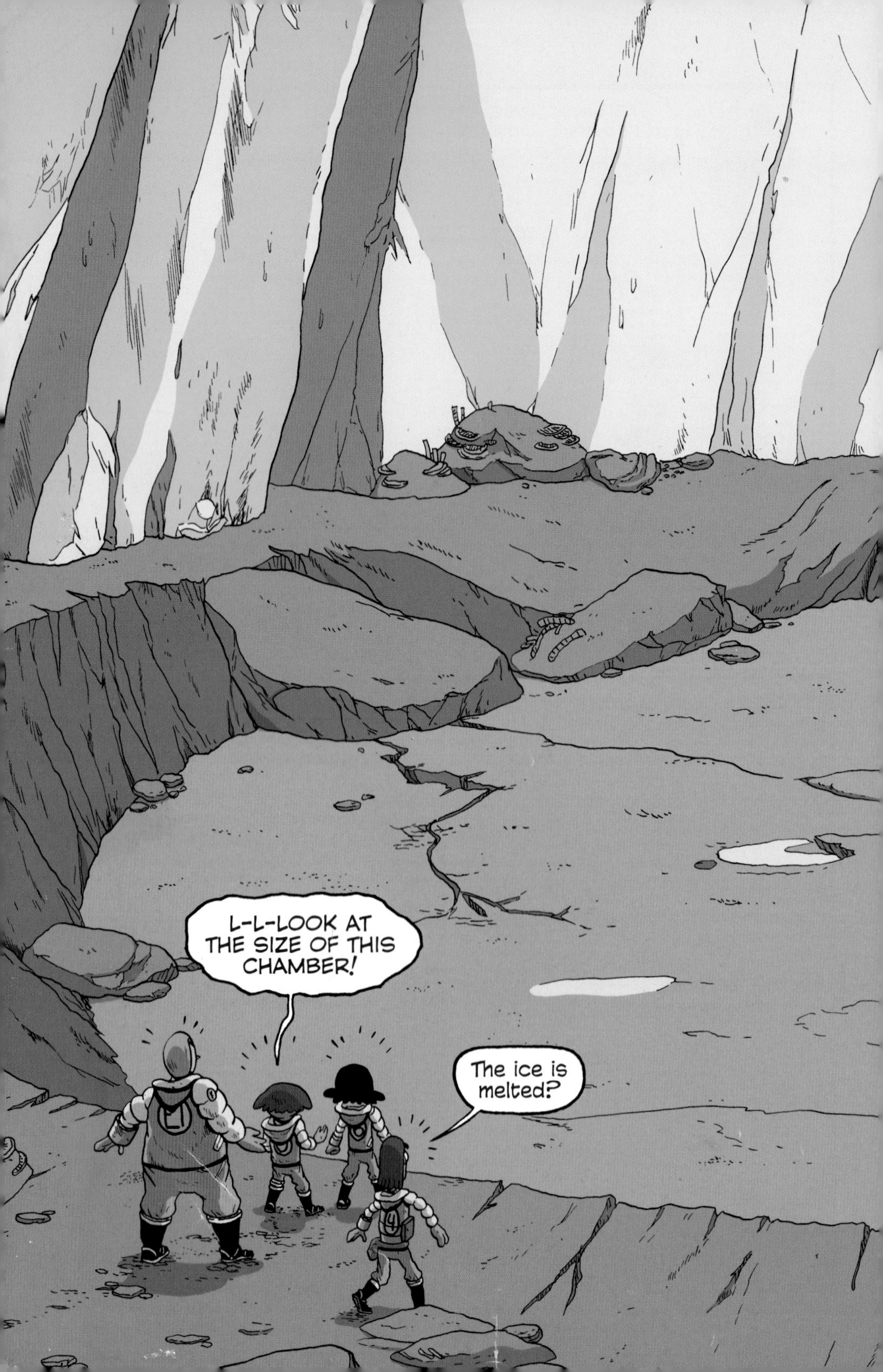
L-L-LOOK AT THE SIZE OF THIS CHAMBER!
The ice is melted?

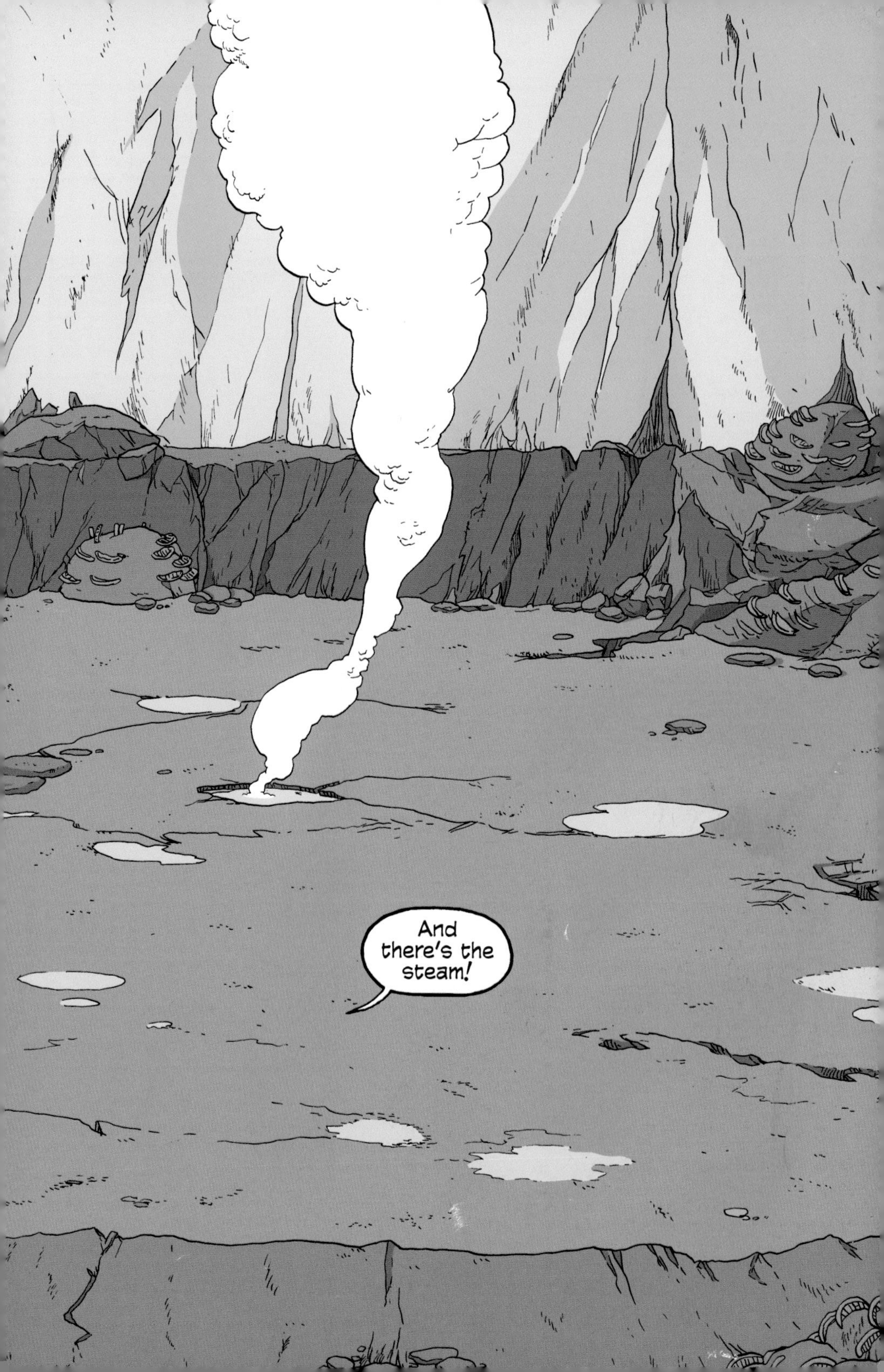
And there's the steam!

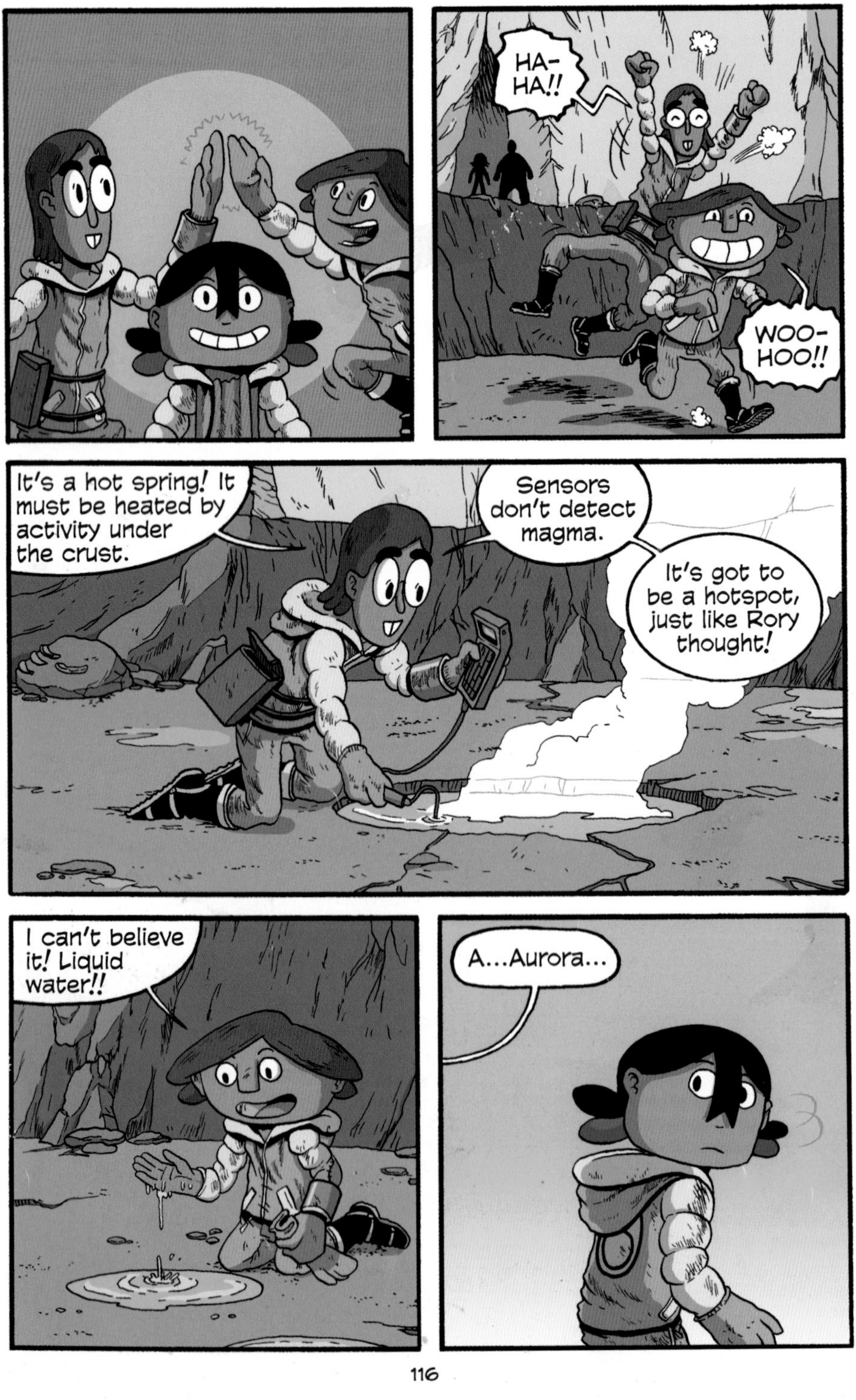
HA-HA!!
WOO-HOO!!
It's a hot spring! It must be heated by activity under the crust.
Sensors don't detect magma.
It's got to be a hotspot, just like Rory thought!
I can't believe it! Liquid water!!
A...Aurora...

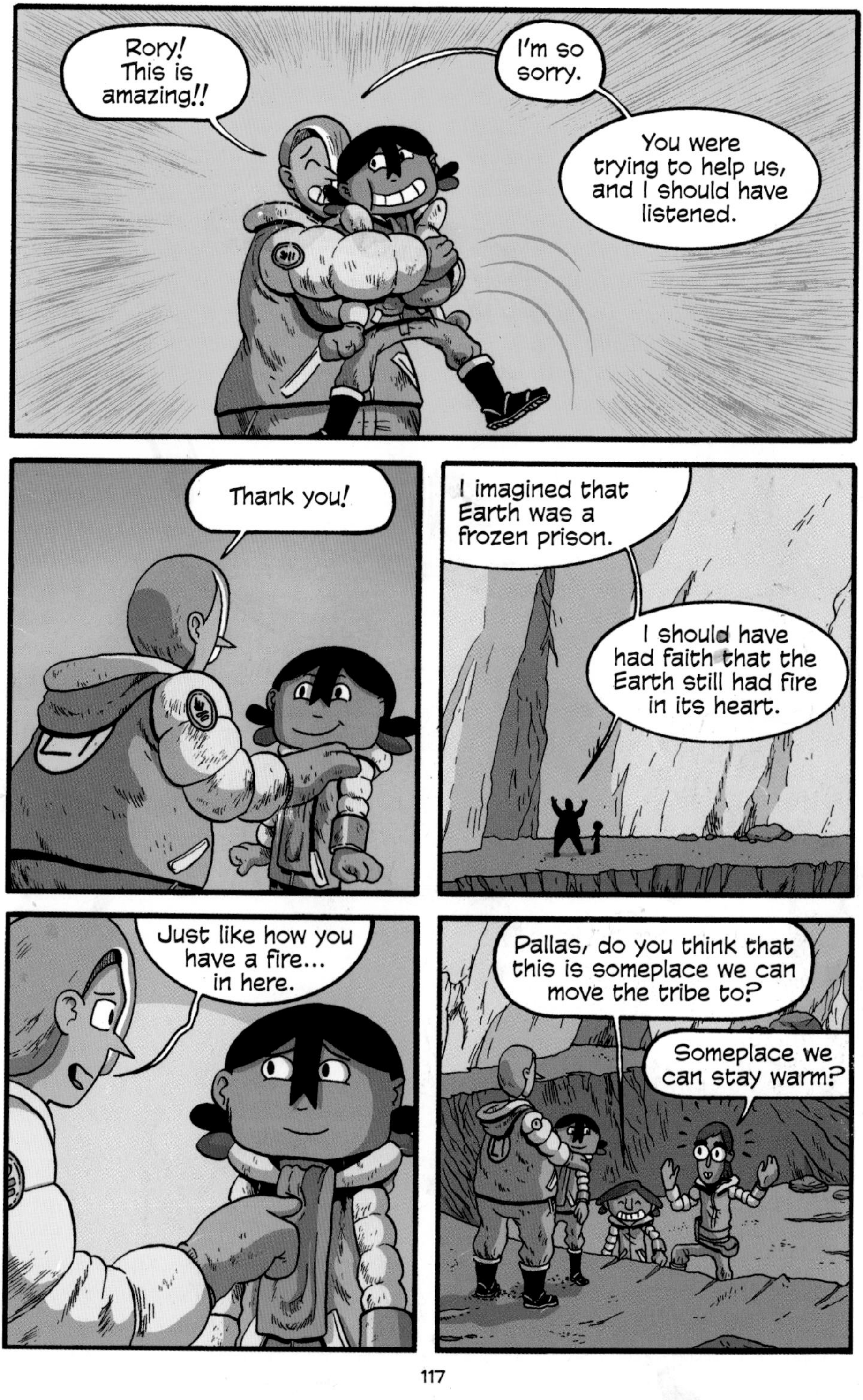
Rory! This is amazing!!
I'm so sorry.
You were trying to help us, and I should have listened.
Thank you!
I imagined that Earth was a frozen prison.
I should have had faith that the Earth still had fire in its heart.
Just like how you have a fire... in here.
Pallas, do you think that this is someplace we can move the tribe to?
Someplace we can stay warm?

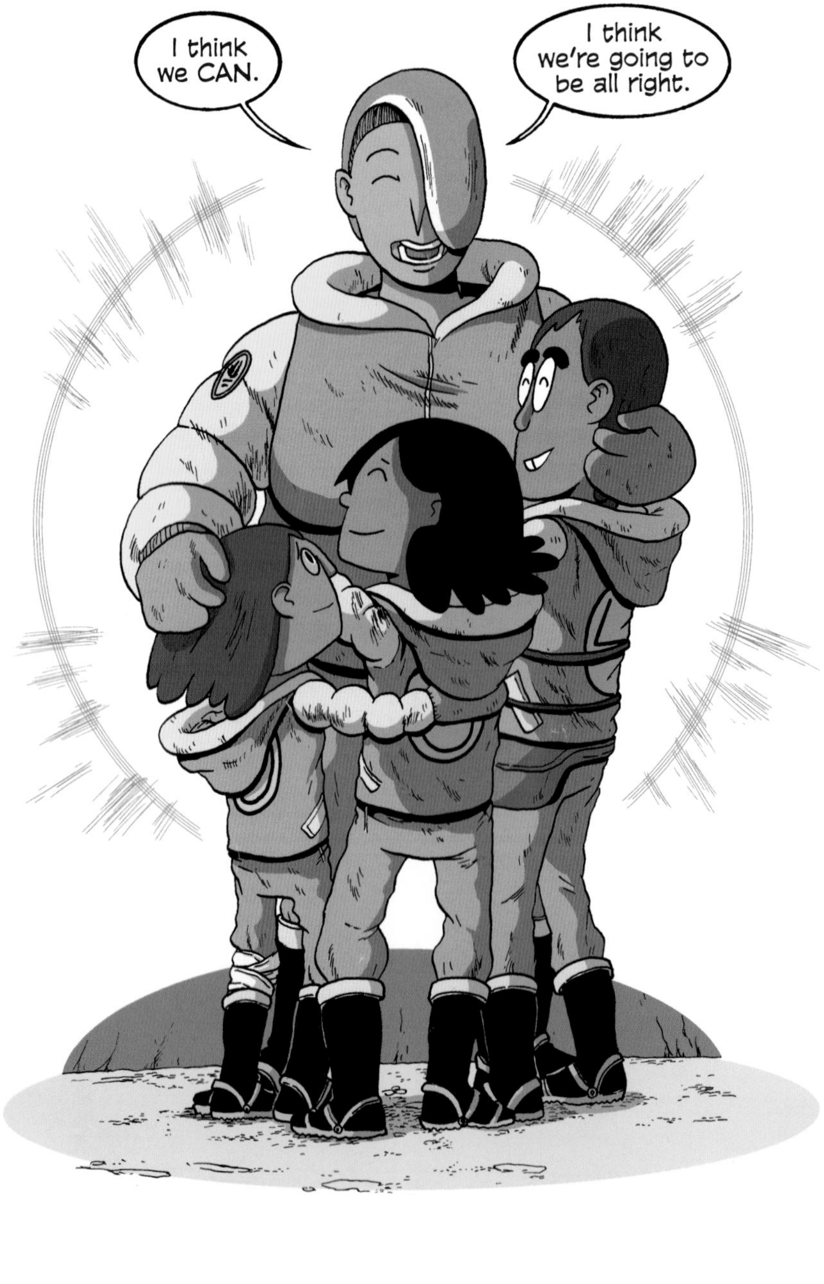
I think we CAN.
I think we're going to be all right.

VOCABULARY

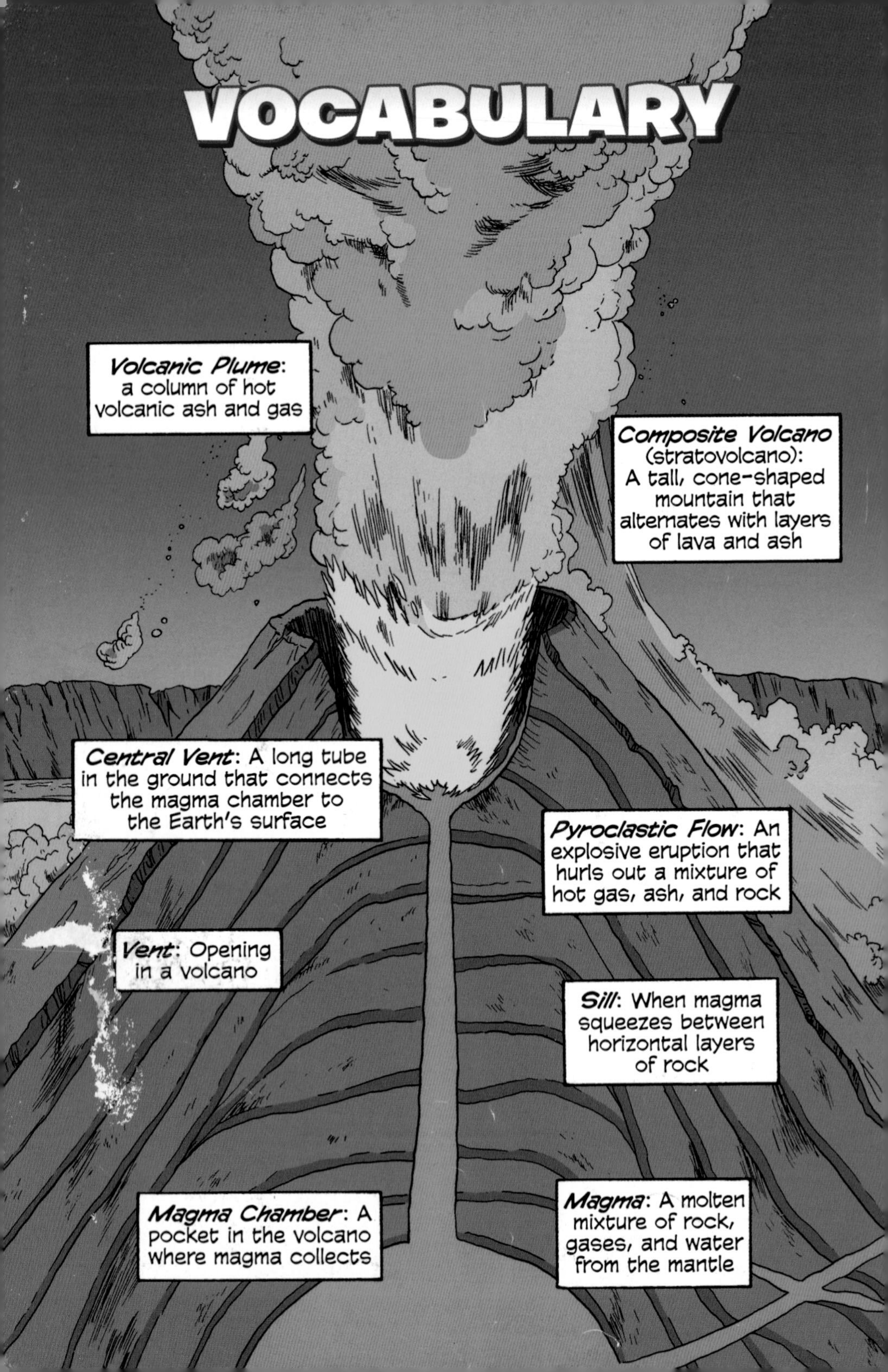
Volcanic Plume: a column of hot volcanic ash and gas
Composite Volcano (stratovolcano): A tall, cone-shaped mountain that alternates with layers of lava and ash
Central Vent: A long tube in the ground that connects the magma chamber to the Earth's surface
Pyroclastic Flow: An explosive eruption that hurls out a mixture of hot gas, ash, and rock
Vent: Opening in a volcano
Sill: When magma squeezes between horizontal layers of rock
Magma Chamber: A pocket in the volcano where magma collects
Magma: A molten mixture of rock, gases, and water from the mantle

Volcano: A weak spot in the crust where magma and gases erupts onto the surface

Ring of Fire: A major volcanic belt that covers parts of Asia, South and North America, and Australia

Island Arc: A string of islands

Hotspot: Where hot magma rises from the mantle/outer core border and through the crust. Unlike other types of volcanoes, these don't occur at plate boundaries.

Crater: Bowl-shaped area that may form around a volcano's central vent

Dormant: A volcano likely to awaken in the future, but currently inactive

Extinct: A volcano unlikely to ever erupt again

Caldera: The huge depression left by the collapse of a volcano with a depleted magma chamber

Cinder Cone: A steep volcano created by layers of ash, cinders, and rocks

Tectonic Plate: A huge portion of the Earth's crust that moves. There are two type of Tectonic Plates: heavier Oceanic Plates and lighter Continental Plates.

Viscosity: Liquid that is LESS viscous is thinner and runnier. Liquid that is MORE viscous is thicker.

Silica: A mixture of silicon and oxygen. More silica in magma makes it thicker and stickier.

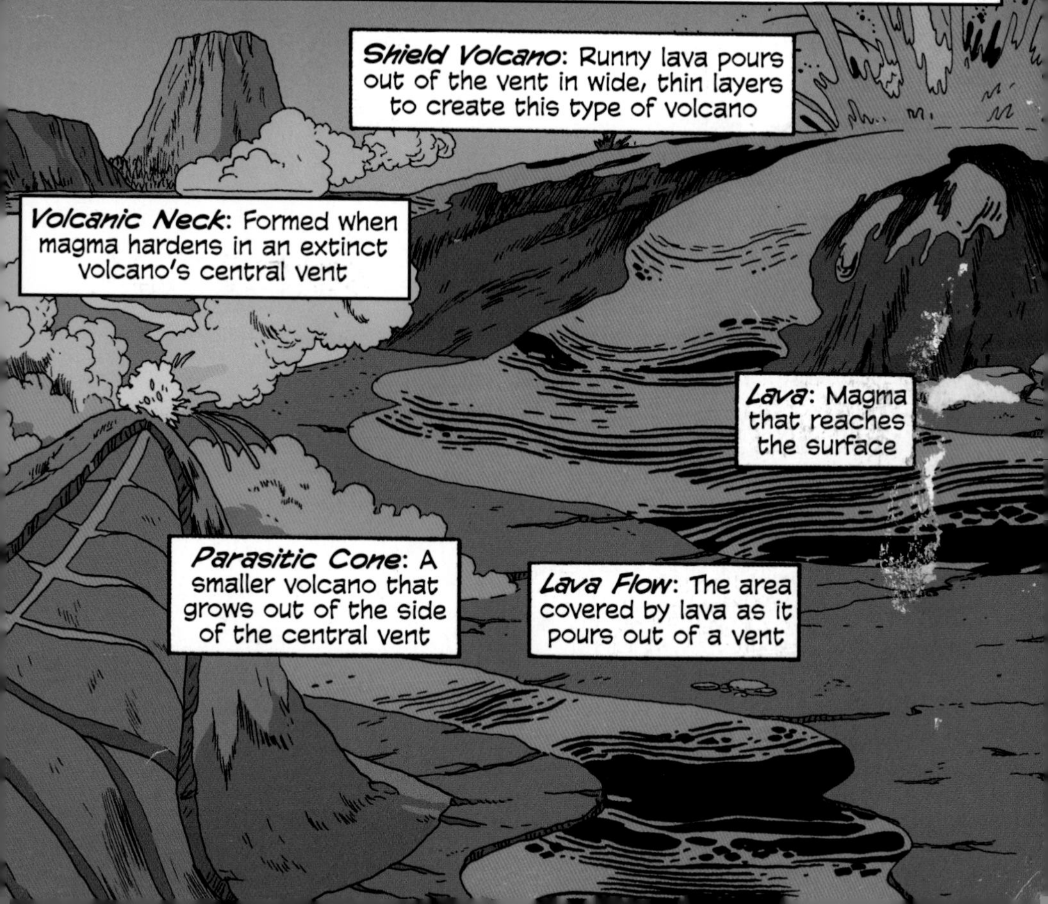
Shield Volcano: Runny lava pours out of the vent in wide, thin layers to create this type of volcano
Volcanic Neck: Formed when magma hardens in an extinct volcano's central vent
Lava: Magma that reaches the surface
Parasitic Cone: A smaller volcano that grows out of the side of the central vent
Lava Flow: The area covered by lava as it pours out of a vent

Interested in learning more about volcanoes?

Check out these cool books!

Gallant, Roy A. *Dance of the Continents*. New York: Benchmark Books, 2000.

Gallant, Roy A. *Plates: Restless Earth*. New York: Benchmark Books, 2002.

Gallant, Roy A. *Structure: Expoloring Earth's Interior*. New York: Benchmark Books, 2002.

Rosi, Mauro, Paolo Papale, Luca Lupi, Marco Stoppato. *Volcanoes*. New York: Firefly Books, 2003.

Stewart, Melissa. *Inside Volcanoes*. New York: Sterling Children's Books, 2011.

Thompson, Dick. *Volcano Cowboys: The Rocky Evolution of a Dangerous Science*. New York: St. Martin's Press, 2002.

Biography

Jon Chad is a cartoonist and illustrator living in Manchester Center, Vermont. He teaches bookmaking and design at the Center for Cartoon Studies and has done illustration work for the Professional & Amateur Pinball Association, *Highlights* magazine, and the FBI, among many others. He's also the author and artist of two other children's books, *Leo Geo and His Miraculous Journey Through the Center of the Earth* and *Leo Geo and the Cosmic Crisis*.

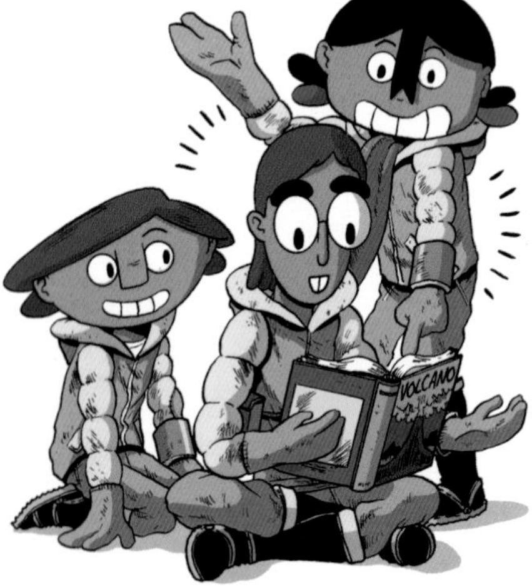

VOLCANO

Sophie Goldstein is a 2013 graduate of the Center for Cartoon Studies. She won two Ignatz Awards for her graphic novel, *The Oven*, in 2015 and one for her mini-comic, *House of Women, Part I*, in 2014. Her work has appeared in various publications including *Best American Comics 2013*, *Fable Comics*, *The Pitchfork Review*, *Maple Key Comics*, *Sleep of Reason*, *Symbolia*, *Trip 8*, and *Irene 3*.

Thanks

Thank you to my friends and family. Thanks to Alec L, Alison W, Calista B, Casey G, Laura T, Luke H, Maris W, MK R, Sophie Y, and Stephen B for their support and guidance. Thanks to Kelly S for her help scanning and ruling out pages. Thank you to Gywn Hughes and Michael Cardiff for their amazing geology expertise, advice, and wisdom. Thanks to Sophie G for making this book come alive, and thanks to Tess Kahn for her love and friendship.